D1592248

DATE DUE

Form & Content In Instrumental Music

Form & Content In

wcb

WM. C. BROWN COMPANY PUBLISHERS

Dubuque, Iowa

Instrumental Music

Gail de Stwolinski
University of Oklahoma

CONSULTING EDITOR

Frederick W. Westphal
California State University, Sacramento

Library of Congress Catalog Card Number: 74-84049

ISBN 0—697—03412—7

Printed in the United States of America

*To the memory of
my mother and my father*

contents

preface

This book has developed out of a personal conviction that musical content creates the form; that many composers have organized musical elements into structures that are aurally discernible at a certain level; and that the level at which these structures are aurally comprehended by an individual can be expanded by guided listening experience. The materials of this book are organized to first provide a means of aurally analyzing form and content as a preliminary to a more cognitive analysis of a score. The fusion of aural analysis, a partially affective response, with visual analysis, a cognitive response, results in a more sensitive understanding of any work.

With full recognition that aural perception intimidates many young musicians, every effort has been made to provide tangible materials for the initial aural experience with each form. In each chapter general expectations about the specific form and its content are discussed and illustrated prior to the assignments. Several analyzed models are included, with a discussion of the ways in which characteristic musical elements are organized to create the structure. Unless otherwise indicated, all the examples in each chapter are drawn from compositions that represent the forms discussed in the respective chapters.

The first assignment at the end of each chapter includes musical indices of illustrative traditional and twentieth century works which are to be used for the aural analysis and diagramming of the structure. Formal diagrams of each of the indexed works are placed in the appendix, and these can be used for self-grading purposes. This will free class time for discussion of the musical content, as suggested by Assignment 2, and for analysis of additional works from the list in Assignment 3. For use as a quick reference, the examples of Assignments 2 and 3 are always ordered alphabetically by composer rather than by chronology or by gradation of difficulty. Every effort should be made to study the full score of all works analyzed aurally. Visual aids such as the overhead projector have revolutionized the world of score reading!

While the text has been designed primarily for the class in formal analysis, it can also be used as a supplementary text in the following classes: a general music literature course; a survey of musical styles; comprehensive musicianship courses; an advanced course in the evolution of larger forms.

The rather unusual ordering of materials in the first half of the book is purposeful. Composers of all periods have extended their musical ideas with the techniques of variation. We recognize continuous variation or transformation as an integral part of many twentieth century works, but we tend to overlook the variation factor in a work of a traditional composer if that work is not cast in the variation form. Variation is a creative force of such impact on the content of all forms that it seems necessary to present these processes early in the book. Contrapuntal techniques have equal historical significance as a means of exploiting musical ideas. When composers of the eighteenth century again embraced counterpoint as a means of linear development in a homophonic texture, these techniques flourished increasingly into our century.

The study of the small units has been moved back from its usual position as chapter one in an effort to first establish habits of listening that will focus on the larger structure. Disproportionate attention to detail may foster the concept that the larger organization is the product of consecutive segments. Music *is* a temporal and sequential art form, but a musical work can only be presented sensitively to others—through performance or teaching—if it is thoroughly comprehended at the level of its highest organization. Each teacher can make a judgement, however, and chapter five can easily be used as chapter two if desired.

The use of a number of twentieth century examples has, I believe, greatly increased the relevance of the book, and I am grateful to the publishers and copyright owners for their permission to use them. The staff of the Music Libraries at the University of Oklahoma has been of great assistance in furnishing scores and recordings, as has my colleague Dr. Digby Bell. Another colleague, Professor Spencer Norton, is always a veritable fount of knowledge, and he has advised me on many occasions.

The support of my own University and School of Music through a semester's sabbatical leave has been a much appreciated necessity.

To three bright and gifted graduate students I owe a particular debt of gratitude. Ann Dotter, Janet Janzen, and Elaine Bittman have supported the project through its final stage with invaluable assistance of a practical and critical nature.

Finally and foremost, this book would never have been realized without my husband's belief in my ability and his unswerving support.

1 . introduction to aural analysis

The musical form of a composition evolves from the manner in which a composer has organized and used his materials. Music is a temporal and audible art, and it is shaped by an organic process involving statement and departure, growth, change, return, and closure. Certain authors, such as Meyer[1] and Beardsley,[2] have advanced very convincingly the proposition that music can convey meanings or kinetic qualities that elicit expectations in the listener. If form is interpreted as inseparable from content, the meaning or formal purpose of a musical passage should become clear to the listener either at the time of presentation or in retrospect. One could even extend this proposition to the level where musical purposes are present in a composition only to the degree that they are audibly apparent to the listener.

Knowledge of musical styles and compositional techniques and an accumulation of aural experiences play important roles in listener response. Musical purpose usually results from the relationship of musical passages in the context of the whole composition. There are, however, certain arrangements of musical materials that announce a musical purpose so directly that it can be understood even though the listener's knowledge is limited and the musical context is partial. Suppose that you know only that two of the common purposes of musical passages are to progress (transition) and to close (conclusion). With each of the following compositions apply this very limited knowledge to selected musical passages that are out of context and out of order, and determine by listening that some passages serve the purpose of transition and others the purpose of conclusion. These purposes may become clear as the passage unfolds or they may only be evident in retrospect.

Ex. 1-1. Mozart: Sonata in C Major, K. 309, II (tempo, andante un poco adagio).

1 a. Transition or conclusion?

1. Leonard Meyer, *Emotion and Meaning in Music* (Chicago: University of Chicago Press, 1956).
2. Monroe Beardsley, *Aesthetics* (New York: Harcourt, Brace and World, Inc., 1958).

Ex. 1-1. (Continued)

1 b. Transition or conclusion?

1 c. Transition or conclusion?

Ex. 1-2. Bartok: *Mikrokosmos*, No. 128 (tempo, moderato, $\quarternote = 112$).
   2 a. Transition or conclusion?

2 b. Transition or conclusion?

2 c. Transition or conclusion?

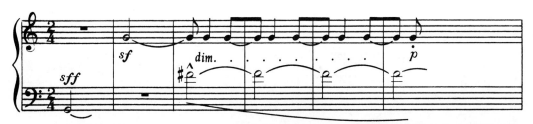

In Ex. 1-1 excerpts 1a and 1c sound like transition, and 1b sounds concluding. The transition passages of Ex. 1-2 are excerpts 2b and 2c, and 2a is concluding. The musical materials which create the effect of each passage can be described as follows.

Musical materials in transition passages:

> Ex. 1-1a—rapid bass rhythm; sequence in the second and third measures; dissonance in the alto suspensions; an open, or progressive, cadence at the end; acceleration of the bass rhythm at the end.
>
> Ex. 1-1c—same materials as Ex. 1-1a except for the omission of the triplets.
>
> Ex. 1-2b—repeated melodic motives that form three-beat patterns within the two-beat meter; bass sequence; ends with the unresolved dissonance of a bitonal chord; tempo slows and dynamics increase.
>
> Ex. 1-2c—repeated pitch in syncopation; dynamics decrease; ends with an unresolved dissonance of a minor second.

Musical materials in concluding passages:

> Ex. 1-1b—repeated melodic pattern and descending line; repeated chord progression throughout that is, coincidentally, an authentic cadence; dynamics decrease; melodic rhythm decreases.
>
> Ex. 1-2a—repeated melodic and harmonic pattern throughout; melodic rhythm decreases; ends with the sound of a modal cadence.

Listen several times to the excerpts within each of the next compositions, determine which ones sound like transitions or conclusions, and notice if any common characteristics begin to emerge from either kind of passage. Some passages sound concluding at the beginning, but the materials change to effect a transition purpose by the time the passage ends. As you listen to such a passage, your response will probably change as it progresses, or your decision may be made in retrospect. Each set of excerpts will continue to be out of context and possibly out of order.

Ex. 1-3. Mozart: Sonata in F. Major, K. 533/499, III (tempo, allegretto).

Ex. 1-4. Brahms: Ballade, Op. 118, No. 3 (tempo, allegro energico).

Ex. 1-5. Shostakovich: 24 Präludien, Op. 34, No. 10. Peters Edition No. 4773A. Reprint permission granted by the publisher. (Tempo, moderato non troppo, ♩ = 108.)

5a.

Ex. 1-6. Hindemith: Piano Sonata No. 2, III (tempo, ♩=100-108)

6 a.

6 b.

Langsam (♪bis 60)

Ex. 1-6. (Continued)

6 c.

Several additional characteristics of transitions may have been noted in some of the preceding excerpts: a tonal instability and an "interruption" process that created an unstable or restless sound.

Expectations about musical materials and purpose could be expanded with the knowledge that the passages in which important musical ideas are stated will be presented through a succession of musical phrases. The next group of musical excerpts will consist solely of thematic sounding materials. Listen to just the beginning of each excerpt to become familiar with the tempo, meter, and beginning key, which will be stated with the title of the composition. Then listen two or more times to the excerpt cited and determine the number of phrases included in each musical idea. Phrases are likely to be at least four measures long, and they sometimes have a pause in the middle of the phrase. When you have listened sufficiently to determine the number of phrases in the excerpt, check your analysis with the phrasing indicated in the appendix example listed, in which the number of phrases will be shown in diagram form.

Excerpts for Aural Analysis of Phrasing

Appendix Example

1. Chopin: Mazurka, Op. 7, No. 2.   Ex. 6-17
   Measures 1-16, repeated; tempo,
   vivo, ma non troppo; meter, 3/4;
   key, A minor.

2. Chopin: Mazurka, Op. 41, No. 2.   Ex. 4-32
   Measures 1-16; tempo, andantino;
   meter, 3/4; key, E minor.

3. Mozart: Symphony in D Major   Ex. 6-19
   (Haffner), K. 385, III.
   Measures 1-8, repeated; tempo,
   moderato; meter, 3/4; key, D major.

4. Hindemith: *Ludus Tonalis*, Interludium   Ex. 4-35
   in F.
   Measures 1-8, repeated; tempo, scherzando
   (♩=96-100); meter, 2/4; f tonality.

5. Schubert: String Quartet in D Minor, III.   Ex. 6-23
   Measures 1-22, repeated; tempo,
   allegro molto; meter, 3/4; key,
   D minor.

Occasionally one of the primary musical ideas will be introduced by a passage whose materials anticipate the accompaniment of the more important musical idea or may establish tonality by sounding tonic and/or dominant harmonies without a melody line. The following examples for aural analysis will illustrate several kinds of introductory passages preceding a primary musical idea. Continue to analyze the phrasing in the latter.

Excerpts for Aural Analysis of Introductory Passages

Appendix Example

1. Chopin: Mazurka, Op. 7, No. 3
   Measures 1-24; tempo, ($\lozenge$=54);
   meter, 3/4; key, F minor.

   Ex. 4-31

2. Chopin: *Grande Valse Brilliante*,
   Op. 18.
   Measures 1-20 with 5-20 repeated;
   tempo, vivo; meter, 3/4; key, E♭ major.

   Ex. 7-13

3. Schumann: String Quartet in A Minor,
   Op. 41, No. 1, II.
   Measures 1-10; tempo, presto; meter,
   6/8; key, A minor.

   Ex. 7-18

4. Bartok: *Mikrokosmos*, No. 128.
   Measures 1-20; tempo, moderato
   ($\lozenge$=112); meter, 2/4; g tonality.

   Ex. 4-28

5. Bartok: Concerto for Orchestra, II.
   Measures 1-24; tempo, allegro scherzando
   ($\lozenge$=74); meter, 2/4; D tonality.

   Ex. 6-13

6. Prokofieff: Violin Concerto No. 2,
   Op. 63, II.
   Measures 1-18; tempo, andante assai
   ($\lozenge$=108); meter, 12/8; E♭ tonality.

   Ex. 6-20

Rarely does a composition contain only one musical idea. More often in a brief, complete work a first musical idea is followed by a second one that either ends the composition or is followed by a restatement of the first idea. The succession of first to second idea is known in formal terms as A B; should the first idea be restated at the end of the composition, this is designated as A B A. When a second musical idea is presented, it will be audible by virtue of some kind of change, possibly in melodic direction, possibly in rhythm. The length of small compositions can be further extended by the inclusion of transition and concluding materials.

Expand the analysis process for the next examples, which will be short, complete compositions. With the first several listenings, note the number of musical ideas stated or restated. In subsequent listenings, diagram the phrases within each musical idea in the manner that you have observed in the appendix examples. Use your accumulated experience of introduction, transition, and conclusion materials to locate these passages, but do not be particularly concerned about the phrasing that might be present there.

Complete Compositions for Aural Analysis of Important Melodic Ideas

	Appendix Examples
1. Beethoven: Eleven Bagatelles, Op. 119, No. 5. Tempo, risoluto; meter, 6/8; key, C minor.	Ex. 4-29
2. Schumann: *Kinderszenen*, Op. 15, No. 8. Tempo, (♩ =108); meter, 2/4; key, F major.	Ex. 4-40
3. Schumann: *Album for the Young*, Op. 68, No. 19. Tempo, non presto (♩ =130); meter, 4/4; key, A minor.	Ex. 4-42
4. Haydn: String Quartet, Op. 33, No. 2, III. Tempo, largo sostenuto; meter, 3/4; key, B♭ major.	Ex. 4-34
5. Shostakovich: 24 Pralüdien, Op. 34, No. 10. Tempo, moderato non troppo (♩ =108); meter, 2/4; c♯ tonality.	Ex. 4-43

The number of different musical ideas that a composer may present in one composition is limited, of course, but not always to two. As an additional experience in aural analysis, use the musical indices of Assignments 1 at the end of some of the succeeding chapters to aurally identify each succeeding idea and any restatements. Use the index numbers to record your analysis of the following suggested examples, which you can then check against the comparable example number in the formal diagrams of the appendix. Musical purpose and formal terminology are not the present concern; aural perception of musical ideas is.

Examples for Aural Analysis of Larger Works

Chapter	Assignment 1 Example Number
6	Ex. 6-18
6	Ex. 6-19
6	Ex. 6-14
6	Ex. 6-16
6	Ex. 6-17
6	Ex. 6-23
6	Ex. 6-24
6	Ex. 6-20
7	Ex. 7-10
7	Ex. 7-16
7	Ex. 7-18

2 ∎ variations

Stated in the extreme, composers have two alternatives: to limit and reuse musical materials in a composition, or to spin out an endless series of new ideas. With few exceptions composers have inclined toward the former alternative and have used the techniques of variation as one means of enhancing recurring materials.

The variation form is one of the oldest of the instrumental forms, dating from the early sixteenth century and continuing to the present time. Variational procedures exist not only in the variation form proper, but they are also represented in many diverse forms, a number of which will be discussed in later chapters. Variation is a creative force of such impact on the content of all musical forms that young composers of the eighteenth and nineteenth centuries were traditionally encouraged to expand their craftsmanship and imaginative powers through the writing of variation sets. Whether or not this was a useful approach to composition can only be judged by an interesting coincidence in the repertoire of today's concert stage: the solo sonatas, chamber works, and symphonies of the traditional period that are still performed and appreciated are often by composers who also have produced fine sets of variations. Most traditional sonatas, chamber works and symphonies begin with a first movement sonata form, a form in which variational techniques are essential.

Variational Techniques

To vary a musical idea is to modify or change any of its elements: pitch, duration, texture, timbre, or intensity. In order to make audible the relationship between a musical idea and its varied restatement, some of its original elements will be retained. Perhaps the most frequently varied element of a musical idea is its pitch, more particularly its melody or harmony.

Variational Techniques Using Pitch

Melodic variants exist in great profusion. Typically, composers of the classic period were inclined toward melodic embellishments that contained much figural and scalar writing, the type of line that derives much of its contour from nonharmonicism and arpeggiation. Ex. 2-1 represents some of the melodic variants present in a theme with variations that Mozart used for the first movement of a keyboard sonata.

Ex. 2-1a. Mozart: Sonata in A Major, K. 331, I, Theme (partial). The first two phrases of the theme are shown with the essential contour indicated by the circled notes.

In variation 1 the melody is altered by neighboring and passing tones in an off-beat rhythm. The skeletal form of the original accompaniment is present in the first phrase, but it is changed to accompany the change of variational procedure used with the second phrase.

Ex. 2-1b. Variation 1.

The second variation also makes use of passing tones to modify the melodic contour of the theme. Increased motion of the bass pattern furnishes more of the musical energy than is generated by the melody line. In this variation, as in variation 1, the basic melodic contour of the theme is still very audible. Another similarity between this variation and the preceding one is the change of variational procedure with the second phrase. A certain synthesis occurs when the arpeggiation of the accompaniment to phrase 1 is combined with the passing tone embellishment to form phrase 2.

Ex. 2-lc. Variation 2.

Ex. 2-1c. (Continued)

In a secondary fashion variation 1 and more particularly variation 2 have also incorporated a slight change of texture from the chordal style of the theme to the style of a single line melody with arpeggiated bass. Variation 3 continues the two voice texture with a change of tonality as a further dimension of pitch variation. A limited amount of chromaticism results from the changing tone contours of measures 55 and 56 and from the altered, lower neighbor tones.

Ex. 2-ld. Variation 3.

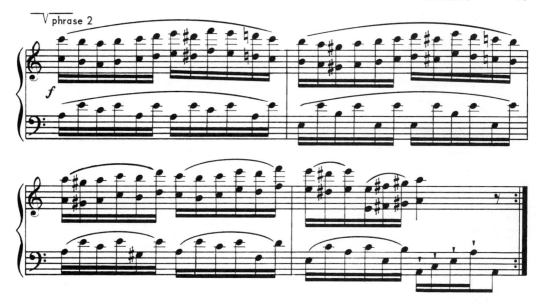

Melodic variational techniques such as those illustrated by Ex. 2-1 are common in classical forms other than the variation form proper. The large ternary form, which is discussed in chapter 4, consists of a first musical idea or theme, a departure theme, and a return to the first theme. In Ex. 2-2 the large ternary form is extended by additional repetition of both the departure theme and the restated first theme, and variational techniques are applied to several of the repetitions.

Ex. 2-2. Haydn: Sonata in E Major (Peters No. 40), III.

First thematic idea

Tempo di Menuetto

Ex. 2-2. (Continued)

A much later example of melodic variation in a non-variational form is shown in Ex. 2-3. The first eight measures of the recurring first theme are melodically varied in much the same scalar and nonharmonic fashion as certain variants in the two preceding examples. Twentieth century emphasis on duration, texture, and intensity, however, add dimensions that are not usually present in variants of the classic period.

Ex. 2-3. Bartok: *Mikrokosmos*, No. 128.

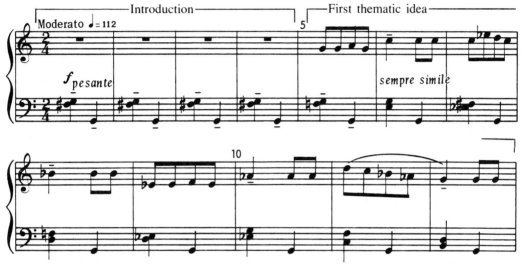

Recurrence of first thematic idea

Another facet of pitch variation concerns the harmony supporting a melodic idea. As a variation technique the substitution of harmonic progression can occur with occasional chords of a supporting progression or, more rarely, it can provide the primary modification of a total variation. Ex. 2-4 illustrates the latter technique.

Ex. 2-4. Beethoven: String Quartet, Op. 18, No. 5, III.

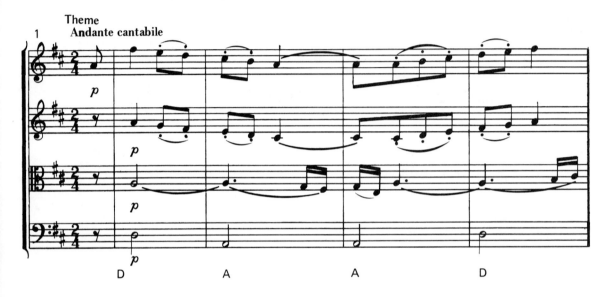

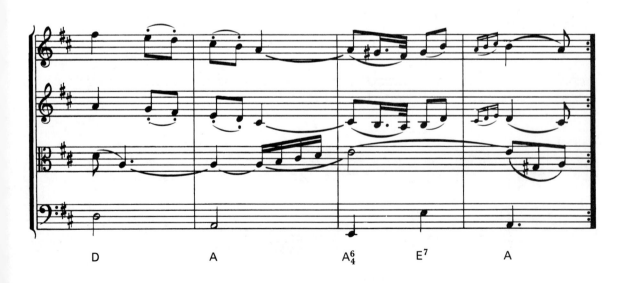

The set of variations from which Ex. 2-4 is taken contains an illustration of a melodic variation technique that became increasingly frequent from the time of Beethoven onward: the technique of motive fragmentation and transformation. The first four notes of the theme shown in Ex. 2-4 are taken out of the melodic context in which they appear, and they are modified and extended into a two measure motive that acts as the basis of variation 1. The texture changes from the four voice homophony in which the theme is set to an imitative texture of two, three, and then four lines.

Ex. 2-5. Variation 1 of the theme in Ex. 2-4.

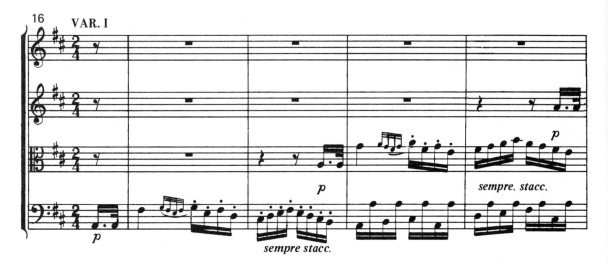

Ex. 2-5. (Continued)

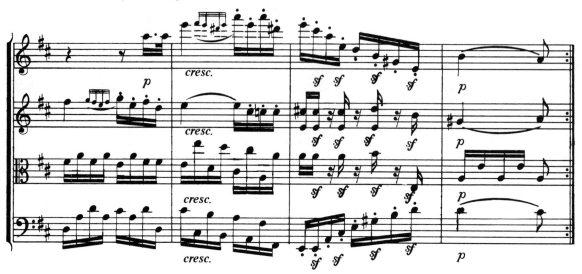

A more extended use of motivic fragmentation and transformation appears in Schumann's *Symphonic Etudes.* Variation sets of the romantic period made considerable use of the technique of creating variations from characteristic fragments of the theme. In Ex. 2-6 the first descending intervals of the theme act as a springboard for seven of the variations, three of which also make prominent use of imitation.

Ex. 2-6. Schumann: Symphonic Etudes, Op. 13.

Ex. 2-6. (Continued)

Ex. 2-6. (Continued)

Motivic fragmentation and transformation have played an extremely important role in another large instrumental form. The sonata allegro form is discussed in chapter 8, but for present purposes it can be defined as a large structure that is divided into three main sections. The first section states musical materials; the middle section manipulates and develops the musical materials of the first section, and the last section restates the original materials of section one. Fragments taken from first section materials are one of the primary sources for the middle section, and in the act of developing the fragments, the composer often transforms them. Ex. 2-7 illustrates this melodic variation technique in a work by Bartok, a composer whose writing exemplifies motivic transformation. The first developed fragment in measures 179-182 is transformed rhythmically and deletes a note. This can also be interpreted as a derivative from measure 7 alone in which the last note is treated with octave displacement. The origin of the passage in measures 190-193 is most clearly seen in measure 191. The original contour of measure 7-8 is transformed with a change of rhythmic pattern and an added note. This grows into further transformations in the following two measures, illustrating one of the differences between the techniques of variation and transformation. The act of varying a melodic motive does not conceal the origin; often transformation does so, and it can act as a process of growth to motivic forms that are quite different than their source. The last derived fragment of measures 204-206 is not truly transformed but is simply varied by inversion.

Ex. 2-7. Bartok: Violin Concerto No. 2, I.

First thematic idea from the beginning section of a sonata allegro form:

Ex. 2-7. (Continued)

Fragments of the first melodic idea developed in the middle section of a sonata allegro form:

Transformation has also been useful in the cyclic treatment of motives or themes, a practice that existed to some degree in the sixteenth and seventeenth centuries but that is more commonly associated with late nineteenth century practices. Cyclic treatment is the use of a motive or theme in more than one movement of a multimovement work, and the material is often transformed as it reappears. To cite a few examples, Berlioz used cyclic techniques in his *Symphony Fantastique*, Franck in his D Minor Symphony and D Major String Quartet, Debussy in his only string quartet, and Richard Strauss used the cyclic principle in his one-movement symphonic poem, "Till Eulenspiegel." As a twentieth century example Bartok's Violin Concerto No. 2 represents cyclic treatment through the use of transformed first movement themes in the last movement. Ex. 2-8 can be compared to the theme of Ex. 2-7 to note the rhythmic and melodic transformations.

Ex. 2-8. Bartok: Violin Concerto No. 2, III.

Variational techniques using duration

Duration is almost automatically affected by melodic variation. The addition of notes to a melodic contour without changing its temporal length will mean that note values are shortened and the melodic rhythm is hastened. In a broader sense, duration represents meter, tempo, and accent as well as note values. Ex. 2-6 illustrates a metrical change from the theme into variation 1. The sequence of metrical markings in consecutive variations of the Schumann *Symphonic Etudes* appears in the following order: Theme, ♩=52; Etudes I, ♩=72; II, ♪=72; III, ♩=63; IV, ♩=132; V, ♩.=108; VI, ♩=60; VII, ♩=96; VIII, ♩=80; IX, ♪=116; X, ♩=92; XI, ♩=66; and XII, ♩=66. Duration is obviously very much a variational factor in this composition, particularly as the beat note in each variation will be divided in a way that is characteristic of that particular variation.

In his Octet for Wind Instruments, Stravinsky has written a second movement theme with variations in which the factors of duration are extremely influential as modifying forces. The tempo of each variation changes from that of the preceding one, and, after variation 1 (A), the meter changes with each successive variation. The fluctuating durational plan is partly due to the unusual large structure of the movement, which is as follows: theme, variation 1 (A), variation 2 (B), variation 1 (A), variation 3 (C), variation 4 (D), variation 1 (A), variation 5 (E). Each time that variation 1 occurs, there is an aural impression of increased rhythmic activity although the tempo marking may be actually slower. The grouping of the notes and the smaller note values of variation 1 characterize it as a passage of rhythmic activity.

Ex. 2-9, ab. Stravinsky: Octet for Wind Instruments, II.

(a) Theme

(b) Variation 1 (A).

The first rhythmic modification of thematic patterns occurs in variation 2 (B) where the change of note values is also combined with a metrical and tempo change. Thus three of the four durational factors affect the variation.

Ex. 2-9c. Variation 2 (B).

The tempo of variation 3 (C) grows out of the metronomic marking of the second variation, and the internal influence of duration on this variant is one of accent. Pitted as it is against a triple background in the accompaniment, the duple meter of the varied theme is heightened by the accentuation. The thematic meter later changes to three, but the accent is still at odds with the accent of the accompaniment.

Ex. 2-9d. Variation 3 (C).

Ex. 2-9d. (Continued)

Tempo more than doubles from variation 3 to variation 4 (D), but the change is smoothly bridged here, as it has been in each successive variation except the recurring variation 1.

Ex. 2-9e. Variation 4 (D).

introduction measures

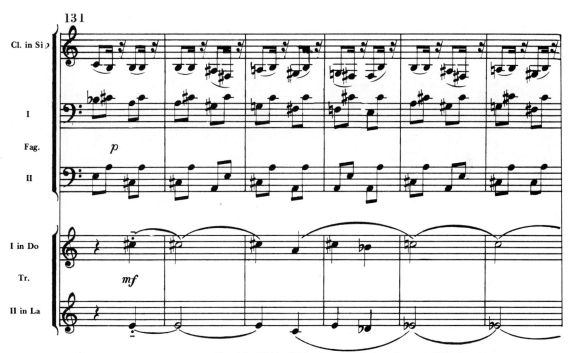

Ex. 2-9 should be studied in full, aurally and with score, as it represents an outstanding example of a twentieth century variation form.

Duration as a variational technique in forms other than the theme with variation is illustrated by Ex. 2-10. Traditional literature is more likely to capitalize on changes of notational value, tempo, and accent than on changes of meter. The third movement of Brahms' Symphony No. 2 is a large rondo, another form that is discussed in a later chapter. The rondo structure is characterized by the alternation of a first theme with other themes, and it is a form that makes good use of variational techniques to modify the recurrence of the first theme. Rhythmic change is used unexpectedly in Ex. 2-10, however, to fashion a second theme from the materials of the first theme rather than to modify recurrence of themes. If Theme II at measures 33-40 is sung or played with the rhythm of the first eight measures of Theme I, the two themes will sound almost identical. A further paraphrase of the original material appears in the cello line of measures 172-175 as part of the recurrence of a modified Theme II.

Ex. 2-10. Brahms: Symphony No. 2 in D Major, Op. 73, III.

Theme II

Presto ma non assai (♩ = ♪)

Part of recurring Theme II

Variational Techniques Using Texture

Texture is here interpreted as the broad distinction between homophonic and polyphonic writing, with certain limited subdivisions in each large category. This is only one of the several current interpretations of the term, but it will serve to distinguish this facet of the variational procedures.

Most themes of a variation form are simple melodies with chordal accompaniment, so they are generally homophonic (harmonic) in texture. The most obvious textural variant is presentation of the thematic materials in some context of imitative statement and answer, a polyphonic (contrapuntal) texture. To the reader who is not familiar with all contrapuntal terms, some simple definitions are listed below:

1. Imitation is a successive statement of a musical idea, each time in a different voice (instrumental line).

2. Canonic imitation is an overlapping of imitative entries.

3. Dialogue is a term to describe the alternating statement of a short musical idea by two voices.

The above definitions are descriptive rather than technical, but they will serve present purposes.

Exs. 2-11 and 2-12 respectively illustrate excerpts from a traditional and a twentieth century set of variations. Of the thirty-three variations that constitute the entire set of Ex. 2-11, almost a third of them are fashioned in a polyphonic texture of some kind. The theme is vertically conceived and very harmonic in style, so the variations with textural changes are a striking contrast. The polyphonic technique that affects each illustrative variation is cited in place.

Ex. 2-11. Beethoven: 33 Variations on a Theme by Diabelli, Op. 120.

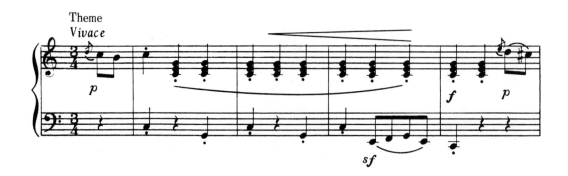

Var. 6
Canonic imitation
Allegro ma non troppo e serioso

Var. 9
dialogue
Allegro pesante e risoluto

Var. 19
Canonic imitation
Presto

Ex. 2-11. (Continued)

Var. 24
Imitation

The third variation of Ex. 2-12 uses a much freer type of canonic imitation than does Ex. 2-11. Nevertheless, the staggered entries and similar lines will create the aural effect of canonic imitation.

Ex. 2-12. From Piano Sonata No. 3, Movement I, by Norman Dello Joio.

Tema

Var. III

The middle, or development, section of the sonata allegro form offers many examples of variation by textural change. Ex. 2-13 illustrates a passage in the development section that uses eight measures of imitation followed by ten measures of dialogue. Musical energy begins to accumulate as the imitative entries grow closer.

Ex. 2-13. Beethoven: Sonata in D Major, Op. 28, I.

First thematic idea of a sonata allegro form

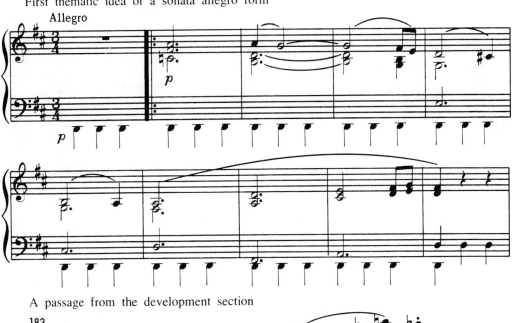

A passage from the development section

Ex. 2-13. (Continued)

Variational Techniques Using Timbre

In discussing instrumental forms, variation in timbre must obviously rely on changes in instrumentation or, in some cases instrumental range. Changes in the tone color of a stated musical idea are extremely effective, and as composers of the nineteenth and twentieth centuries explored the furthest limits of the orchestra as a performing medium, the use of timbre as a variational technique expanded. A notable variation set of the twentieth century appears as the second movement of the Bartok Violin Concerto No. 2. The theme of the variations is a very lovely and poignant melody in the solo violin, accompanied by strings, harp, and timpani. The plan of orchestral accompaniment proceeds along the same line with each variation: the beginning accompaniment is thin and limited to a few instruments; midway through each variation the texture is thickened by other instruments in the same orchestral section which began the variation. With the exception of the horns, which are often scored with winds, no brass instruments are used. Through most of the variations the orchestral instruments function in either an accompaniment or a punctuation role, and there is very little use of countermelody or doubled solo melody. Variation 6 is an exception. The string section doubles the line of the solo or carries the theme as the solo violin performs a countermelody. At the end of the movement the solo violin states the theme with less adornment than the original statement, the orchestration thins to beginning proportions, and the movement concludes at the lowest possible level of intensity. Changes in intensity are associated with changes of timbre and of style, and contribute to the effectiveness of the composition.

It is of particular importance that the full score of Ex. 2-14 be heard and seen, as timbre is one of the more difficult of the musical elements to hear with the ''inner ear.''

Ex. 2-14. Bartok: Violin Concerto No. 2, II.

Ex. 2-14. (Continued)

Ex. 2-14. (Continued)

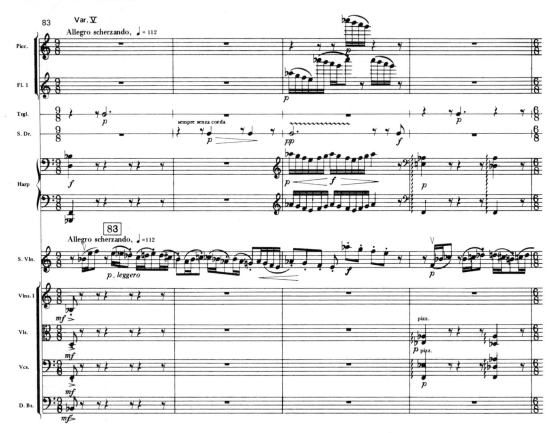

* with wooden sticks, to be played at the edge of the head   ** at the edge of the head

Var. VII (Theme)

Examples of timbre as a variational technique in forms other than the variation form proper can be found in almost any twentieth century work that involves restatement of ideas and that is written for instrumental groups. For example, the first movement of the Prokofieff Symphony No. 5 introduces the beginning theme with flutes and bassoons marked *piano* and restates it at measure 165 with a *fortissimo* brass section.

Variational Techniques Using Intensity

This element of music has long been exploited as both a distinguishing and a modifying factor. In the eighteenth century the Mannheim symphonists made an important contribution to the expressiveness of music with their use of dynamic extremities and their sudden contrasts of *forte* and *piano*.

As a variational factor, intensity usually supports other musical elements rather than acting as an independent catalyst for change. Some of the variations of the set illustrated again in Ex. 2-15 show an interrelatedness of tempo, style, and dynamics. In the first variation of Beethoven's Diabelli Variations, Op. 120, the dynamic indications of *forte* and *sforzando* are very appropriate to the angular chordal style and the march-like character of the variation. As can be noted, the theme of this set of variations begins in a staccato style marked *piano* and ends at a dynamic level of *forte,* so its dynamic contrast with the first variation is not at the point where they meet but between the beginnings of each. The second variation also seems to have an appropriate relationship between the dynamic level and the style, and it does furnish an immediate dynamic contrast to variation 1 which ends at the level of *forte* where it began. The seventh variation shows a compatibility of intensity and style that is similar to that of the first variation, and again it appears that intensity is supportive of other musical elements. In variation 8, however, the actual effect of intensity on style is clearly demonstrated. The style of the eighth variation could be adapted to either a *forte* or *piano,* and the fact that *piano* is marked seems to indicate that contrast of intensity between consecutive variations is important and perhaps is even part of the overall plan.

Ex. 2-15. Beethoven: 33 Variations on a Theme by Diabelli, Op. 120.

Ex. 2-15. (Continued)

Var. I
Alla Marcia maestoso

Var. II
Poco allegro

Var. VII

Un poco più allegro

Var. VIII

Poco vivace

sempre legato

The String Quartet No. 1 of Debussy provides several examples of the use of intensity to modify the character of a restated musical idea. The composition is cyclic, and the cyclic motive appears in the first, second and fourth movements. Changes in pitch, duration, texture, timbre, and intensity all effect the motivic transformations, some of which are illustrated in Ex. 2-16.

Ex. 2-16. Debussy: String Quartet No. 1, Op. 10.

First movement
cyclic motive

Ex. 2-16. (Continued)

Second movement

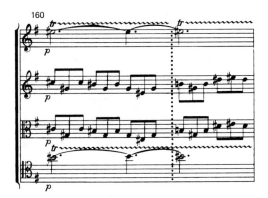

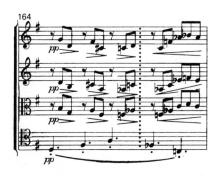

Fourth movement

Ex. 2-16. (Continued)

Variation Forms

Nearly all compositions in a variation form could be placed in one of two broad categories: the variation form in which an initial melody or harmony is repeated without essential changes throughout the set, or the variation form in which the initial melody and other associated elements are treated with modification throughout the set. Compositions in the first category are either called *cantus firmus* variations because of the fixed element or *continuous* variations because of the relative absence of pause between individual variations. Compositions in the second category are variably named *independent* or *sectional* variations.

Sets of variations appear as independent compositions or they may form a movement or section of a multimovement work. The writing of variations has had such a universal appeal that virtually every composer has written at least one work in the variation form. The form itself has an inherent quality of unity and variety, and it permits a composer to develop a single musical thought with all the ingenuity and creativity that he possesses. Thus the form holds the aesthetic potentials of balance and of risk, two vistas that have always had an allure to creative people.

Variation Forms with a Fixed Melody or Harmony

The variation form with a fixed melody has come to be considered a *passacaglia,* although when baroque composers wrote a variation set with either fixed melody or harmony, their designated name for the work might be either *passacaglia* or *chaconne.* The present interpretation of the chaconne is a composition where a harmonic progression is repeated without essential change or interruption throughout the set of variations.

The melodic theme of a passacaglia ranges from four to eight measures in length, it is presented in an unaccompanied form in the bass, and it remains in the bass line much of the time. Traditionally the mode was minor and the meter was triple. The texture through which the continuous theme sounds is more often contrapuntal than it is harmonic, possibly because the effect of forward motion must be generated by accompanying voices, and linear writing is tantamount to motion. At times the bass melody is moved to an upper voice; occasionally it is ornamented without changing its basic contour or accent. One of the most magnificent of the baroque passacaglias is from Bach's *C Minor Passacaglia and Fugue* for organ, excerpts of which appear in Ex. 2-17.

Ex. 2-17. J.S. Bach: Passacaglia for Organ in C Minor.

Ex. 2-17. (Continued)

Var. 2

Var. 5

Var. 12

The fixed bass melody is used in a different context in the finale of Brahms' *Haydn Variations*. The five bar melody acts as a ground bass above which a series of miniature variations are presented. Forward momentum is assisted by the elision of the cadence which overlaps the beginning of each next statement of the ground bass. Despite the duple meter and major mode, there is much about this excerpt that resembles the passacaglia form. The melody is stated without interruption until measure 85 of the finale and much of the texture is polyphonic.

Occasionally the ground bass is ornamented without any alteration of the essential contour, and several statements of the melody appear in upper voices. Toward the end of the finale, the bass melody is abandoned, and the original theme returns.

Ex. 2-18. Brahms: Variations on a Theme by Haydn, Op. 56 b.

Ex. 2-18. (Continued)

*Measure numbers are consecutive from the beginning of the finale.

In the last fifty years composers have again begun to write in the passacaglia form, and several of the twentieth century passacaglias are very much like the Bach excerpt of Ex. 2-17. A twentieth century passacaglia that is strikingly like the Baroque model is in the final section of Barber's First Symphony. The typical characteristics of a minor melody, a triple meter, and an imitative texture are all present in the Barber passacaglia.

In the fashion of the Baroque composers, Vaughan Williams has named the last movement of his Symphony No. 5 a passacaglia, which is something of a misnomer. Using extremely ingenious means the composer has created the aural effect of a passacaglia, when in reality only the first forty-one bars use the ground melody in a consistently recurring pattern. At measure 8 the violins introduce above the bass melody a melodic phrase that will act interchangeably or in conjunction with the bass melody throughout the entire composition. In spite of real differences of direction and contour, these two melodies have enough in common that the ear eventually accepts the presence of either one as a ground melody. The characteristic rhythm of ♩ ♪♩ ♩ appears in the fifth measure of each melody; the lengths differ by one measure, but the effect of the bass melody is that of a six bar phrase that goes through an evaded cadence in measure 7 and that progresses to an elided authentic cadence in measure 7-8. The violin phrase is actually a six bar melody with an elided cadence into a seventh bar. From measure 42 to the end of the composition, transformed derivatives of both melodies are contrapuntally developed in a series of small, free variations. The two melodies and the broad structural plan of melodic materials are shown in Ex. 2-19 as a guide to a preliminary aural analysis of the composition.

Ex. 2-19. Vaughan Williams: Symphony No. 5 in D Major, IV.

Ex. 2.19. (Continued)

Structural Plan of Melodic Materials

Passacaglia section
mm. 1 - - - - - - - - - 8 - - - - - - - - - 14 - - - - - - - - - - 28 - - - - - - - - - - 41
                     melodic phrase 1   melodic phrase 1
     bass (ground) melody---

Development of both melodies in a series of small variations.
mm. 42-67
    Transformed fragments of the ground melody and phrase 1.

mm. 68-90, Allegro (one in a bar) $\downarrow$. = 60
    Phrase 1 which has been transformed durationally.

mm. 91-113
    Transformed fragments of the ground melody.

mm. 114-152, Tempo primo (moderato) (3 beats in a bar)
    Transformed fragments of phrase 1 and the ground melody.

mm. 153-185
    Transformation of the ground melody with pitch (mode): phrase 1 transformation
    is associated in a subordinate capacity.

mm. 185--199 ---
    Motive of the ground melody;   transformed motive of phrase 1;
207 ---216.
    motive of the ground melody.

mm. 217-236, Tempo del Preludio
    Skeletal outline of the ground motive combined with a transformed motive of
    phrase 1.

mm. 236, Final measure
    Closing section using phrase 1.

Example 2-20 illustrates a variation form that is based on a fixed harmonic progression. Bach's Chaconne in D Minor for unaccompanied violin is a classic example that demonstrates an incredible wealth of variational techniques. The creative abundance is particularly astonishing under the circumstances of the medium of solo violin and by the fact that the more than 250 measures of the chaconne are divided into variations that are usually four measures in length. The work is continuous, and most of the harmonic substitutions that occur are either added to embellish the original progressions of the harmonic theme or are substitutions of a chord that has a comparable function to the chord that is replaced. This work is readily available in current anthology form so the limited excerpts shown in Ex. 2-20 are intended to illustrate only two of the many facets of the form: the type of harmonic substitutions that replace chords of the fixed harmonic progression and the manner in which many of the four bar variations evolve out of the material of the preceding four bars. This last is a common technique in variation forms whose thematic basis is brief.

Ex. 2-20. J.S. Bach: Chaconne from Partita No. II in D Minor for Unaccompanied Violin.

Part of the reason that harmonic substitutions do not appreciably disturb the original harmonic progression stems from the harmonic ambiguity of this type of writing. For example, most of the diminished triads imply incomplete dominant seventh sounds to many listeners, and patterns such as the one in measure 39 can imply several different harmonic progressions.

Although the chaconne as a variation form was not generally used by composers of the eighteenth and nineteenth centuries, there are some interesting similarities between the Bach chaconne and a set of variations by Beethoven. In Ex. 2-21 it can be noted that the harmonic substitutions in the first several variations are no more extensive than those in the Bach chaconne. Also the "variation on a variation" principle illustrated in Ex. 2-20 is present again in Ex. 2-21.

Ex. 2-21. Beethoven: 32 Variations for Piano.

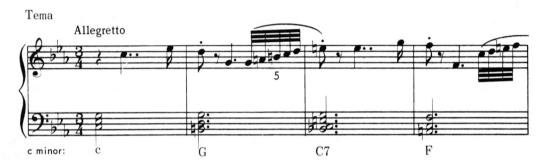

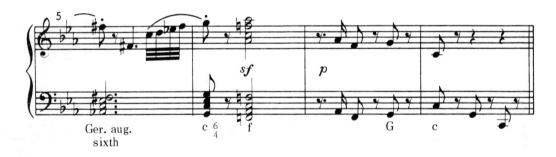

F   Ger. aug. $c^{\,6}_{\,4}$ f
      sixth

15

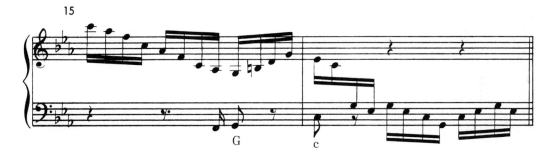

G   c

Var. II

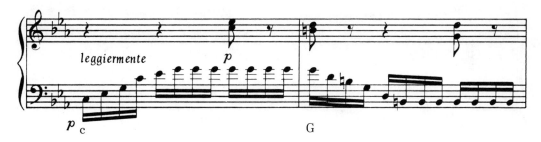

leggiermente

c   G

20

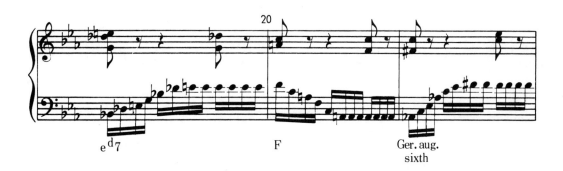

$e^{\,d}7$ F   Ger. aug.
                                                sixth

Ex. 2-21. (Continued)

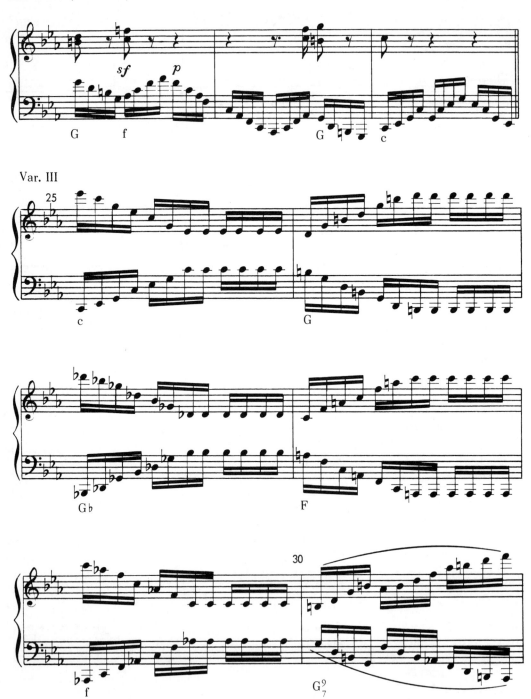

c

Variation Forms with Modification of the Melody

Most of the variation sets of the eighteenth and nineteenth centuries can be placed in the second broad category which is characterized by modifications of the initial melody and other associated elements. Variations of the classical period are likely to adhere rather faithfully to the entire melody of the theme, however extensive the modifications might be; variations of the nineteenth century are more often constructed from characteristic fragments of the theme that are transformed in different ways to form the set. In the latter circumstances the basic structure of the theme will prevail as the unifying factor throughout the consecutive variations.

Twentieth century composers who have written in the variation form have used any and all of the techniques of preceding centuries. Their contributions to the variation forms have been primarily in the areas of greater thematic transformation, greater exploitation of duration and timbre, and more distant extensions of tonality.

Analysis Models

The theme of the ten variations of Ex. 2-22 is an aria taken by Mozart from Gluck's opera *Die Pilger von Mekka*. The three phrases of the theme form a pattern of statement (phrase 1), departure (phrase 2), and return (phrase 3), and the simplicity of thematic style adapts well to variational techniques.

The variation set is fashioned primarily from the elements of pitch. Melody, harmony, and the bass line act in turn as the fixed, or partially fixed, elements of each variation, and they also serve as the basis of different variants. Duration enters into the variational process in two ways: melodic embellishment of the theme always changes its melodic rhythm; and there are some changes in harmonic rhythm and in the actual meter. The use of imitative patterns in variations 2,4,6 and 8 changes the homophonic texture of the theme, and a change of dynamic relationships in the ninth variation modifies intensity. Of the five basic elements of music, only timbre does not contribute to the variational processes in Ex. 2-22.

Ex. 2-22a. Mozart: 10 Variations on an Air of Gluck, K. 455, Theme.

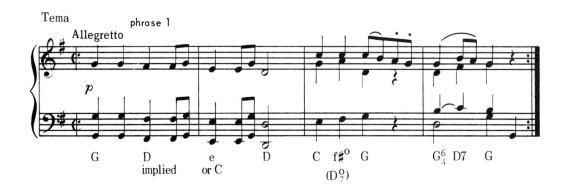

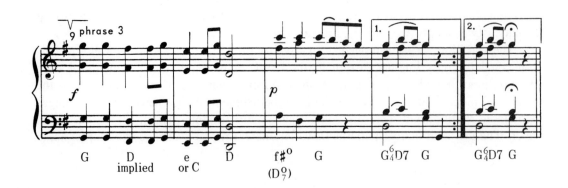

In the first variation the harmonic progression acts as a fixed element, and the bass line is partially fixed. Neighbor tones, passing tones, and appoggiaturas create the figural variation of the melody whose basic contour alternates between the original contour of the theme and an arpeggiation of the harmony. A slight growth pattern is shown in phrase 3 which incorporates the broken octave with the figural embellishment.

Ex. 2-22b. Variation I.

(phrase 3 will be shown only when it differs from phrase 1)

The harmony of variation 2 continues as a fixed element, and the melody is partially fixed. The variational techniques applied to the bass line are directly derived from the melodic embellishments of variation 1.

Phrase 2 of this variation introduces a textural change from the pure homophony of the theme. Between the bass and melody of alternating measures there is established a free imitation of sorts. The bass contour of measure 29 is answered by a modified and inverted form in the melody of measure 30.

Ex. 2-22c. Variation 2.

In variation 3 the harmony and bass are only partially fixed, and the melodic variant incorporates a new figure that is introduced as an ornamented suspension in measure 38 and that becomes a freely-approached changing tone figure in phrase 2. Between them the two lower lines simulate the contour of the theme, although certain of the thematic pitches are touched by the upper line, as shown by the circled notes.

Ex. 2-22d. Variation 3.

Variation 4 begins as though the bass and the harmony will be fixed elements. The repetition of phrase 1, however, initiates a harmonic substitution of a secondary dominant between the two implied C chords of measures 54 and 55, and comparable harmonic substitutions occur in the second and third phrases. The harmonic ambiguity of the first chord in measure 2 of the theme allows the substitution of different dominant sounds in the harmony preceding this beat. There is a kind of contrapuntal dialogue established by the upper and lower voices at the beginning of the variation, and the contour of the theme is fairly evident in the first phrase. The second phrase forms an expanding wedge between outer voices, but the thematic contour is absent.

Ex. 2-22e. Variation 4.

Change of mode in variation 5 triggers additional harmonic substitutions. This often occurs when there are altered chord progressions in a variation theme of major mode, as all of Mozart's fifteen variation sets are keyed. A harmonic progression of secondary dominants in a major key is not usually as successful when transposed into the parallel minor mode, and many composers later than Mozart chose to substitute harmonies under such circumstances. Except for a few chromatic passing tones in the bass, the harmonic progression of phrase 1 is a literal transposition into the parallel minor key. Phrase 2, however, substitutes tonic and dominant harmonies for the original altered chord progression, and the phrase sounds very much like phrase 1 with the voices switched. Possibly because of the similarity of phrases 1 and 2, phrase 3 is a rhythmically modified return of the first phrase.

Ex. 2-22f. Variation 5.

Ex. 2-22f. (Continued)

For the first time since the statement of the theme, the first phrase is stated clearly and without embellishment in variation 6. An inner voice states the phrase; the upper voice states the phrase repetition. The associated trill serves a more functional purpose in phrase 2, which replicates in the lower voices the rhythm, but not the pitches, of the phrase. The line of each half of phrase 2 originally spanned an octave, respectively from e^1 to e^2 and from d^1 to d^2. Association of the rhythmic pattern with the trilled e^2 and d^2 creates an aural effect that sounds curiously like the original phrase 2. In the recurrences of phrase 2, voices are switched as they were in the repetition of phrase 1, and a touch of chromaticism in the upper line anticipates the chromatic embellishment of phrase 3 as it recurs.

Ex. 2-22g. Variation 6.

Ex. 2-22g. (Continued)

Variation 7 is a fine blend of variational techniques that accumulate successively. Phrase 1 states the melody line with harmonic substitutes that accelerate the harmonic rhythm of the first half of the phrase. A suspension figure ornaments the second half of phrase 1, and this too will be carried forward. Only the prominent pitches of phrase 2 are present, and the variational technique is that of imitation (statement and answer in another voice). In phrase 3 the staccato-legato line of phrase 2 accompanies the melodic line, and the eighth note motion of the lower line combined with the suspensions of the upper line creates an aural effect of an even greater acceleration of harmonic rhythm than existed in phrase 1.

Ex. 2-22h. Variation 7.

Phrases 2 and 3 are restated with voices switched.

Imitation is again an important technique in variation 8. The harmonic progression remains absolutely fixed until the recurrence of phrase 3. Here the cadential goal is evaded, and a passage much like a cadenza follows. The long dominant harmony at the end has an effect of slowing the brisk rhythm of variation 8 and preparing for the change of tempo in variation 9.

Ex. 2-22i. Variation 8.

Ex. 2-22i. (Continued)

Durational change is the primary technique of variation 9. In all of the phrases the harmonic rhythm is doubled, which doubles the phrase lengths. One additional chord is added to the otherwise unchanged progression of phrase 1: in the location that is comparable to the last beat of measure 3 in the theme, a supertonic chord is inserted to fill out the measure. This does not essentially alter the progression, however, as the same chord could have been implied by the single line of the theme at this location.

The highly embellished melodic line touches on the essential notes of the thematic contour, but this is not aurally apparent at all times because of the florid line. Each time that a phrase recurs, the embellishment of its melodic line changes and becomes more ornate, until the end of the restatement of phrase 3. The melodic line then returns to a much more simple rhythm in anticipation of variation 10.

Ex. 2-22j. Variation 9.

Ex. 2-22j. (Continued)

Ex. 2-22j. (Continued)

Ex. 2-22j. (Continued)

Variation 10 returns to a style which is so relatively simple that the theme is very audible despite the changes. Duration again affects the variation but in a completely opposite fashion than the durational modification of variation 9. The meter signature changes to triple meter and the tempo changes from adagio to allegro. The contrast is so great that variation 10 has the effect of a diminutive version of the theme, separated as it is from the beginning allegretto.

Melodic line, harmonic progression, and bass line are quite faithful reproductions of these elements in the theme until the recurrence of phrase 3. As in variation 8, the cadential goal here is evaded, and phrase 3 is extended by an imitative pattern in the bass. This is followed by a passage that sounds very much like an orchestral preparation for the solo cadenza of a concerto, even to ending on the traditional tonic six-four chord under a fermata. A short cadenza does indeed follow. One needs to recall that Mozart wrote variations and concertos throughout all of his short career. A passage such as this might seem strange and out of place in a variation set by Beethoven or Brahms, but in this context and from this composer, the passage somehow seems perfectly appropriate.

Measure 268 to the end constitutes a closing or final section that quite typically ends a set of variations. In the first part of the finale a diminutive form of the beginning motive is developed through imitation, repetition, and sequence. The allegretto marks the second subdivision of the finale, and one final, clear statement of the first thematic phrase leads into repeated statements of the cadence.

Ex. 2-22k. Variation 10 and finale.

Ex. 2-22k. (Continued)

Ex. 2-22k. (Continued)

Ex. 2-22k. (Continued)

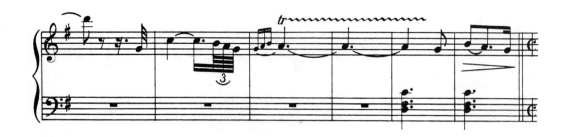

section 2
Allegretto

Ex. 2-22k. (Continued)

Twentieth century extension of duration as a variational factor is represented by Stravinsky's Octet for Wind Instruments, Ex. 2-9, which also extends formal process and tonality. Extensions of timbre and tonality as variational factors are represented by the second movement of Bartok's Violin Concerto no. 2, Ex. 2-14. Neither composition, however, represents serial composition[1] which is uniquely twentieth century in character and which is integrally bound to the variation process. Ex. 2-23 is not a serial composition but it employs many of the serial techniques: inversion and retrograde of motives, transposition, a texture that is often transparent and pointillistic, limited basic materials, and a mixture of horizontal and vertical presentation of thematic pitches. The theme itself is a miniature set of variations, as illustrated in the reduction of Ex. 2-23 b.

1. The Harvard Dictionary of Music, edited by Apel, gives a general description of serial composition, and writings by Krenek, Babbitt, and others explore this technique in depth.

Ex. 2-23a. Copland: Piano Variations, Theme.

* ◇= press down silently

Ex. 2-23b. Measures 1-11, reduction of the theme to its basic contour.

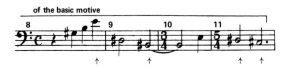

In variation 1 the theme is presented more simply than it was at the beginning. Copland has stated in his book, *What to Listen for in Music,* that it was his intention to begin with the more striking form of the theme, and he surely has done so. Changes in duration and intensity are effected in this variation as they are throughout the work. The texture changes from the almost monophonic form of the theme to a two voice texture that uses canonic imitation for the first half of variation 1. The introduction of a repeated figure in measure 16-17 is an unessential change in this variation but will become a prominent pitch variant in later variations.

Ex. 2-23c. Variation 1.

Variations 2 and 3 demonstrate characteristics that resemble the techniques of se-rial composition. The first half of the theme will be clearly heard as stated in the inner voice of the excerpt from variation 2. However, when the pointillistic fragments are combined with the inner and lower voices, two lines emerge that look very much like serial presentation of rows with the notes used in both horizontal and vertical patterns. This abstraction is shown in Ex. 2-23e following the excerpt of variation 2.

Ex. 2-23d. Variation 2.

Ex. 2-23e. Abstractions of lines from variation 2. (compare to Ex. 2-23b)

In the lower voices of the third and fourth variations there is a reversal of the two halves of the basic motive, a technique that simulates retrograde.

Ex. 2-23f. Variations 3 and 4.

The beginning of each remaining variation and the coda are shown in Ex. 2-23g as a guide to aural identification of each section. The notes of the basic motive are marked as an indication of their use in the variation. The primary focus of a first hearing can be the notes of the theme, their displacements and their repetitions. The composition is a fine illustration of motive transformation and of changes in duration, intensity, and texture.

Ex. 2-23g. Variations 5 through 20; coda.

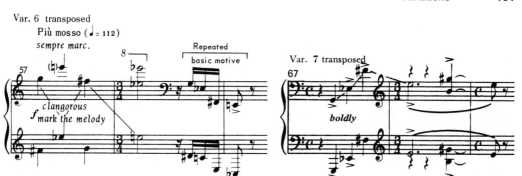

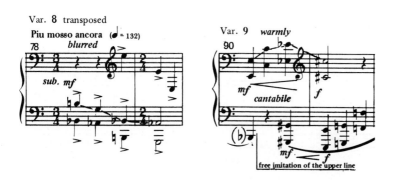

Ex. 2-23g. (Continued).

Var. 11 transposed

Var. 12 transposed

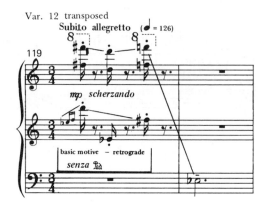

Var. 13 transposed

Var. 14

Var. 15

Var. 16

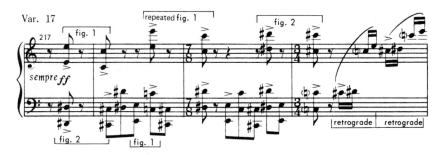

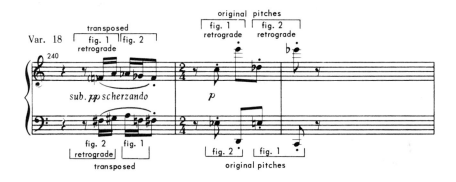

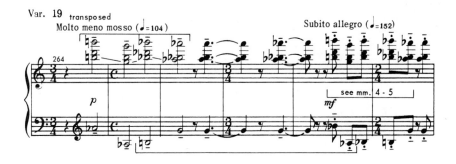

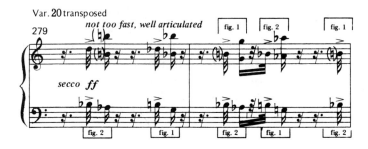

Ex. 2-23g. (Continued).

■ **Assignment 1 - *Aural analysis of form***

Using the aural analysis process begun in Chapter 1 analyze the variation set for each of the themes shown in Exs. 2-24 to 2-30. The primary focus of the analysis is to determine similarity or difference in the number and order of melodies within each variation and the number of phrases within each melody. You are to be concerned only with the comparative *structure* of each variation to its theme. Following the score of the theme as each variation is heard will assist you in recognizing when a melody has been extended, abbreviated, or omitted. If a set of variations ends with a coda, a finale, or a fugue you need not analyze these sections.

Ex. 2-24. Bartok: Violin Concerto No. 2, II. (Theme and 7 variations) *Appendix page—555*

Ex. 2-24. (Continued)

Ex. 2-25. Beethoven: String Quartet, Op. 18, No. 5, III. (Theme, 5 variations, and coda)
Appendix page—555

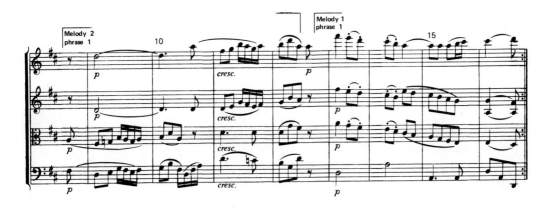

Ex. 2-26. Brahms: Variations and Fugue on a Theme by Handel, Op. 24. (Theme, 25 variations, and fugue)
Appendix page—555

Ex. 2-26. (Continued)

Ex. 2-27. Mozart: Sonata in A Major, K. 331, I. (Theme, 6 variations, and small coda)
Appendix page—555

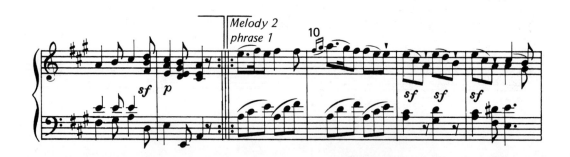

Ex. 2-28. Schubert: String Quartet in D Minor, Op. posth. II. (Theme, 5 variations, and small coda)
Appendix page—556

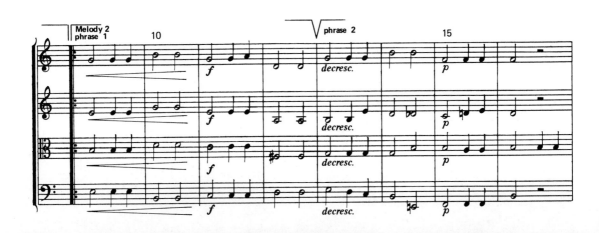

Ex. 2-28. (Continued)

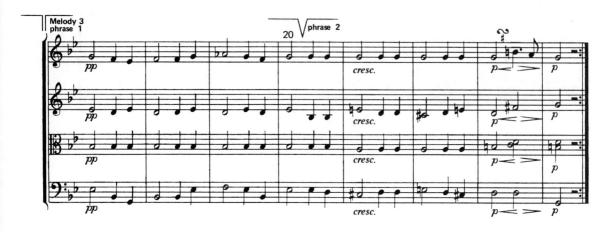

Ex. 2-29. Schumann: Symphonic Etudes, Op. 13. (Theme, 11 etudes, and finale)
Appendix page—556

Ex. 2-30. Shostakovich: String Quartet No. 1, II. (Theme and 3 variations)
    Appendix page—556

Ex. 2-30. (Continued)

■   **Assignment 2 - *Aural analysis of content***

1. After completing assignment 1 could you rank or group Exs. 2-24 to 2-30 according to the extent of melodic modification of each theme in its variations?

2. Memorize the sound of the themes in Exs. 2-27 and 2-28 in order to describe the processes of variation in each set as you hear them again. For example in the first variation of Ex. 2-28, the Schumann string quartet, the melody is taken by the second violin in a triplet pattern and this is accompanied by a violin obligato.

3. Study the recorded works of Exs. 2-9 and 2-24 to identify aurally the instrumentation of each. In the case of Ex. 2-9, the arrangement of instruments into soloists and

accompanists will be the focus; in Ex. 2-24, determine combinations of instruments that accompany the solo violin.

4. Of the traditional compositions in assignment 1, Exs. 2-26 and 2-29 make the greatest use of transformed motives of their themes. Arrange to stop the recording or tape at the end of each variation so that you can write about or discuss the source of the motive and the means of transforming it. The discussion needn't be particularly technical nor profound as long as the description of the variational techniques represents the sound of them.

As a brief summary, the variation techniques that are likely to be used in a traditional work will modify any of the following elements of the theme:

a. Pitch—melody, harmony or tonality.

b. Duration—rhythm, meter, tempo or accent. (You have already discussed changes in temporal span as part of assignment 1.)

c. Texture—involves a basic change from a homophonic texture to a polyphonic texture. There also may be changes within each category such as a change from a chordal theme to a variant that uses only melody and one accompanying voice; changes to a polyphonic texture might also expand or decrease the number of voices, or telescope imitative entries until the texture becomes canonic imitation.

d. Timbre—neither of the assigned works is orchestral so any changes here will be related to the difference in timbre of the ranges in the instruments or the special effects that can be realized with four stringed instruments.

e. Unless changes in dynamic level are abrupt and adjacent, it is difficult to hear the effect of intensity on a work. If the work is heard at the level of its broad structural plan and if note is made of successive extremes of intensity, the effect of intensity on the overall structure of the variations might be discernible.

■ **Assignment 3 - *Analysis with score***

As a preliminary step to the analysis of any of the examples for additional study it will be helpful to become aurally familiar with the theme. Most of the compositions listed are variation forms in which any of the elements, including the structure, might be modified. If a composition is based on a fixed harmonic progression or fixed bass melody, it is noted after the title.

Examples for further study

BACH
: C Minor Passacaglia for Organ; Chaconne from Partita No. 2 in D Minor for Unaccompanied Violin.

BARBER
: Excursions for the Piano.
Symphony No. 1, final section (passacaglia).

BARTOK
: *Mikrokosmos*, No. 87; Sonata for Piano, III.

BEETHOVEN
: Sonatas, Op. 14, No. 2, II; Op. 26, I; Op. 57, II; Op. 109, III.

String Quartets, Op. 74, IV; Op. 127, II; Op. 131, IV.

Symphonies, No. 3 in E♭, Op. 55, IV; No. 5 in c, Op. 67, II.

Variations, 33 on a Theme by Diabelli, Op. 120; 32 in C minor

BRAHMS
: Clarinet Quintet, Op. 115, IV.

Sonata, Op. 1, II.

String Quartet, Op. 67, IV; String Sextet, Op. 36, III.

Symphony No. 4 in e, Op. 98, IV (chaconne).

Variations on a Theme by Haydn, Op. 56.

BRITTEN
: Variations, Op. 10, on a Theme by Frank Bridge,
Young People's Guide to the Orchestra.

CARTER
: Variations for Orchestra

DELLO JOIO
: Piano Sonata No. 3, I.

Variations, chaconne, and finale (the first and last movements are also used in the outer movements of the Piano Sonata No. 3. The work is listed to note the chaconne).

FRANCK
: *Symphonic Variations* for piano and orchestra (mm. 99-246).

HAYDN
: Sonatas (Peters ed.), No. 12 in G, III; No. 13 in E♭, III; No. 28 in D, II; No. 31 in D, III; No. 36 in A, II.

String Quartets, Op. 64, No. 2, II; Op. 64, No. 4, III; Op. 74, No. 2, II; Op. 77, No. 2, III.

Symphony No. 94 in G, II.

HINDEMITH	Theme and Four Variations.
MOZART	Sonatas, K. 284 in D, III; K. 498a in B♭, II.
	String Quartets, K. 421 in d, IV; K. 464 in A, III.
	12 Variations on "Ah, vous dirai-je, Maman," K. 265.
PROKOFIEFF	Piano Concerto No. 3, II.
RAVEL	Piano Trio, III (passacaglia).
SCHÖENBERG	Variations for Orchestra, Op. 31.
SCHUBERT	Piano Quintet (Trout) in A, Op. 114, IV.
SHOSTAKOVICH	String Quartets, No. 2, IV; No. 6, III (passacaglia).
STRAVINSKY	Octet for Wind Instruments, II; Septet for Three Winds, Three Strings and Piano, II (passacaglia).
TSCHAIKOVSKY	Variation on a Rococo Theme, Op. 33, for cello and orchestra.
VAUGHAN WILLIAMS	Symphony No. 5, IV (passacaglia).

3 ∎ fugue

Part of the fascination of discovering the form and musical content of compositions is the insight gained when we relate what we find in the music with what we know about the culture in which it was created. Many cultural periods seem to progress through a cycle of rejecting a heritage, pursuing the new, and ultimately accepting heritage as a gift and not a burden. When the composers of the early Classic period rejected the Baroque techniques of polyphony in favor of the homophonic style, musical form could have ceased to evolve in the direction that it did had not certain composers recognized the value of using contrapuntal techniques in homophonic forms, particularly in the sonata form. It is true that the supremacy of homophony during the eighteenth and nineteenth centuries relegated polyphony to a subordinate position, and it was only in the twentieth century that the fugue, as one of the great formal vehicles of Baroque polyphony, was fully reinstated as a musical form. Nevertheless, the contrapuntal techniques of the Baroque period have contributed a great deal to the evolution of homophonic forms, and these techniques have enriched the compositional style of many composers of the past and present centuries.

Contrapuntal Techniques

The technique of *imitation* is fundamental to all polyphonic compositions, and it can be defined as a successive statement of a musical idea, each time in a different voice. Ex. 3-1 illustrates imitation in a Baroque fugue at tonal intervals that are typical of the key relations of that period. Several other generalizations about Baroque imitative techniques can be abstracted from Ex. 3-1, in which only the imitating voices are shown:

1. The overall tonal plan stays within a closely related circle of keys.

2. Often successive entries are either in the same keys or they show a tonic-dominant relationship. The former is called *imitation at the octave* and the latter is called *imitation at the fifth*, meaning the fifth above the immediately preceding tonality.

3. Some of the imitative entries are slightly modified versions of the preceding

117

statements. Numbering the scale steps of the primary melodic idea, which is named *subject* in a fugue, assists in noting these modifications and it can be an aid in determining tonality at various internal points.

4. Imitative entries can overlap, as is done in the statements beginning in measures 17 and 28. This technique is defined as *stretto*.

5. More than two voices can state the subject in a texture of stretto, as is illustrated in the excerpt beginning at measure 28.

6. And finally, some of the entries may be incomplete, as in the lowest voice of the excerpt beginning in measure 28.

Ex. 3-1. Bach: *Well Tempered Clavier*, Book I, Fugue No. 16.

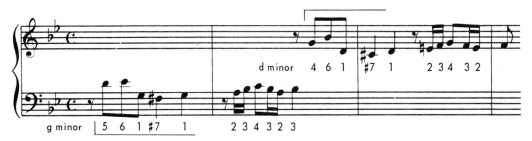

Ex. 3-1 illustrates imitation of a single musical idea, as is typical of fugal writing. Another type of imitation is used in a *canon* in which the melodic line is constantly changing and unfolding throughout the composition. The melody is duplicated by one or more voices that enter later than the first voice. The popular ''round'' illustrates canonic imitation of a type called *circle* or perpetual canon. Other types of canons are described by the temporal or intervallic distance between the first voice and the imitating voices, or are named according to special contrapuntal techniques that are included.

Canonic imitation is more often used for sections of a composition than as the basis of an entire work, but in the period of the Baroque canons were written as independent compositions. If you have never written a traditional canon, you must do so in order to appreciate the difficulty of maintaining the musical interest and avoiding the tonic-dominant cycle in which most popular rounds are caught. Bach was a supreme master of all polyphonic techniques, and he has written a number of canons that are exemplary. Ex. 3-2 is an excerpt taken from Bach's *Art of the Fugue*, and it illustrates the greater tonal freedom in imitative entries that is typical of canonic imitation. The lower voice begins as the leader and thus the initiator of each new melodic direction that is imitated by the upper voice. At almost the exact center of the composition the upper voice assumes the leadership and the lower voice follows to the end. An interesting, and technically rather spectacular, feature of the materials from the midpoint on is the reuse of the melodic line from the first 35 measures with a different interval of imitation.

Ex. 3-2. Bach: *Art of the Fugue*, Canon at the Tenth.

Canon

Ex. 3-2 (Continued)

The intervals of imitation in successive entries of the Baroque fugue are most often the octave and the fifth, although other intervallic relationships are explored to a lesser degree in the middle of the fugue. In his *Goldberg Variations* Bach wrote canons in which the interval of imitative entry ranged from a second to a ninth, and, generally speaking, canonic writing traditionally allows greater range of intervallic relation between imitating voices than does fugal writing. The great changes in the concept of consonance and dissonance that have taken place since the Baroque period have affected twentieth century use of all the musical forms and techniques from the traditional periods. Canonic writing is no exception. In the following example of canonic imitation Bartok has used very traditional intervals of imitation but with a bitonal effect in the passages marked. The composition from which Ex. 3-3 is taken is not a canon per se, but it does illustrate canonic writing in a twentieth century imitative work. The example also demonstrates that slight modifications in the voice that imitates are not aurally perceptible.

Ex. 3-3. Bartok: *Mikrokosmos*, No. 94.

As a term, *dialogue* is not usually included in counterpoint texts, but it is a very useful term that has been assimilated into the descriptive vocabulary of music. It can be defined as the alternating and successive statement of short musical ideas by two voices. In polyphonic compositions dialogue is often found in linking passages between areas of subject entry, and the material stated in dialogue will be derived from a fragment of the subject materials. The dialogue that begins in measure 5 of Ex. 3-4 uses two different fragments for the statement and answer pattern; the materials are identical in the second passage of dialogue, and so it is a form of imitation in this passage. Both passages effect a modulation through sequence.

Ex. 3-4.　Bach: *Well Tempered Clavier*, Book I, Fugue No. 2.

Ex. 3-4. (Continued)

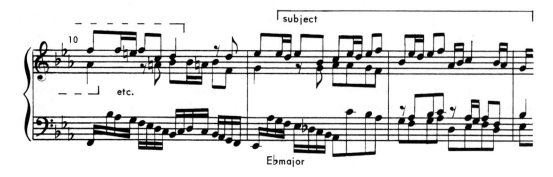

Ex. 3-5 illustrates dialogue in a contemporary fugue, and here the pattern is less regular than the dialogue pattern of Ex. 3-4. Materials are not derived from the subject but are taken from lines that accompany the third subject entry.

Ex. 3-5. From *Fuguing Set*, "Fugue in G", by John LaMontaine.

To summarize the contrapuntal techniques discussed thus far, the next example illustrates imitation of a subject, canonic imitation developing out of the second subject
entry, and, several measures later, dialogue in a passage that leads to subject entries in
stretto.

Ex. 3-6. Hindemith: *Ludus Tonalis*, Fugue No. 2 in G.

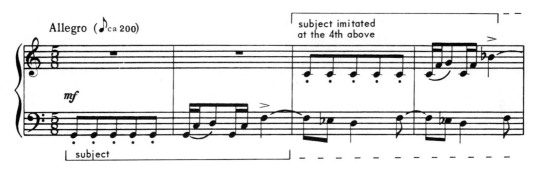

Ex. 3-6. (Continued)

When the musical subject of a composition is presented upside down, it is defined as *inverted.* This does not refer to the kind of inversion associated with interval inversion where the numerical quantity changes, but it is literally turning a melody over. The contour and numerical quantity of the subject remain although direction is completely inverted. Sometimes when a subject is inverted the quality of an interval is modified from major to minor or from perfect to diminished, for example, but the essential shape of the subject is still visually and aurally present. This technique and the device of stretto are used more often in the middle and final sections of a fugue rather than at the beginning. Exs. 3-7 and 3-8 illustrate inversion used respectively in a Baroque and a twentieth century fugue.

Ex. 3-7. Bach: *Well Tempered Clavier*, Book I, Fugue No. 13.

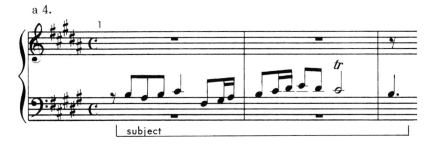

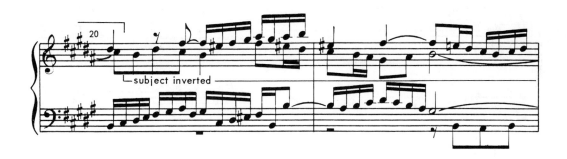

Ex. 3-8. Hindemith: *Ludus Tonalis*, Fugue No. 10 in D♭.

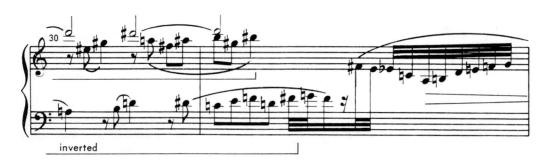

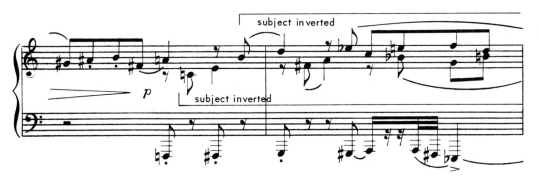

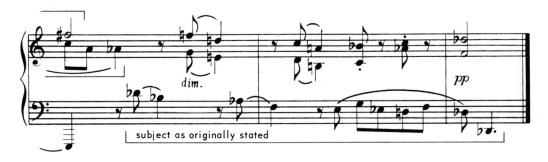

It can be noted in the two preceding examples that the Hindemith fugue made more extensive use of subject inversion than did the Bach fugue. Present century concepts of consonance and dissonance have expanded so drastically that stretto and other contrapuntal modifications of a musical subject are more easily incorporated into a twentieth century work than it was possible to do in the established tonal framework of a comparable Baroque work.

Another pitch modification with which a subject may be treated is *retrogression*, in which a musical idea is stated in reverse. This technique is rarely used outside of serial composition, and when a retrograde form of a musical idea appears in a score it is doubtful that many listeners are really aware of it. If one is inclined toward musical analysis it is intellectually intriguing to discover retrograde in a nonserial composition, and such a discovery invariably sets in motion a thorough and usually fruitless search for further instances of retrograde in the same work. Ex. 3-9, however, illustrates only one of several retrograde appearances of the subject in this fugue.

Ex. 3-9. Hindemith: *Ludus Tonalis*, Fugue No. 3 in F.

(upper voices are also a retrograde of measures 23-30)

subject retrograde (of the transposed subject

entry in measures 24-30)

If the element of duration modifies the subject of a fugue, it is used to lengthen or shorten its note values. These techniques are named respectively *augmentation* and *diminution*. Exs. 3-10 and 3-12 illustrate a typical combination of several contrapuntal techniques into one compressed area, and Ex. 3-11 simulates combined techniques by using the head of the subject with the augmented version in the bass. Stretto combined with other modifying techniques has the musical effect of generating tension and, for this reason, these devices are likely to appear later in a polyphonic composition rather than at its beginning. Ex. 3-10 appears to be an exception to this practice, but it is the sixth fugue of a monumental work of twenty odd fugues and canons, all written by Bach on the same subject and ranging through a literal catalogue of imitative devices. The fugue of Ex. 3-10 represents characteristics of a section in a very large development of one subject rather than typifying an independent single fugue.

Ex. 3-10. Bach: *Art of the Fugue*, Fugue No. 6.

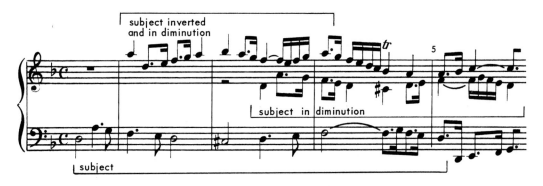

Ex. 3-11. Brahms: Variations and Fugue on a Theme by Handel, Op. 24, Fugue.

Ex. 3.11. (Continued)

Ex. 3-12. Hindemith: *Ludus Tonalis*, Fugue No. 9 in B♭.

subject inverted

A type of texture that is very typical of polyphonic writing exists when two or more melodic lines that have been stated simultaneously can successfully exchange horizontal positions in later simultaneous presentations. An upper voice becomes a lower voice, and vice versa. *Invertible counterpoint*, as this is designated, is based on well defined principles of Baroque composition, principles whose rather extensive details will be found in any good counterpoint text. In fugal writing, invertible counterpoint is often used for a secondary melodic line that is presented with the primary subject near the beginning of a fugue. With successive statements of the subject the secondary line can be presented simultaneously in a position that is above or below the voice in which the subject appears. If the secondary melodic line is present with the primary subject extensively throughout the fugue, it is called a *countersubject*. Invertible counterpoint in any polyphonic form functions as an additional means of presenting material in new contexts. Invertible counterpoint used in the countersubject in a fugue can complement the character of a primary subject (as it does in Ex. 3-13), it can furnish additional material for development, and it can strengthen the aural perceptibility of any successive subject entry because of initial association with the subject.

Ex. 3-13. Bach: *Well Tempered Clavier*, Book I, Fugue No. 12.

Ex. 3-13. (Continued)

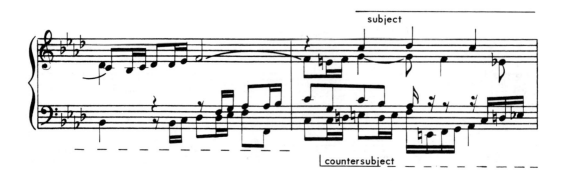

The fugue subject of Ex. 3-14 sounds like a simple little tune that might develop into a jazz improvisation and be harmonized with I, IV, and V. One contrast between the use of a countersubject in this fugue and the preceding one is the difference of intervallic relationships between voices. It can be noted in Ex. 3-13 that the vertical intervals formed by the subject and countersubject are either the same or they are literal intervallic inversions. Thus in measures 7 and 13 of Ex. 3-13 the beginning vertical sounds of subject and countersubject are respectively a major third and its inversion. A comparison of the two examples reveals expanded interval relationships in the use of "invertible" counterpoint in Ex. 3-14.

Ex. 3-14. Dmitri Shostakovich: 24 Preludes and Fugues, Op. 87, Fugue No. 5.

Ex. 3-14. (Continued)

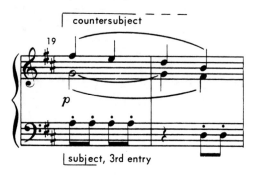

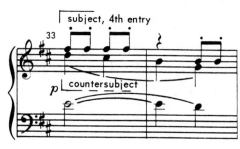

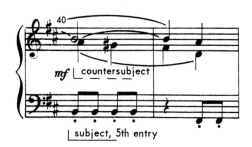

The pedal tone commonly functions as a concluding device in fugues of both periods. Pedal can act as a generator of musical tension and as a reinforcer of central tonality; both effects are characteristic sounds at the end of a polyphonic composition and both are illustrated in Exs. 3-15 and 3-16. The dissonance of the Bach example is created by the accompanied subject above the pedal. In the Hindemith fugue, the repeated subject is also the pedal, and dissonance is formed by the accompanying voices.

Ex. 3-15. Bach: *Well Tempered Clavier*, Book I, Fugue No. 2.

Ex. 3-16. Hindemith: *Ludus Tonalis*, Fugue No. 2 in G.

© Schott and Co., Ltd., London, 1943, renewed 1971. With permission by B. Schott's Söhne, Mainz.

Contrapuntal Techniques in Homophonic Forms

Linear writing has the musical effect of motion, and musical tension accumulates from the simultaneous use of several contrapuntal techniques. The musical tension is generated under these circumstances partly from sheer activity and partly from an effect of concentrating a sequence of musical events into a shorter temporal span. Musical tension and energy are effects that are particularly appropriate to the middle section of the sonata form. This form was briefly described in the preceding chapter as being divided into three sections, with materials being stated in the first section, developed in the middle section, and restated in the last section.

Many composers of the eighteenth and nineteenth centuries have used contrapuntal techniques in their homophonic compositions, but particularly in the mature compositions of Beethoven and Brahms it is possible to see a real synthesis of homophony and polyphony. Excerpts from Beethoven's early and late periods are shown in Exs. 3-17 and 3-18 to illustrate in brief the evolution of this synthesis in his own writings. Even in the early work of Ex. 3-17 there is a prediction of the polyphonic mastery that Beethoven was to achieve. Notice the gradual transformation of the repeated octave pattern of measure 110 to become the basis for the canonic imitation.

Ex. 3-17. Beethoven: Sonata in C Major, Op. 2, No. 3, I.
Middle section, development

The difference between the techniques of sequence, imitation, and dialogue is illustrated in the preceding example: sequence is a transposition of a musical idea presented in a single voice, where imitation and dialogue involve two or more voices.

There were twenty odd years between the writing of the sonata in Ex. 3-17 and the one in the following example. The contrapuntal writing in the development sections of Ex. 3-18 forms a *fugato*, a passage in fugal style. The materials are derived from the beginning theme of the composition, a theme that is purely homophonic in character, and the treatment of these materials in the middle section is almost as purely polyphonic. Ex. 3-18 shows the beginning excerpts of each imitative area to illustrate the gradual changes in texture.

Ex. 3-18. Beethoven: Sonata in B♭ Major, Op. 106, I.

Beginning theme

Two voice canonic imitation

Two voice canonic imitation with accompanying lower voice

Two voice canonic imitation between pairs of nonadjacent voices

Two voice canonic imitation between pairs of adjacent voices

Simultaneous imitation of a motive and its inversion

In Ex. 3-19 the beginning measures of the development section illustrate the rapidity with which musical energy can accumulate through the use of stretto and diminution.

Ex. 3-19. Brahms: String Quartet, Op. 51, No. 2, I.

Beginning theme

Ex. 3-19. (Continued)

Passage preceding the middle section, imitative entries in stretto

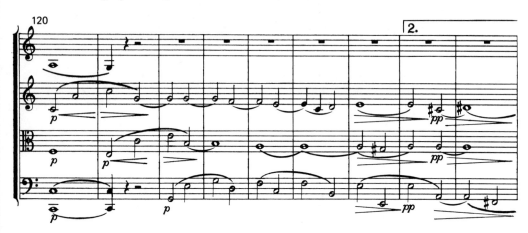

Beginning of the development section

End of the development section: two planes of canonic imitation between pairs of nonadjacent voices. The viola inverts the line of the first violin.

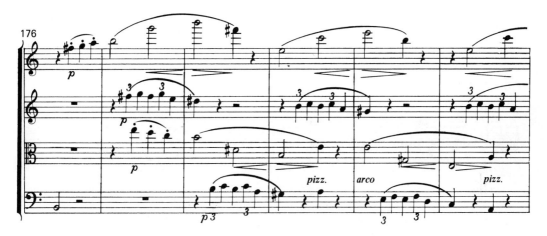

Materials developed contrapuntally in a homophonic texture are likely to be fragments rather than complete musical ideas. When there is no rhythmic distinction between fragments and if successive fragments alternate between voices, there is an aural effect of dialogue rather than imitation even though the line of either voice might have a certain melodic distinction if heard alone. The dialogue excerpt in the preceding work by Brahms illustrates this point. The next example provides an interesting paradox. The texture and sound of measures 57-59 resemble dialogue that merges into continuous rhythmic activity in measure 59. The two measures that follow use material that is no more distinctive than the fragments of dialogue, yet the motive fragment of descending semitones suddenly assumes shape and line through the rhythmic arrangement of measures 60-61. The effect of duration on pitch is well illustrated here, and there is a brief impression of canonic imitation with nonadjacent pairs of voices. Adjacent pairs of voices form simultaneous imitation in contrary motion. From this complex emerges another line of descending dialogue with the voices so closely spaced that it sounds very much like a single line. Ex. 3-20 is a fine study of the effects of rhythm and spacing in an imitative texture.

Ex. 3-20. Barber: Sonata for Piano, Op. 26, I.

Beginning theme

Development section

Fugue

The Baroque fugue is the apex of polyphonic principles, and, as such, it will here represent the other imitative forms of the preclassic period. The essence of the fugue form is the imitative development of a single musical idea and any of its melodic associates. A few generalizations can be made about the structure of the fugue form, but definitive statements beyond this level are more relevant to particular fugues than to the fugue as a form.

Exposition

The beginning exposition of the Baroque fugue has been the prototype for succeeding generations. Since the fugue is constructed from a single musical subject and any of its melodic associates, its aural effectiveness depends on listener recognition of the subject as it is developed. The exposition plan of the Baroque fugue is ideally suited to this end. The subject is announced alone, then stated successively in the remaining voices. If the texture of the fugue is three-voice, then at least three clear and unaltered statements of the subject will be heard before imitative development begins. The number of voices in the texture of a fugue assures that same minimum number of successive statements of the subject in the exposition. If the listener is ever going to become familiar with the fugue subject, he will have done so by the end of the exposition.

Listener recognition of a musical subject is also related to the nature of the subject. Fugue subjects are usually brief, and many of them are characterized by a distinctive rhythmic pattern that can be remembered and recognized when heard again and that is capable of clearly articulating a subject entry in the most complex of polyphonic textures. The following fugue subjects illustrate rhythmic distinctiveness, and a number of them have striking melodic lines as well. It is interesting to note that melodic distinction in a fugue subject is sometimes the result of a certain unexpected awkwardness of contour. Play through the original form and the paraphrase of Ex. 3-21 to hear that the angularity of the original is infinitely more attractive than the melodic paraphrase with its expected linear progression.

Ex. 3-21. Bach: *Well Tempered Clavier*, Book I, Fugue No. 3.

(author paraphrase)

Ex. 3-22. Bach: *Well Tempered Clavier*, Book I, Fugue No. 18.

Ex. 3-23. Handel: *Messiah*, No. 52 final chorus, "Amen."

Ex. 3-24. Mendelssohn: 6 Preludes and Fugues, Op. 35, No. 1.

Ex. 3-25. Hindemith: *Ludus Tonalis*, Fugue No. 10 in D♭.

Ex. 3-26. Bartok: String Quartet, No. 5, V, fugato.

p, oscuro

cont.

The order in which the voices successively state the subject in the exposition will probably not be highest to lowest or vice versa, but any other order is possible. The tonal pattern of the Baroque fugal exposition is oriented to tonic and dominant, and

the second subject entry is transposed to the key of the dominant. The third subject
entry returns to tonic tonality and, if there is a fourth voice, the fourth subject entry
may be in the dominant or the tonic tonality. The pattern of I - V - I - V is the basis
for the terms "subject" and "answer", terminology that can become so complicated
to use in the middle section of the fugue that "subject entry" is a better designation
there. Modulation to the dominant key is very transient, and the answer often sounds
as though it has simply been transposed to a different position in the same key. The
tonality of the answer in Ex. 3-27 is indicated as E♭ major, but it is not a particularly
convincing modulation to many ears. However, most of the notes of the answer are
transposed to the same scale steps in E♭ major as the scale steps on which the subject
first appeared in A♭ major, and the short *bridge*[1] passage that follows the answer goes
through the gestures of modulation back to the first key.

Ex. 3-27. Bach: *Well Tempered Clavier*, Book I, No. 17.

1. A bridge is an internal link between successive subject entries that are grouped.

Curiously, the fifth relationship between subject entries of the fugue exposition continues to prevail in many twentieth century fugues, although the traditional tonal relations have been greatly expanded in other twentieth century forms. Ex. 3-28 illustrates that same relationship of subject entries as Ex. 3-27, although a couple of centuries separates them. In the fugues of his *24 Preludes and Fugues* Shostakovich shows the same preference for a traditional tonal plan in fugal expositions as is illustrated in the string quartet excerpt of Ex. 3-28.

Ex. 3-28. Shostakovich: String Quartet No. 8, V.

Ex. 3-28. (Continued)

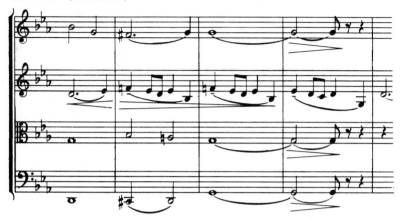

In Ex. 3-29 the terms "subject" and "answer" no longer seem appropriate because of the tonic - dominant connotations of the terms. As one of the nontraditional features of this fugato, the subject entries relate to one another at the interval of a tritone which is really the only logical alternative within the tonal orientation of the ostinato pattern. The stretto between the beginning of each subject entry and the end of the preceding one is also atypical of the Baroque exposition plan. The countersubject spins forth from the end of each subject entry in a manner that is typically Baroque, and also typically, the melodic modifications that take place in the exposition do so in the countersubject rather than in the subject.

Ex. 3-29. Bartok: String Quartet No. 5, V, fugato.

subject, 2nd entry   [counter subject, Viola]

Subject, 3rd entry

Ex. 3-29. (Continued)

(Counter subject, Violin II)

p, oscuro
Subject, 4th entry

(Counter subject,
violin I)

A number of the examples thus far have exhibited slight modifications of the exposition answer. The linking of the first tonality to the second often results in a *tonal* answer, which is somewhat modified, instead of a *real* answer, which is an exact transposition of the subject. The basis for the tonal answer seems to have been a desire of the Baroque composers to move smoothly from one tonality to the next. Tonal adjustments usually take place in the beginning notes of the answer, after which the transposition continues to be exact. It is worth noting here that the kind of melodic or rhythmic embellishment of the subject that may take place in the middle section of a fugue does not denote a "tonal" subject entry unless the embellishment also involves essential changes of the numerical interval pattern. Later subject entries in the opposite mode will change the quality of certain intervals, but the description of "tonal" is reserved for subject entries whose intervallic contour is numerically changed. The following examples illustrate the types of subjects that are likely to receive a tonal answer. They can be categorized as subjects that begin on the fifth scale step, that begin with tonic to leading tone or dominant, or that modulate.

Ex. 3-30. Bach: *Well Tempered Clavier*, Book I, Fugue No. 12.

Ex. 3-31. Bach: *Well Tempered Clavier*, Book I, Fugue No. 13.

Ex. 3-32. Bach: *Well Tempered Clavier*, Book I, Fugue No. 23.

Ex. 3-33. Bach: *Well Tempered Clavier*, Book I, Fugue No. 18.

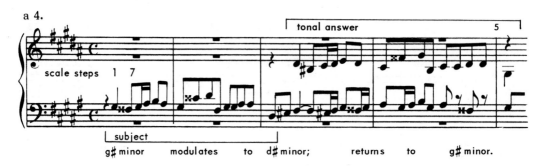

The key oriented basis for the tonal answer is not valid in the twentieth century, and contemporary fugues will probably have real answers in the sense of exact transposition.

The conclusion of the fugal exposition is either rounded out by a short cadential passage or it is followed by a modulatory passage leading to the next group of entries in the development section.

Development Section

The remaining measures of the fugue develop the exposition materials, and it is here that the form of a fugue becomes very individual. The subject, and the countersubject if there is one, are developed through subject entries in a tonal organization that generally avoids the tonic key and connecting passages named *episodes*. Most of the contrapuntal techniques contribute to the subject development: imitation, stretto, subject inversion, and subject augmentation are the commonly used techniques of the Baroque fugue. In passages of three or more subject entries in stretto, it is not uncommon for the last voice to present an incomplete form of the subject.

Sometimes tonality fluctuates within the subject itself although it may not have originally modulated. This, in turn, may bring about tonal adjustments in the subject contour.

The general effect of the development section is one of increasing complexity of texture and device. Since the actual number of voices will not increase, an impression of increasing texture can be made by closer stretto entries which gives an effect of greater density.

Fugues are compositions that depend on an almost continuous motion, and there are few internal cadences that create more than a temporary cessation of this motion.

Typically all Baroque music is less regularly phrased than music of the eighteenth and nineteenth centuries, and cadences are more often elided than terminated. In stretto passages cadences are particularly elided because of the overlapping of subject entries. There is a fluidity of sound to the fugue that comes from its essential character. The episodic passages contribute much to the musical flow, and an examination of several examples will illustrate the characteristic features of the episode.

In Ex. 3-34 the episode that follows the exposition leads to a *counter-exposition* in which the three voices again present the subject in succession using the same tonal plan but a different order of voice entries than the order of the first exposition. The materials of the episode in measure 13 are taken from both the subject and the countersubject. The upper line uses the first three-note motive of the tonal answer with displacement of accent, and the middle line follows in canonic imitation. The source of the lower line is measure 4 where the subject and countersubject link. The second episode again pits the two upper lines against the lower line, and the "head" and the "tail" of the subject are the sources of material. A free inversion of the first two measures of the subject form the bass line, and the end of the subject forms canonic imitation in the upper lines. A distinction needs to be made between episodes and the cadence measures that sometimes round out a subject entry because the musical purpose of each differs. Episodes are passages of motion, often by sequence as well as imitation, and cadences serve the usual purpose of cessation or slowing of motion. At measure 44 a subject entry has concluded in the lowest voice, and the next three measures effect greater conclusion through a cadential pattern. This particular subject anyway has an inconclusive cadence sound on the third of the tonic, and an extended cadence is again used to end the fugue.

Ex. 3-34. Bach: *Well Tempered Clavier*, Book I, Fugue No. 11.

Exposition, first episode and beginning of counter-exposition

Ex. 3-34. (Continued)

Second episode

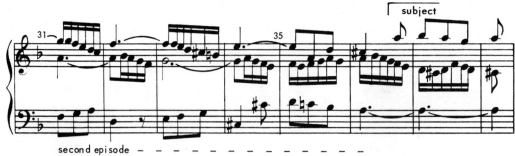

Cadential extensions

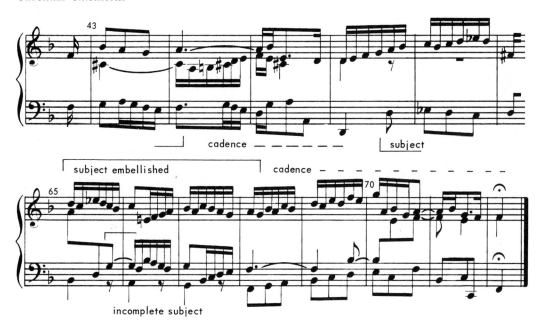

The next example of episodic material from a development section illustrates the same unusual contrapuntal technique that is used for all the subject entries in the last half of the fugue: the technique of retrogression. One of the passages of retrograde subject was illustrated in Ex. 3-9 where it was noted that the entire passage was a total retrograde of the previous seven measures. The second of the two episodes in this fugue is also a complete retrograde of the first one. The fugue is structured in almost a perfect arch, which is shown in brief diagrammatic form following the episodes.

Ex. 3-35. Hindemith: *Ludas Tonalis*, Fugue No. 3 in F.

Episode 1, and episode 2 as its retrogression

Ex. 3-35. (Continued)

Diagram of Hindemith's Fugue No. 3 in F

Measure	1	7	13	20	23	24
Formal content	Subject 1st entry	Subject 2nd entry	Subject 3rd entry	Episode 1	Subject 4th entry inverted	Subject 5th entry
Beginning and ending pitches	F – D	D – Db	F – F	F { B–D / A / B	E – A	A – A

Measure	31	38	41	47	53
Formal content	Retrograde of 4th and 5th subject entries	Retrograde of episode 1	Retrograde of 3rd subject entry	Retrograde of 2nd subject entry	Retrograde of 1st subject entry
Beginning and ending pitches	A – E A – A	D–B} A {F B }	F – F	Db – D	D – F

At the end of the development area the Baroque fugue returns to tonic tonality, and final subject entries may be stated. Cadential extensions, as illustrated in Ex. 3-34, and pedal tones, as illustrated in Exs. 3-15 and 3-16, are common techniques for effecting closure.

The following analyzed models illustrate contrapuntal techniques in the context of a fugal development.

Analysis Models

Ex. 3-36. Bach: *Well Tempered Clavier*, Book I, Fugue No. 8.

Ex. 3-36. (Continued)

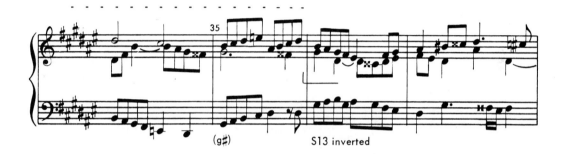

Ex. 3-36. (Continued)

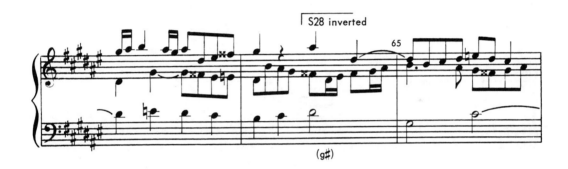

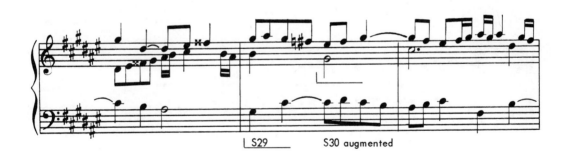

Ex. 3-36. (Continued)

The development of the preceding fugue subject is divided into four sections, at measures 19, 30, 52, and 61. Cadence articulation and a concentration of particular contrapuntal techniques group the entries within each section. Not all fugues illustrate the cumulative effect in development to the degree that is present in Ex. 3-36. In the final section all the contrapuntal techniques previously used in preceding groups of entries are joined with the augmented forms of the subject, and the musical tension is most concentrated just prior to the extended cadence.

Modifications of the subject in Ex. 3-36 take the form of tonal entries and incomplete entries. Each time the subject begins with a fourth rather than a fifth it must be considered "tonal."

Ex. 3-37 represents a fugue written in the second half of the nineteenth century, and the effect of the pervading homophonic style is particularly evident in the development of the subject. Comparing this fugue to the preceding fugue reveals some essential differences: an increase in the amount and development of episodic materials; the use of a greater variety of contrapuntal techniques in the episodes; and a complete lack of stretto, although there are several instances of simultaneous imitation between the subject and its inversion.

The Brahms fugue demonstrates a synthesis of polyphony and homophony that was anticipated in the late works of Beethoven and that has a twentieth century successor in the last movement of the Barber Piano Sonata, Op. 26. More often twentieth century composers have chosen the earlier polyphony of the Baroque period as a model.

Ex. 3-37. Brahms: Variations and Fugue on a Theme by Handel, Op. 24.

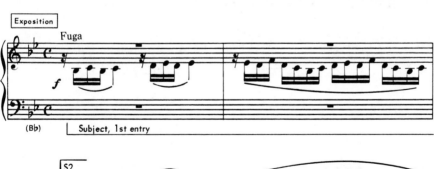

Ex. 3-37. (Continued)

episode using m. 2

p leggiero

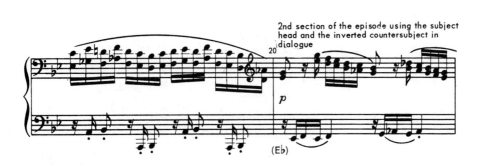

2nd section of the episode using the subject
head and the inverted countersubject in
dialogue

(E♭)

Ex. 3-37. (Continued)

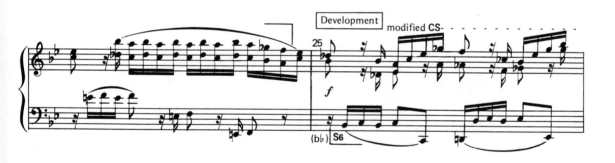

Episode using a motive from No. 2 of the subject and an augmented motive from the counter subject.

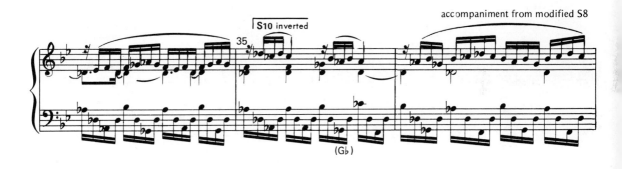

Ex. 3-37. (Continued)

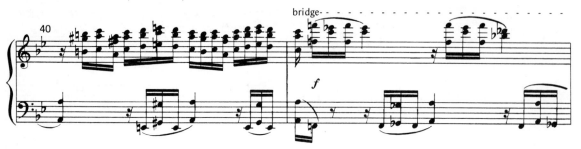

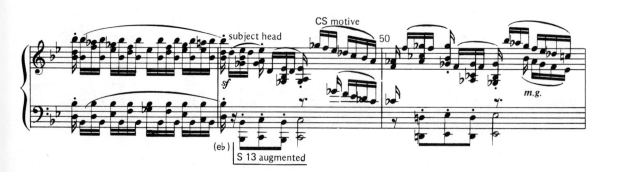

episode using a motive of measure 2
and its inversion.

Ex. 3-37. (Continued)

2nd section of the episode using the head of the subject
and its inversion in dialogue.

Subject in simultaneous imitation with its inversion

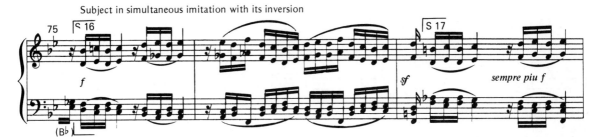

sequence leading to the cadence - - - - - - - - - - -

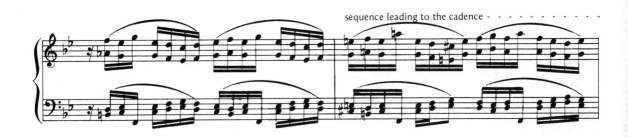

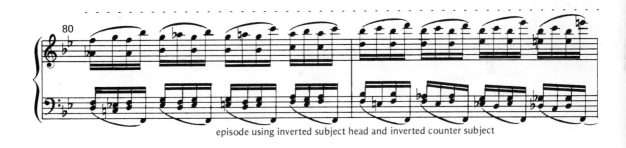

episode using inverted subject head and inverted counter subject

Ex. 3-37. (Continued)

The counterpoint of measures 83 — 86 is inverted

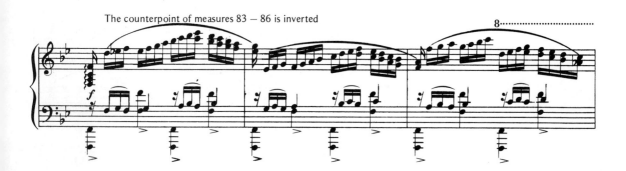

from CS

dialogue using subject head and inversion

The final section is a very extended cadence.
The use of the subject head substitutes for a final subject entry.

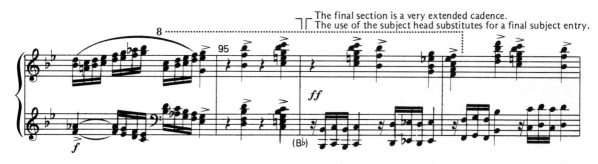

Composers of all periods have occasionally written fugues with two or more subjects. There are two alternatives for the broad structure of the fugue with multiple subjects: separate expositions for each subject and combination of the subjects somewhere in the development; or a simultaneous presentation of subjects in one or more expositions and some additional combination of the subjects in the development. Ex. 3-38 is a triple fugue that represents the first alternative. Each subject is presented and developed separately, to be followed in turn by a development area that is progressively cumulative. The growth process in a structure like this would be almost overwhelming if there were not the occasional plateaus of released tension and lightened texture such as the entrance of the third subject.

Ex. 3-38. Hindemith: Sonata in C for Violin and Piano, III.

First subject and real answer

Second subject

Second subject developed in stretto

First and second subject developed together

Ex. 3-38. (Continued)

Third subject

Third subject developed in stretto

First, second, and third subjects developed together

■ Assignment 1 - *Aural analysis of form*

In aural analysis of imitative compositions the activity within certain areas of the music may become so complicated that it is impossible to hear everything at once. Even with score, analysis should be a process of comprehending the larger structure before determining internal details; and the following suggestions are intended to guide the aural analysis along the same lines. The melodic excerpts will note the number of voices present in each composition listed, and this information will augment the expectations derived from your reading and a study of the analysis models. For example, if you were making an aural analysis of the fugue in Ex. 3-1, and if you knew that it was a four-voice fugue, you would expect to hear each of the four voices present the subject in a succession that would probably not move from highest to lowest voice or the reverse but in a more random order. What you would actually hear is the following plan of subject and countersubject entries in the exposition of Ex. 3-1:

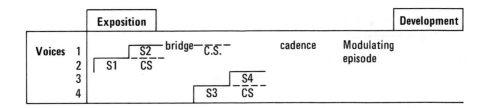

It is very likely that in the first listening you will be able to hear and record only the subject entries and their relative position in the polyphonic texture. Even though the subject entries may be in a "subject-answer" pattern, it is recommended at this stage of the analysis that clusters of subject entries be noted in a simple, numerical order. Subsequent listenings can be directed toward hearing and noting the following elements, perhaps one at a time: passages in which subject entries overlap in stretto; cadential and episodic passages; the presence of countersubject with subject entries; and modifications of the subject with tonal changes, inversion, augmentation, or abbreviation.

Musical Excerpts

Ex. 3-39. Bach: *Well Tempered Clavier*, Book I, Fugue No. 18. (four voices)
   Appendix page—557

The countersubject of this fugue is used less frequently and with more modification than the countersubject of Ex. 3-40. It does, however, appear with the subject entries of the exposition, and it furnishes much of the accompanying counterpoint thereafter.

Ex. 3-40. Bach: *Well Tempered Clavier*, Book I, Fugue No. 23. (four voices)
    Appendix page—557

Ex. 3-41. Bach: Two Part Invention No. 5. (two voices)
    Appendix page—558

The Two and Three Part Inventions of Bach represent more a style of writing than a form.[2] An example of each has been included for comparison to the fugues.

Ex. 3-42. Bach: Three Part Invention No. 3. (three voices)
    Appendix page—558

2. See the article entitled "Invention" in the *Harvard Dictionary of Music*, edited by Apel.

Ex. 3-43. Hindemith: *Ludus Tonalis*, Fugue No. 9. (three voices)
Appendix page—558

As illustrated in Ex. 3-12, the subject of this fugue is developed through the techniques of augmentation and inversion. The subject is also treated with retrogression. To assist aural analysis in passages where the modified subjects enter in stretto, it is suggested that the inverted and retrograde forms of the subject be written on the scores below the subject and that you familiarize yourself with the sound of all three forms.

Ex. 3-44. Mendelssohn: 6 Preludes and Fugues, Op. 35 Fugue No. 2. (four voices)
Appendix page—559

Several unusual features of this fugue should be noted. The countersubject is clearly present only with the first four subject entries, although much of the later accompanying counterpoint resembles the countersubject. Secondly, one of the internal subject entries and the final subject entry are extended versions as the result of sequence and repetition of a motive. And finally, the fugue seems to fall into three sections that are articulated respectively following the sixth entry and at the eleventh entry. An examination of the score will reveal that neither of these locations is in the tonic key although one might expect the first and last sections of a fugue to be tonic oriented.

Ex. 3-45. Dmitri Shostakovich: 24 Preludes and Fugues, Op. 87, Fugue No. 5. (three voices)
Appendix page—559

The treatment of this fugue subject includes variational as well as contrapuntal techniques. At different points in the development the subject is tonally altered or abbreviated, or it is extended in length either in the voice of entry or by imitative patterns in another voice.

■ Assignment 2 - *Aural analysis of content*

Use the recorded compositions of Assignment 1 for further analysis of the content. Stopping the record or tape at various points in a composition will permit you to verbalize or note your responses to the following suggested areas of focus.

1. Subject entries
   a. In the fugues determine any tonal modifications of subject entries, including those that take place in inverted subjects.
   b. Compare the handling of the countersubject in Exs. 3-39, 3-40, 3-42, 3-44, and 3-45. Note particularly if the countersubject is modified and if it is presented in a voice that has just completed a subject entry.
   c. Ex. 3-41 uses invertible counterpoint in the exposition. Determine if this process continues in the next pair of entries.

2. Episodes
   a. Determine the source of material for each episode in the fugues.
   b. Identify those episodes that make particular use of sequence, imitation, or dialogue.

c. In Ex. 3-43 determine which of the episodes end with an abrupt tonal shift up or down a third.

3. Final area

At the end of a fugue there is generally a sound of conclusion that is effected in one of several ways: the last subject entry or entries are in the tonic tonality; an extended cadence in the tonic tonality may follow the final subject entry or may be substituted for a final entry in the tonic; a pedal tone may be used with the final entry or cadence to further deplete the musical energy. In each fugue determine the means of effecting conclusion and the return to tonic tonality.

■ Assignment 3 - *Analysis with score*

Most of the examples for further study are multimovement works in which one or more complete movements is a canon or a fugue. The particular movement will be denoted either by the title or by the number of the movement following the title.

Examples for further study

BACH	*The Art of the Fugue.*
	Organ fugues, Fantasia and Fugue in G Minor; Passacaglia and Fugue in C Minor; Prelude and Fugue ("St. Anne's") in E♭ Major.
	The Well Tempered Clavier, Books I and II (48 Preludes and Fugues for keyboard).
BARBER	Sonata for Piano, Op. 26, IV.
BARTOK	Music for String Instruments, Percussion and Celesta, I.
BRAHMS	Thirteen Canons, Op. 113, for Women's Voices.
BRITTEN	Prelude and Fugue for String Orchestra.
FRANCK	Prelude, Chorale and Fugue for Piano.
	Prelude, Fugue and Variations, Op. 18, for Organ.
HARRIS	Quintet for Piano and Strings, III.
HINDEMITH	*Ludus Tonalis.*
	Piano Sonata No. 3, IV.

Sonata for Two Pianos, II (canon) and V (fugue).

Sonata in C for Violin and Piano, III.

HONNEGER   Prelude, Fugue and Postlude for Orchestra.

LISZT   Fantasia and Fugue on the name of Bach, for Organ.

MENDELSSOHN   6 Preludes and Fugues for Piano, Op. 35.

3 Preludes and Fugues for Organ, Op. 37.

MOZART   Adagio and Fugue in C, K. 546, for String Quartet.

Fantasy and Fugue in C, K. 394, for Piano.

Fugue in C, K. 426, for Two Pianos.

PISTON   Prelude and Fugue for Orchestra.

RIEGGER   Canon and Fugue for Strings

SCHUMANN   Six Etudes in Canonic Form for Organ, Op. 56.

Four Fugues for Piano, Op. 72.

SHOSTAKOVICH   24 Preludes and Fugues for Piano, Op. 87.

String Quartet No. 8, Op. 110. V.

STRAVINSKY   *Symphony of Psalms*, II.

4 ∎ part forms

There is a prevailing structural principle of division in musical forms: division of a work into two or more consecutive areas by means of cadences, of musical ideas, and of musical purpose. Within these structural areas there are further subdivisions into consecutive small units, such as phrases or motives.

If a series of two or more consecutive musical phrases adhere to one another in some manner as to attain partial independence and melodic significance, the total constitutes a single *part*. Even a phrase alone can create a part, usually by virtue of its location, or of its departure and restatement qualities. If two or more consecutive parts occur in a composition, they constitute a *part form* (sometimes called a *song form*) or *theme*. The hierarchy of structural divisions thus far described can be shown by the illustrative diagram below:

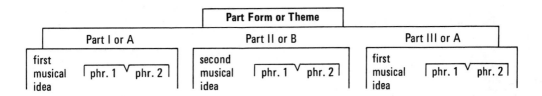

Three-Part Form (Ternary Form)

The number of consecutive parts which create a part form or a theme is practically and aesthetically limited, as is shown by a study of literature. Ranging from the usual limits of a one-part form to a five-part form, the three-part form emerges as the structural unit that composers have used most often. The term *three-part form* rarely means the successive presentation of three different musical ideas. Rather the term commonly means the presentation of two musical ideas followed by a recurrence of the first one—statement, departure, and return is a prime principle of musical structure. The recurrence of the first musical idea may be complete and quite literal or it may simply initiate the opening measures of the first idea with somewhat different material following. Examples 4-1 and 4-2 illustrate each of these possibilities.

Ex. 4-1. Haydn: Piano Sonata in A Major (Peters No. 33), III.

Ex. 4-2. Bartok: *Mikrokosmos*, No. 128.

Part A¹

However literal or modified the recurrence of the first part is, the tonality throughout the recurring part will generally be the initial tonality, thus reinforcing the sound of return after the sound of departure created by the middle or second part.[1] A formal means of conveying that melodic, rhythmic, or tonal changes in length have taken place in the recurring first part is to use the letters ABA¹ for the three parts rather than the letters ABA which would denote a virtually unchanged recurrence of the first musical idea.

Tonality and Final Cadences of the Parts

The tonality of the first musical idea (Part A) has followed one of two patterns: Part A begins and ends in the first tonality, or it modulates to and ends in a second tonality, usually closely related if the work is a traditional one. If there is a modulation to a second key encompassed within Part A of a traditional ternary form, the most probable tonal changes appear to have been tonic to dominant or tonic to the related major or minor mode. Often the modulation of a short Part A takes place toward the end of the part, and the sound of tonality change is very transient indeed.

---

1. Exceptions to this principle of reprise in the first tonality will be discussed later in the appropriate context.

Some type of terminating cadence in the prevailing tonality is commonly found to conclude the first Part A, thus giving it a sound of temporary closure. There are, of course, exceptions to this practice, and in these instances the musical distinction of a next consecutive part is usually strengthened beyond the distinction of a next part that follows a substantial terminating cadence.

The probable tonality at the beginning of Part B rests considerably on the tonal pattern of Part A and on the degree to which musical ideas of Part B are distinctive from those of Part A. It is possible for Part B to begin in the first tonality or to continue in the second tonality of a Part A, or even to initiate a tonal center not used by Part A. In a traditional work the extensive use of altered chords can create the aural impression of transient modulations, even though none have taken place. All these tonal possibilities exist between Parts A and B in the countless examples of ternary form that are to be found.

Part B of a ternary form often ends with an open, or progressive, cadence because of its dependence on the recurring Part A for conclusion. A common traditional cadence at the end of Part B is the dominant chord in the key of Part A. This is most apt to occur if the ternary form is fairly small and compact with not too much difference in style between parts. Also if Part A is initiated with a tonic chord, a linking of Part B to the return of Part A can be effected by the tendency of a dominant cadence to progress on to a tonic chord. The length of Part B and the extent to which it had tonally departed from Part A apparently influences its dependence on or independence from the recurring Part A which follows. There are examples of three-part forms whose Part B seems almost as independent as the first Part A by virtue of style change, tonality change, or a concluding terminal cadence in a key other than the beginning tonality. Under these circumstances Part B may be followed by a modulatory area called "retransition" to lead back to the tonic key or the original tonality in which the past Part A is stated. At other times the addition of a few notes added in the last measure of Part B will accomplish the return to the first tonal center.

The most likely tonal relations and cadences of traditional works can be summarized as follows:

(1)	B cadence— V, or other progressive cadence of the first tonality		A returns in the first tonality
(2)	B cadence— terminal cadence in a second or third tonality	retransition	A returns in the first tonality
(3)	B cadence— terminal cadence in a second or third tonality		A returns in the first tonality

One expects certain rather stereotyped key relationships in the forms of traditional works. In a twentieth century work that is tonally oriented (although not in major or minor keys), the delineation of the structure is more often reliant on musical elements other than tonality: for example, texture, line, or dynamics. If there is a clear tonal relationship between parts of a twentieth century work it is apt to be a more remote one, as is Ex. 4-5 where Part B centers on C♯ as a contrast to the beginning tonality on A. A further expectation about twentieth century part forms is that the recurrence of a part may be transposed as well as considerably modified, as illustrated by Ex. 4-27.

Formal Contents of a Part

Any of the three parts of an ABA form may contain one or more phrases. Each of the parts may have the same number of phrases as the other two parts, or the phrase content of each may be different. There seem to emerge, however, several patterns of balance that appear very commonly in the three-part form and that can be depicted by the following ratios of length (not number of phrases): 2:1:1, 2:1:2, and 1:1:1. The temporal balance of parts is sometimes achieved and at other times changed or lost by the use of repeat marks with Part A, or Parts B and A¹ together, or with both. For example, all three parts might be one phrase each in length with repeat marks used as follows: ‖:A:‖BA¹‖.[2] The temporal ratio then changes from 1:1:1 to 2:1:1 or A--1:BA--1. It should be noted that repeat marks rarely surround Part B alone. It should be noted further that ‖:A:‖:BA¹:‖or a ternary form with the repetition of parts written out (AABA¹BA¹) is still considered essentially a three-part form.[3]

It is extremely important to bear in mind that formal analysis of a musical work is most comprehensive and sensitive when it is approached from the larger structure inward to the smaller. The location of the part should precede any consideration of the manner in which the interior phrases of the part relate to one another.

Stylistic Relationship of Parts

Composers have used a variety of compositional devices to make audible that the first of three parts has ended and the second part has begun. The usual terminal cadence at the end of the first Part A signals a closure, temporary or otherwise, of the first musical idea. The ensuing musical idea of Part B holds sufficient contrast to fur-

---

2. Explanation may be made of the following terms not used in this discussion: rounded binary and incipient three-part form.

3. The ABA¹B¹A¹ form with a transposition of the second Part A or Part B is sometimes considered to be a five-part rather than a three-part form.

ther strengthen the aural impression that a "statement" has ceased and that a "departure" has been initiated. The stylistic contrast in Part B often serves as well to heighten the unity of the composition as a whole because the materials of Part B are so frequently drawn from the materials of Part A, but used in some different manner. The following listing is representative of common musical relationships in the ternary form.

Part B can be related to Part A by:

1. A texture common to both (Ex. 4-3).
2. An accompaniment pattern common to both (Ex. 4-4).
3. A prominent melodic motive of Part A which may appear in Part B in a different location, with a different rhythmic pattern, or with a motive inverted (Exs. 4-4 and 4-5).
4. A rhythmic figure or motive from Part A which may be associated with a different melodic contour or a different accentual placement in Part B (Exs. 4-6 and 4-7).
5. Prominent reuse of a characteristic nonharmonic tone from Part A (Ex. 4-8).
6. Reuse of the microstructure of Part A, such as phrases formed by two equal halves or semi-phrases (Exs. 4-8 and 4-9).
7. An almost literal restatement of Part A in a different tonality (Ex. 4-9).
8. A musical mannerism which punctuates all or most of the cadences of both parts (Ex. 4-10).

Ex. 4-3. Bartok: *Mikrokosmos*, No. 81.

Ex. 4-4. Brahms: Intermezzo, Op. 76, No. 4.

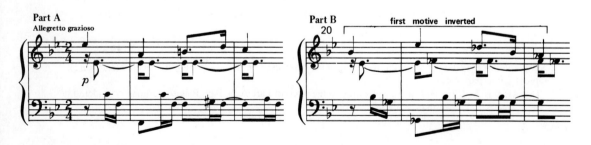

Ex. 4-5. Kennan, Kent: Two Preludes, No. 2.

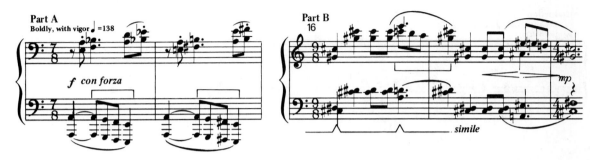

Ex. 4-6. Chopin: Mazurka, Op. 6, No. 4.

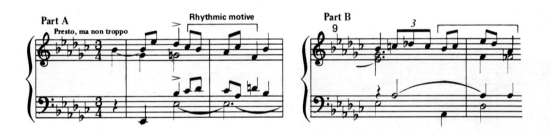

Ex. 4-7. Hindeminth: *Ludus Tonalis*, Interludium in G.

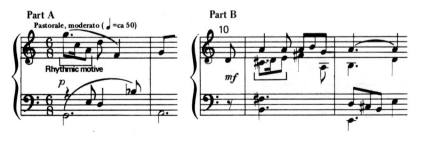

Ex. 4-8. Schumann: *Davidsbündler*, Op. 6, No. 1.

Ex. 4-9. Chopin: Mazurka, Op. 7, No. 5.

Ex. 4-10. Schumann: *Carnaval*, Op. 9, No. 2.

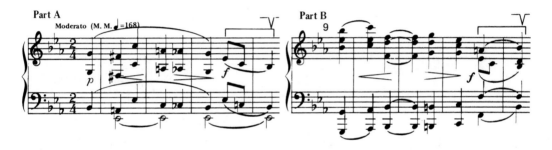

In a limited number of three-part forms there is no overt relationship between Parts A and B, or the relationship is so subtle that it cannot be adequately verbalized. Here the common meter, the common key signature and, more significantly, the return of Part A are the cohesive elements that bind together the parts of the ternary form.

Modulation, or an impression of modulation, always heightens the sound of departure in Part B. Further departure is established by the modifications with which materials borrowed from Part A are reused in Part B. As a general principle the greater the temporal space allotted to a three-part form, the greater may be the digression of a Part B from a Part A.

If the return of Part A is modified rather than literal, several kinds of modification may have taken place. The length, melodic contour and even the harmonic progression of the initial Part A may be evident in its recurrence, but the composer may have elaborated the melodic contour with additional nonharmonic tones, filled-in arpeggios, and the like. Modifications such as those shown in Ex. 4-11 are prevalent in works of the classic period.

Ex. 4-11. Haydn: Piano Sonata in E♭ Major (Peters No. 35), II.

Ex. 4-12 illustrates a ternary pattern in which a modulation has taken place in measure 10 of Part A. The recurring and abbreviated Part A¹ uses essentially the first eight measures of Part A¹ which do not modulate. Toward the end of Part A there is a slight modification to accommodate a terminal cadence in place of the progressive cadence used originally in measure eight.

Ex. 4-12. Beethoven: Six Bagatelles, Op. 126, No. 5.

In other ternary examples such as Ex. 4-13 only the beginning of the first part may have been restated, after which there is new material in a similar style. (See also Ex. 4-2.)

Ex. 4-13. Schumann: *Album for the Young*, Op. 68, No. 17.

Ex. 4-13. (Continued)

At times these digressions of Part A¹ appear necessary because of a difference in tonal objective that may exist between a first and a third part. At other times the motive behind the modification of a restated musical idea may have been simply that human inclination to elaborate or expand a musical idea, an inclination which has apparently existed through all of music history.

Auxiliary members: Introduction, Retransition, Transition, and Codetta

The function of Part A of a three-part form is to present a musical idea which has sufficient inner cohesion to sound at least modestly independent and whose rhythmic and melodic pattern are distinctive enough to be aurally recognized when Part A recurs after the departure of a Part B. The function of Part B is to depart from Part A, and thus to highlight the return of Part A. Parts are generally cast in a series of regular phrases, which may be extended but which are still audible as phrase units. Areas that are not clearly expository and whose phrasing may be ambivalent or nonexistent are auxiliary to the parts. The *introduction*, *retransition*, *transition*, and *codetta* are the four auxiliary members that may occur in the part forms. They each serve a distinctive musical function of their own which differs from the expository nature of the part.

An *introduction* is a preparatory area that precedes the melodic line of the first phrase of Part A. Introductions of part forms range in length from a partial measure to eight measures, and their harmonic equipment is often limited either to the tonic chord or to an alternation of tonic and dominant. As in Ex. 4-2 most introductions to a three-part form simply anticipate the accompaniment pattern of Part A, although Ex. 4-8 which anticipates forthcoming melodic and rhythmic patterns is illustrative of another common introduction characteristic. These two types of introductions are generally without a true melodic line, and they must not be confused with a Part A that begins with a bar or so of unaccompanied melody, as in Ex. 4-1. There are less common instances of part forms whose first essential melody is preceded by a contrasting sound that intensifies the entrance of the first Part A.[4] In Ex. 4-14 the aural contrast between the three-measure introduction and Part A is created by differences of dynamic level, tempo, and texture. If the bracketed areas are compared, however, the introduction is not as contrasting to Part A as a first hearing might indicate.

Ex. 4-14. Dello Joio: Suite for Piano, IV.

4. Sometimes a distinction is made between the terms *introduction* and *prelude*.

If the tonality at the end of Part B differs from the original tonality or, more rarely, if the style of Part B differs considerably from that of Part A, a *retransition* may
occur between the end of Part B and the recurrence of Part A. The cadence ending this
type of Part B and preceding the retransition is usually terminal, or potentially terminal
but evaded. Examples 4-15 and 4-16 illustrate the usual function of the retransition,
which is to bridge the tonal and/or style difference from Part B to the return of Part A.

Ex. 4-15. Brahms: Intermezzo, Op. 19, No. 3.

Ex. 4-16. Dello Joio: Suite for Piano, III.

Because the part form is the small structure, the temporal space allotted to the retransition is usually brief. Sequence and the use of motivic fragments are two common sounds in this area, and the materials of the retransition sometimes anticipate the materials as well as the tonality of Part A. The harmony at the end of the retransition is some sound which leads appropriately into the first harmony of the return of Part A. Rather infrequently *transitions* occur from the first Part A to Part B. The function of the transition is identical with that of the retransition—to bridge tonality and/or style differences—and the materials are similar.

The *codetta* appears at the end of the part form and only rarely at the end of the first Part A. In part forms of the traditional style the usual purposes of the codetta are to emphasize closure or to deplete musical energy. In such works the cadence which ends the part and which precedes the codetta is generally authentic, but closure may be avoided here by weakened or evaded forms of the cadence or by continued motion of the melodic line or accompaniment in the cadence measure. The prevailing tonality of a codetta will be the same as the key of the part that precedes it; a codetta does not modulate although it may contain altered chords. A common harmonic basis for a codetta is an extended form of a cadence ending Part A. For instance, a cadence which is V-I may be expanded in a codetta to IV-I$^6_4$-V-I. Another possible harmonic direction is toward emphasized subdominant harmonies, a technique which resembles an expansion of the plagal cadence which follows the authentic cadence of a hymn. Examples 4-17 through 4-19 illustrate the following materials and techniques that traditional composers have used to create a codetta at the end of a part form:

1. One of more restatements of the cadence which ends the part, often expanded (Exs. 4-17 and 4-18)
2. Prominent use of subdominant harmonies (Exs. 4-19 and 4-20)
3. Use of a pedal tone (Exs. 4-18 and 4-20)
4. A generally descending melodic line (Exs. 4-17 and 4-20)
5. Repetition of a motive that ends the preceding Part A (Ex. 4-18)
6. Reuse of a motive from Part B (Ex. 4-19)
7. A style that is independent of but related to Parts A and B (Ex. 4-17)
8. Less distinction or less energy in the rhythmic patterns than in the preceding part (Ex. 4-19)
9. A lowering of the dynamic level (Exs. 4-18 and 4-20)
10. A thinning of the texture (Exs. 4-18 and 4-20)

Ex. 4-17. Schumann: *Kinderszenen*, Op. 15, No. 8.

Ex. 4-18. Chopin: Mazurka No. 16, Op. 24, No. 3.

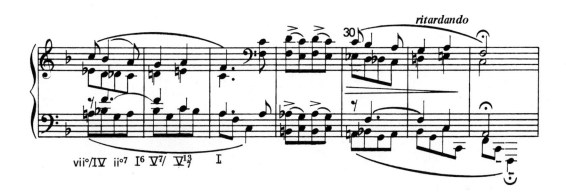

Ex. 4-18. (Continued)

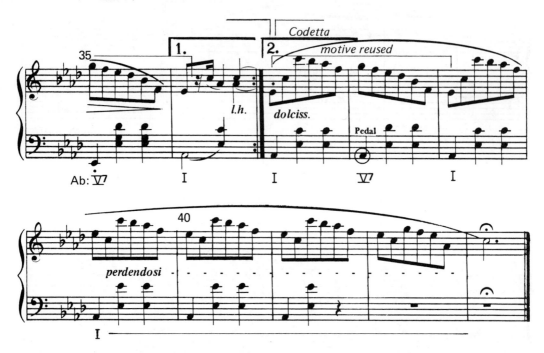

Ex. 4-19. Mozart: Piano Sonata in C Major, K. 545, II.

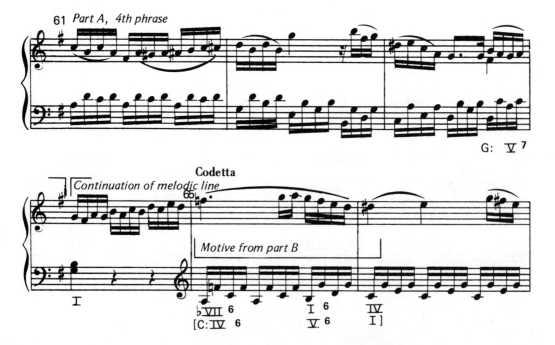

I^6 ii^6 I^6_4 V^7 I

17   *Part B (motive used in measures 65-66)*

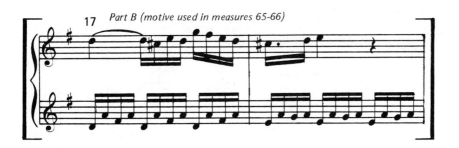

Ex. 4-20. Beethoven: Seven Bagatelles, Op. 33, No. 6.

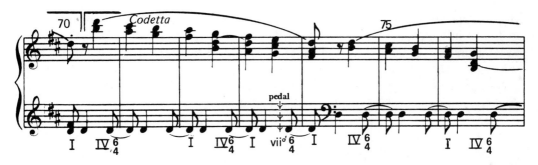

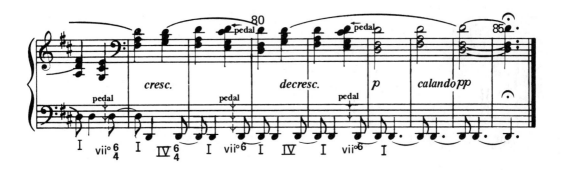

Quite often short twentieth century works end with codettas that reveal techniques resembling those found at the end of more traditional works. In Ex. 4-22 the cadence that ends the last phrase of Part A¹ is extremely traditional. The cadence extension that follows in measures 43-48 again reaches a dominant sound in measure 48, a sound whose resolution is evaded by a series of triad and diad sounds that serve as upper and lower leading tones to the C♯ tonal center. For example, in the upper line the F major triad outlined in measure 50 and the C major triad outlined in measures 51 and 52 each have a multiple semitone relationship to the C♯ minor triad of measure 53 as shown in Ex. 4-21. The diad in the lower voice of measures 49-52 serves the same function of upper and lower leading tones to tones of the C♯ minor chord.

Ex.   4-21.

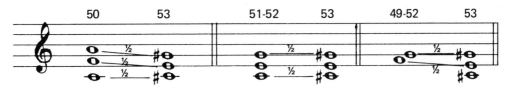

The concept of semitone relationship to the original cadence chord of measure 42 is continued in the codetta of Ex. 4-22. In the lower voices of measure 55 the open fifth on G natural serves aurally as a lower leading tone to the implied G♯ dominant chord of measure 57, and the upper line C natural on measures 59 and 61 highlights the C♯ minor center in the same manner. Thus the codetta should be described as several expanded restatements of the cadence that ended Part A¹.

Ex. 4-22. Shostakovich: 24 Präludien for Piano, Op. 34, No. 10. Peters Edition No. 4773A.

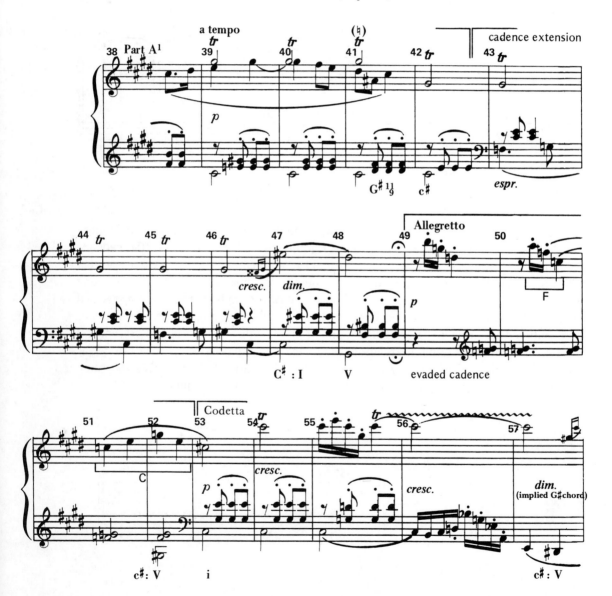

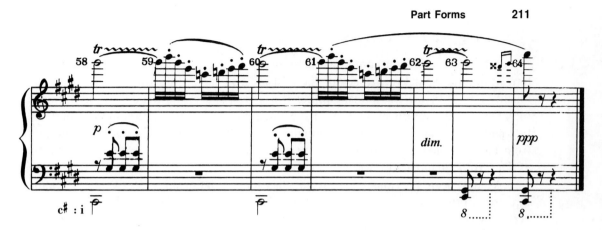

Reprint permission granted by the publisher.

Smaller and Larger Part Forms

Part forms with fewer or more divisions than the three-part form are less common in both traditional and twentieth century examples. The one-part form as the basis of a complete work or movement can be found in the larger sets of short compositions such as the 24 Preludes, Op. 28, of Chopin; the *Mikrokosmos* of Bartok; and 24 Preludes, Op. 34, of Shostakovich. Possible arrangements of the musical ideas within the part forms of two, four, and five divisions can be depicted as follows:[5]

Two Part	Four Part	Five Part
AB	ABCA	ABACA
		ABCDA
		ABCBA

These part forms have many characteristics in common with the three-part form, and individual differences among them can be identified by comparison to the expectations about the ternary form.

5. When they occur, seven-part forms are usually arranged as ABA[1]CABA[1], with Part C quite divergent in style. Many of these forms more nearly resemble a song form with trio, although a few quite authentic seven-part forms will be listed at the end of this chapter.

Tonality and Final Cadences

In the two-part form composers have used tonality to create the aural sense of return without an actual recurrence of the first musical idea.[6] Regardless of its beginning tonality Part B of the traditional two-part form will end in the tonic key and terminate fully, as did the return of Part A in the three-part form. In the traditional four- and five-part forms, all Parts A will continue to recur in the tonic key and all departures from Part A (Parts B, C, or D) are open to the same tonal and cadential possibilities as Part B of a three-part form.

As has been previously discussed, the tonal relationships of twentieth century three-part forms are much less crystallized than those of the eighteenth and nineteenth centuries. This situation exists also in the two-, four-, and five-part forms of the twentieth century.

Formal Contents of a Part

Any of the parts of these smaller or larger forms may contain one or more phrases. Because the four- or five-part form tends to be longer than the binary or ternary form, proportions in general will increase with numbers of parts, and the part that is only a single phrase in length is unlikely in these larger forms. Any of the four- or five-parts may be repeated, but it is not probable that all of them will be in a single work. To understand this discretionary measure of composers, one has only to consider the potential monotony of the sound of Part A if each part of an ABACA form were repeated.

An interesting difference between traditional and twentieth century part forms is the manner in which recurrence of parts is presented. Repeated parts in the traditional two- and three-part form present this appearance:

$$\|: A :\|: B :\| \text{ and } \|: A :\|: BA^1 :\| .$$

Because twentieth century composers have been and are inclined toward continuous development throughout a work, the thematic recurrences of twentieth century two- and three-part forms are more likely to be thus: ABA^1B and $ABA^1B^1A^2$.

Stylistic Relationships of Parts

The same compositional devices that relate the two musical ideas of a ternary form will be found to relate the parts of smaller or larger part forms. The principle

6. The two-part form here referred to has two successive musical ideas only. The binary form that occurs in the Baroque period and before is based more on tonality than on melody. A definition of this older form can be found in the *Harvard Dictionary of Music* under the headings of "Binary and ternary form" and "Sonata form II."

that greater temporal span permits greater digression from the initial musical idea becomes more prominent as additional parts increase the length of a composition. One is tempted to seek confirmation of symmetrical balance in a part form so that, for instance, it could be expected that Part C of an ABCBA form would be stylistically most divergent. This expectation is often not confirmed, and it is wiser simply to identify each successive musical idea and then to look for the relationships and musical purposes that actually exist in the music.

Location of Part Forms

The part form as the basis of a complete work was a common structural vehicle for the nineteenth century salon pieces for piano. These were given descriptive names in a set of short pieces or they were designated as bagatelles, preludes, mazurkas, etudes, nocturnes, intermezzi, capriccio, and so forth. Although less common in the twentieth century, comparable examples of sets for piano can be found in the works of Bartok, Hindemith, Shostakovich, Bloch and others. Only occasionally is a complete work of a solo sonata or a chamber work structured in a single one of the part forms. On the other hand, the part form plays a very important role as the basis for thematic sections of a movement in these larger works. One example will suffice for the present. The last movement of a solo sonata, chamber work, or symphony is often a rondo, which is a large form presenting themes in alternation. A typical rondo could be described successively as theme 1, theme 2, theme 1, theme 3, and theme 1 with any of the themes composed of the one-, two-, or three-part forms. At this level there are forms within a form.

Analysis Models

The last movement of Haydn's Piano Sonata in A Major is illustrative of a clearly articulated and simple ternary design. Part A is constructed of two phrases that are very similar except for the final difference of direction and the cadence at the end of each. Part B is only a single phrase, but a rough temporal balance with Part A is achieved by extending this phrase with a repeated measure and an extended restatement of the cadence. Stylistically Part B grows out of the descending scale passage that begins Part A; Part B then affords a contrast with the disjunct patterns of measures 11 and 12, and with a change of tonality from that of Part A. Two characteristics of the retransition that are both audible and visual are the modulation back to A major and the fragmented lines. With one exception the return of Part A is virtually the same as its presentation. In the absence of a codetta that could deplete the musical energy, the dynamic level of the last two measures (one of them modified) is suddenly lowered to create the effect of greater conclusiveness.

Ex. 4-23. Haydn: Sonata in A Major (Peters No. 33), III (ABA).

Part A - period

Part B - phrase

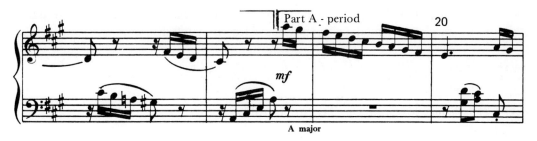

A major

The next example has attained considerable length with repeated structures at several levels. What is essentially a four part form (ABCD) will have the aural impact of the following: two phrases and a repetition of them (AA); at measure 17 two more phrases, again repeated (BB); repetition of the entire material thus far presented with a cumulative aural effect of AABBAABB. The ensuing Parts C and A¹ are each constructed of four phrases that sound like repeated two-phrase patterns except for the difference between the second and fourth cadence of each four-phrase span. From the total and final aural effect emerges the primary technique of repetition.

Additionally it can be noted that while Parts A and C are related stylistically by the rhythmic pattern of ♪ 𝄽 ♪, Part B has no overt relationship to either of the other parts. Again repetition serves as a covert unifying technique. The first half of every phrase of Part B is constructed of the repeated two-beat pattern that begins with the triplet, and the first and third phrases of Part C are created of repeated two-measure motives.

The half cadence at the end of Part A is more articulative of the section change than a dominant chord usually is because of the abrupt modulation that follows. The last cadence of Part B stands in dominant relation to the E♭ major tonality that follows, and the pause of measure 32 is broken by an anacrusis at the end. The modulation at the end of Part C is incorporated into the last cadence measure, and here again there is no need for a modulatory passage such as a retransition.

Ex. 4-24. Chopin: Mazurka, Op. 24, No. 1 (ABCA¹).

Part A - repeated period

Part C - double period

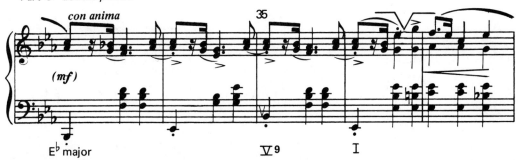

Ex. 4-24. (Continued)

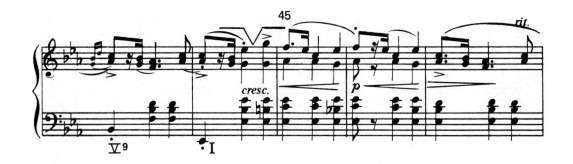

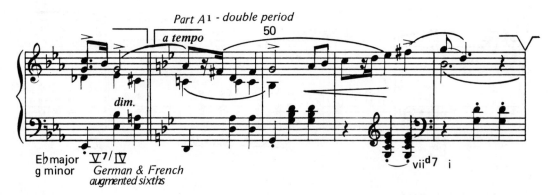

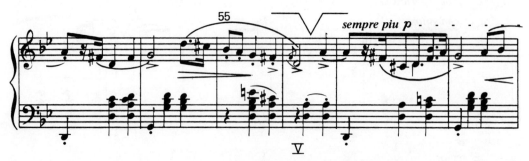

As a contrast to the eighteenth and nineteenth treatment of tonality, Ex. 4-26 illustrates a tonal pattern that does not return to the beginning sound. This process of continuous growth is supported by the lengthening of Part A with each of its returns. The diagram below illustrates the "openness" of the structure rather than the "closed" character typical of most traditional part forms.

part	A	B	A^1	B^1
content	phrase	4 phrases	2 phrases	4 phrases
length	4 measures	18 measures	8 measures	17 measures
tonal center	E	E	E	G

part	A^2	B^2	A^3 and codetta	
content	2 phrases	4 phrases	2 phrases—extension plus a phrase like A^3	
length	10 measures	21 measures	16 measures	
tonal center	C♯	A/B	A	

Part B is stylistically related to Part A by the reuse of measure 1 to form the bracketed line of measures 7 and 8. Further relationship comes from the nonthematic use of repeated pitches in Part A and sustained pitches in Part B. On the whole, however, stylistic contrast is more prominent in this work than is stylistic similarity. The obvious contrasting feature between Parts A and B is rhythm. A much more subtle distinction is illustrated by Ex. 4-25. Part A uses only symmetrical scales, and Part B is fashioned from modes. The choice of Dorian mode in each instance but one dissipates some of the scalar dissimilarity as this is the only one of the modes that effects mirror symmetry from a central axis. The few pitches that are not derived from the scale bases in Ex. 4-25 are circled on the full score of Ex. 4-26. It is interesting to note that most of these "altered tones" act as leading tones to the prevailing tonality.

Ex. 4-25. Scale bases of Ex. 4-26.

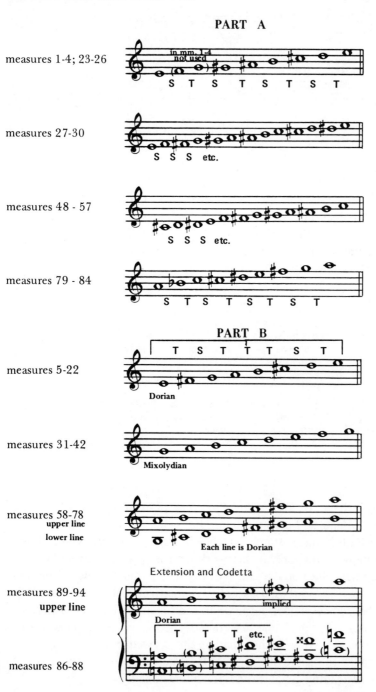

Ex. 4-26. Bartok: *Mikrokosmos*, No. 150 (ABA¹B¹A²B²A³ codetta).

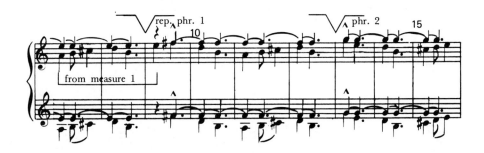

Ex. 4-26. (Continued)

Ex. 4-26. (Continued)

The previous example illustrates many of the fascinating motivic transformations of which Bartok seemed infinitely capable. Both parts are subjected to increasing modification with each return. Ex. 4-27 shows the transformations of Part A which are both cumulative and progressive. In measure 24 the first two notes are a substitution for the first two notes of the repeated motive of measure 2; measure 27 grows out of measure 24 with a single note substitution (see author modification). The first six bars of Part A² are based on measures 23 and 24, and the changes are chromatic: each interval larger than a minor second is contracted by a half step. In measure 54 the second phrase of Part A² appears to begin like measure 1, but the last two notes of the five-note motive exchange places and initiate the upward motion of the second phrase. As can be seen in Ex. 4-26 Part A³ combines the motive of Part A with the first transformation of part A.[1]

The energy that is rhythmically generated by the last appearance of Part A is depleted by the three-bar extension. This is followed by a final lowering of the dynamic level plus a straight descent to the final keynote in measures 92-94.

Ex. 4-27. Motivic transformations of Part A of Ex. 4-26.

■ Assignment 1 - *Aural analysis of form*

Using the aural analysis process presented in Chapter 1, analyze Exs. 4-28 to 4-43 as two-, three-, four-, or five-part forms. The musical ideas of the indices may begin an introduction, one of the parts or its recurrence, a transition, a retransition, or a codetta. Use the knowledge thus far acquired from your reading to make formal designations according to arrangement, content, and apparent purpose of a musical idea. For example, if the initial listening revealed that the musical ideas were arranged in order of 1-2-1, the form would be an ABA or ABA¹ form with no auxiliary members. As a more complex example, musical ideas arranged in an order of 1-2-3-1 would present the formal options of an ABCA form or a ternary form with AB retransition A. The choice between the two options will be governed by the character and purpose of the third musical idea. Should it be modulatory, fragmented, sequential, and relatively brief, this third musical idea is probably a retransition rather than a Part C which would tend to be tonally stable and to fall into regular phrases. Some of the possibilities suggested by different sequential patterns of musical ideas are shown below:

Order of musical ideas	*Possible formal patterns*
1-2-1	ABA or ABA¹
1-2-1-2-1	ABA¹BA¹
1-2-3-2	introduction ABA¹
1-2-3-1	AB retransition A¹, or ABCA
1-2-1-3	ABA¹ codetta
1-2-3-2-4	Introduction ABA¹ codetta
1-2-3-1-4	AB retransition A¹ codetta, or ABCA codetta
1-2-1-3-1	ABACA
1-2-3-2-1	ABCBA
1-2-3-4-2-5	Introduction ABCA¹ codetta, or introduction AB retransition A¹ codetta

After three to five listenings to a work, the analysis should reveal the following structural information: (1) the number and arrangements of parts; (2) the number of phrases within each part; (3) any use of auxiliary members. The accuracy of your aural analysis can be checked against the formal diagrams of Appendix I.[7]

If thorough aural analysis of a work fails to reveal at least the larger structure, a study of the musical index and formal diagram of the work as it is heard will accrue considerable knowledge and aural experience in musical form.

---

7. Attention should be given to the small unit term (phrase, period, etc.) that defines the contents of a part, but, for present purposes of aural analysis, only the number of phrases within a part needs to be indicated.

Musical Indices

Ex. 4-28. Bartok: *Mikrokosmos*, No. 128.
   Appendix page—560

The canonic imitation in the fourth musical idea will disturb the aural clarity of the phrasing. Since the upper line of a two-voice canon is usually the more audible voice, the phrasing of the formal diagram in Appendix I is based on this premise.

Ex. 4-29. Beethoven: Eleven Bagatelles, Op. 119, No. 5.
   Appendix page—560

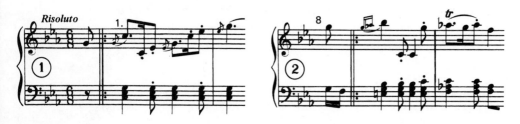

Ex. 4-30. Brahms: Piano Quintet in F Minor, Op. 34, II.
   Appendix page—560

In formal analysis of the music of Brahms, take into consideration the efforts made by this composer to break down the "bar line barrier." These efforts resulted in phrases of irregular lengths, cadences on weak beats, and cadences that were often evaded or elided.

Ex. 4-30. (Continued).

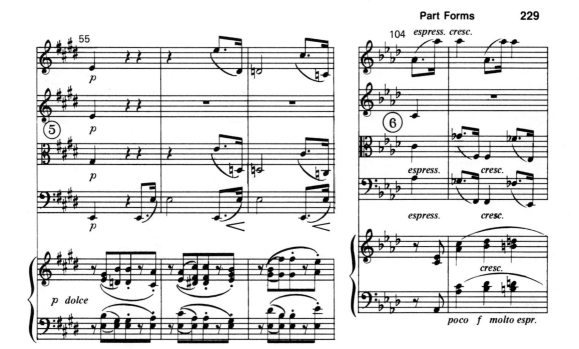

Ex. 4-31. Chopin: Mazurka, Op. 7, No. 3.
Appendix page—561

Ex. 4-32. Chopin: Mazurka, Op. 41, No. 2.
Appendix page—562

Ex. 4-33. Haydn: Sonata in E♭ Major (Peters No. 32), II.
    Appendix page—562

This excerpt uses canonic imitation which lengthens most of the regular four measure phrases to five. It also causes upper and lower voices to cadence a measure apart so that one voice is in the state of anacrusis while the other voice is completing the cadence.

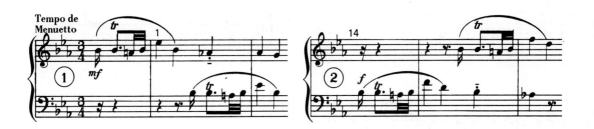

Ex. 4-34. Haydn: String Quartet in E♭ Major, Op. 33, No. 2, III.
    Appendix page—563

Ex. 4-35. Hindemith: *Ludus Tonalis*, Interludium in F.
    Appendix page—563

     Although the structural delineation is clear, this work presents an unusual order of parts and tonalities.

Ex. 4-36. Kabalevsky: 24 Preludes, Op. 38, No. 6.
    Appendix page—564

Ex. 4-37. Kennan: 2 Preludes (1951), No. 2.
    Appendix page—564

Ex. 4-38. Mozart: Sonata in C Major, K.309, II.
    Appendix page— 565

  This work provides an excellent illustration of the embellishment, or variation, with which classic composers often treated recurring musical ideas.

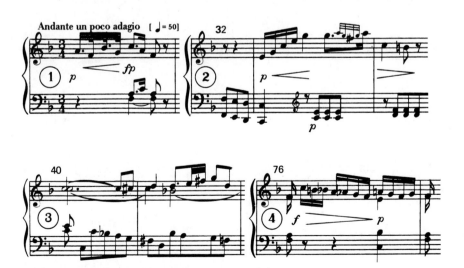

Ex. 4-39. Schumann: *Kinderszenen*, Op. 15, No. 2.
   Appendix page—565

Ex. 4-40. Schumann: *Kinderszenen*, Op. 15, No. 8.
   Appendix page—566

Ex. 4-41. Schumann: *Album for the Young*, Op. 68, No. 7.
   Appendix page—566

Ex. 4-42. Schumann: *Album for the Young*, Op. 68, No. 19.
   Appendix page—566

Ex. 4-43. Dimitri Shostakovich: 24 Präludien, Op. 34, No. 10.
  Appendix page—566

■ Assignment 2 - *Aural analysis of content*

In the aural analysis of the form of Exs. 4-28 to 4-43 many of your decisions grew out of an instinctive or conscious recognition of the musical relationships and purposes present in the works. To strengthen your aural perception of musical process and purpose, analyze certain of the works again and verbalize your responses to the musical effects. This can be done aurally or with scores. Questions such as the following will focus attention on particular aspects of a work:

1. What is the stylistic relationship of Part B to Part A in Exs. 4-28, 29, 33, 36, 37, 39, 40, 42, and 43? Ex. 4-28 reveals an extremely close relationship between Parts A and B with the use of a four-bar melodic idea as the primary basis for both parts. In a monothematic work such as this the analysis focus could be the stylistic *differences*, such as texture, dynamics and tonality, as well as the stylistic similarities.

2. In the codettas of Exs. 4-28, 29, 34, 38, 40, and 43, what musical elements contribute to the depletion of musical energy or to the concluding effect? Contrast the endings of these works to the concluding passages of Exs. 4-36, and 4.37.

3. In Exs. 4-28, 30, 31, 34, 36, 38, and 43 which transitions and retransitions contain tonal instability and key change, and which also anticipate musical elements of the forthcoming parts? For instance, as a result of an evaded cadence the retransition of Ex. 4-28 be-

gins with the G tonality of the Part A¹ that follows. There is in the retransition, however, anticipation of the repeated note pattern that is so characteristic of Part A. As an interesting contrast to Ex. 4-48, the retransition of Ex. 4-43 contains considerable aural preparation for the forthcoming tonality of Part A¹ without actually containing a tonality change.

■ Assignment 3 - *Analysis with score*

Each of the examples for further study is one of the part forms, and certain works contain one or more auxiliary members. For several reasons the process of analysis with score should continue to be preceded by a certain amount of aural analysis: the visual impact of a score tends to distract aural concentration; as teachers and performers, musicians must often grasp the large structural elements of a work without benefit of a score; the increasing ability to aurally comprehend structure and content saves an enormous amount of time for the student of forms.

A valuable tool of formal analysis is the ability to make a musical index of the ideas contained within a work. No doubt small forms could be analyzed without benefit of an index because they do not overtax musical memory. As the formal structures grow larger, however, the need for this research tool increases. The process of making an index of the musical ideas is more easily mastered with small forms, therefore the following process is suggested for the analysis of selected additional part forms.

1. With the first listening, check those places on the score where a sectional separation results from a strong cadence plus an ensuing new musical idea. The beginning tendency will be to mark these locations excessively. A second listening with score may reduce the number of sections.

2. Copy the first one or two measures of the musical idea at the beginning of each section. Do not copy recurrences of ideas. Note on the score the measure number and key that begin a section, and the key and cadence that ends the section. Number the ideas consecutively.

3. Use the index to listen an additional time without score, making note of the arrangement of ideas and of any additional formal factors that can be detected aurally.

Each individual will evolve his own continuing process for completing the analysis. The results should include an analysis comparable to those in the appendix as well as a cognitive response to the combined effect of musical elements, techniques, and purposes contained in the work.

Examples for further study

Each of the following works or movements is comprised of one of the part forms. Specific numbers in a set are indicated as "no. 1," etc.; movements of a sonata, quartet, or symphony are indicated by Roman numerals. Unusual arrangements of parts are noted and the auxiliary members are indicated in parenthesis after the citing of the work.

Two-part Forms

BARTOK   *Mikrokosmos*, Nos. 126 and 139.

BEETHOVEN   Bagatelles, Op. 119, No. 8.

BERNSTEIN   *Seven Anniversaries*, No. II.

BRAHMS   Waltzes, Op. 39, Nos. 5 and 6.

DELLO JOIO   Suite for Piano, 1945, No. IV (introduction AB introduction AB combined, codetta of introduction material).

HAYDN   Sonatas (Peters ed.), No. 7 in D, II; No. 37 in G, III (codetta).

HINDEMITH   *Ludus Tonalis*, Interludia in E and in A♭.

MUCZYNSKI   Six Preludes for Piano, Op. 6, No. 4 (AB retransition A¹B¹ codetta).

SCHUMANN   *Kinderszenen*, Op. 15, No. 10.

Three-part Forms

ADLER   *Capriccio*, 1954, (retransition).

BARTOK   *Mikrokosmos*, Nos. (40 (introduction), 47 (introduction), 81, 94, 97 (introduction), 125 (introduction), and 138 (introduction).

BEETHOVEN   Bagatelles, Op. 119, Nos. 2 (codetta), 4, 9, and 11 (ABC codetta).
                Bagatelles, Op. 126, Nos. 1 (codetta), 3 (retransition, codetta), and 5.

BERNSTEIN   *Four Anniversaries*, Nos. I, II (codetta), and IV (codetta).
                Seven Anniversaries, Nos. I, V, and VII (ABC).

BLOCH   *Poems of the Sea*, No. II (transition, retransition).

BRAHMS   Intermezzi, Op. 76, No. 4 (codetta); Op. 119, No. 1 (retransition); Op. 119, No. 3 (retransition).

Waltzes, Op. 39, Nos. 1, 2, 3 (retransition), 4, 7, and 8.

CHOPIN   Mazurkas, Op. 6, No. 4; Op. 7, No. 5 (introduction); Op. 17, No. 2 (retransition); Op. 24, No. 3 (codetta); Op. 30, No. 1; Op. 33, No. 3; Op. 41, No. 3; Op. 59, No. 2 (retransitions, coda); Op. 63, No. 2; Op. 67, No. 2 (retransition); Op. 67, No. 3; Op. 68, No. 4.

Nocturnes, Op. 9, No. 2 (codetta) and Op. 15, No. 3 (ABC codetta).

DEBUSSY   *Images* (First Suite) for Piano, *Reflets dans l'Eau* (retransitions).

DELLO JOIO   Suite for Piano, 1945, No. III (introduction, retransition).

FINE   Music for Piano, 1949, No. 1.

GINASTERA   12 American Preludes, No. 7.

HARRIS   American Ballads for Piano, Set I, No. I (monothematic, ABA¹).

HAYDN   Sonata (Peters ed.), No. 11 in G, II (codetta); No. 30 in D, II; No. 31 in D, II (codetta); No. 38 in D, II (codettas, retransitions).

String Quartet, Op. 54, No. 2, II

HINDEMITH   *Ludus Tonalis*, Interludia in G and in D.

KABALEVSKY   24 Preludes, Op. 38, Nos. 4 and 8.

MUCZYNSKI   Six Preludes for Piano, Op. 6, Nos. 3 (transition), 5 (codetta), 6 (introduction, codetta).

PROKOFIEFF   Classical Symphony, Op. 15, III.

ROREM   Barcarolles, 1949, Nos. 1 and 2.

SCHUMANN   *Davidsbündlertänze*, Op. 6, Nos. 1, 2, 4 (codetta), and 5.
Carnaval, Op. 9, Nos. 2 (codetta), 3, 4, 5, 10, 11, 13, and 18.
Kinderszenen, Op. 15, Nos. 1, 3, 4, 6, 7, 9, and 13.
Album for the Young, Op. 68, Nos. 1, 2, 3, 5, 6, 8, 9, 10, 13, 14, 15, 16 (codetta), 17 (codetta), 20, 21, 22, 24, 25, 26, 27, 28, 30, 34, 36 (introduction, codetta), 38, 41, and 43.

Scriabine   Etudes, Op. 2, No. 1 (ABA¹BA²) and Op. 8, No. 12 (introduction).

Shostakovich   24 Praludien, Op. 34, Nos. 6 (ABC), 10 (codetta) and 13 (retransi-
                tion).

Four-part Forms

Bernstein   *Five Anniversaries*, No. II (codettas).

Chopin   Mazurkas, Op. 30, No. 2 (ABCB); Op. 33, No. 1; Op. 63, No. 3.
                Nocturne, Op. 15, No. 2 (codetta).

Schumann   *Kinderszenen*, Op. 15, No. 12.

Scriabine   Etude, Op. 8, No. 10 (ABAB¹C retransition ABC¹A¹ codetta).

Five-part Forms

Beethoven   String Quartet in E♭, Op. 74, II (retransitions, codettas, coda).

Brahms   Intermezzo, Op. 76, No. 7 / alternate analysis: prelude, ABA codetta,
                postlude.

Chopin   Mazurkas, Op. 6, No. 1; Op. 6, No. 2 (introductions); Op. 6, No. 3
                (introductions); Op 7, No. 1; Op. 7, No. 4; Op. 24, No. 4 (introduc-
                tions, coda); Op. 30, No. 3 (introduction); Op. 41, No. 4; Op. 56,
                No. 2; Op. 68, No. 3 (introduction).

Ginastera   12 American Preludes, No. 3.

Hindemith   *Ludus Tonalis*, Interludia in A (retransition) and in E♭.

Mozart   Sonata in C, (K.545), II (codetta).

Schumann   *Album for the Young*, Op. 68, Nos. 18 and 33.

Seven-part Forms

Beethoven   Bagatelles, Op. 33, Nos. 1 (codetta) and 6 (codetta).

Chopin   Mazurka, Op. 50, No. 1 (ABACAD coda like A).
                Waltz, Op. 69, No. 2.

Rochberg   Twelve Bagatelles for Piano, No. 12.

Schumann   *Carnaval*, Op. 9, No. 15.

                  Kinderszenen, Op. 15, No. 11.

                  Album for the Young, Op. 68, No. 37 (ABACAB[1] codetta like A).

Chain of Parts

Bartok   *Mikrokosmos*, No. 151 (retransitions).

Rorem   Barcarolles, 1959, No. 3 (introduction, retransitions).

5 . small formal units

The small units of musical structure can be likened to the words and sentences within a discourse. Linked together into a temporal span, small formal units contribute internal order and growth to a larger expression of musical or verbal thought.

A vocabulary of definitive terms that describes the small formal units in music has become more or less standard, and this chapter will be directed toward the meaning of these terms and the musical devices for fulfilling the meanings. The vocabulary is fairly limited; the musical possibilities inherent in each term of the vocabulary are fairly extensive. So we shall begin with the vocabulary itself which is listed below:

1. Motive   4. Period
2. Figure   5. Double period
3. Phrase   6. Phrase group

Motive and figure

The *motive* is the smallest structural unit in music that has the potential for significant development in the larger structure. By description, the motive is a musical fragment of linear pitches formed in a rhythmic pattern, a fragment that may or may not have a distinction in isolation. The determination that a melodic fragment has the potential for generating larger musical patterns is often made only after one sees and hears the ways that the composer has used the fragment. As an illustration Ex. 5-1 shows the following uses that Beethoven made of a beginning fragment that is really nothing but a broken arpeggio with irregular rhythm.

Ex. 5-1. Beethoven: Sonata in C Minor, Op. 10, No. 1, I.

Motive repeated to form a longer unit within the phrase

Motive with octave displacement, added notes and changed rhythm to form a later phrase

Motive transformed further to form later structural areas

Through its use by the composer the fragment at the beginning of Ex. 5-1 has gained motivic distinction and has shown a potential for significant development. Later in the composition the same motive is used in a manner that would be described as *figural*. If there is a distinction between the terms ''motive'' and ''figure''—and many musicians do not acknowledge this difference—it would depend in a large measure on the use of the melodic fragment. In the last excerpt of Ex. 5-1 the broken arpeggio motive that was expanded so significantly in the melodic line is used in a completely subordinate way to form an accompaniment figure.

The Phrase Cadence

The basic small formal unit is the *phrase*, which is analagous to a clause in verbal expression and which ends with a relative cessation of musical activity. This cessation of motion occurs at the cadence, and the degree of repose at this point depends on the context in which the phrase appears. Because the cadence is so essential to the articulation of a phrase, the means of effecting cadences will be examined.

Traditional cadences exploit harmonic clichés and harmonic rhythm. One becomes so conditioned to cadential formulae in traditional compositions that the sound of a I_4^6, for example, can immediately suggest that the musical activity will slow or cease altogether and that the following chords will form a half cadence, a deceptive cadence, an authentic or a plagal cadence. These terms are familiar from the study of harmony. Associated with the cadential formulae will be a slowing of the melodic rhythm and very often a descending melodic line. These are the obvious characteristics of traditional cadence points.

A number of other musical techniques are perhaps less obvious but equally effective in articulating the end of a phrase. In Ex. 5-2 the slowing of the harmonic rhythm, and coincidentally the bass, at the cadence point is the only cessation of motion in a melodically incessant passage. The harmonic analysis of the phrase is open to a number of possibilities, but the slowing of harmonic rhythm from a chord each half measure to a single chord of a measure's length is evidenced by the temporary cessation of bass motion in measure 4. This example also illustrates a means of enunciating a cadence point in retrospect. In measure 5 the melodic line begins a restatement of the first four bars an octave higher, and the aural announcement of a next phrase strengthens the cadential effect of the preceding measure.

Ex. 5-2. Schumann: *Kreisleriana*, Op. 16, No. 1.

A small musical mannerism can announce the beginning or the ending of a phrase, and thus reinforce a cadence on either side of it. Ex. 4-10 in the preceding chapter illustrated this type of phrase and cadence articulation, as does Ex. 5-3 in this chapter. At measure 8 of Ex. 5-3 the repeated pitches could be associated with either the phrase that precedes or follows, but it becomes clear in measure 12 and 13 that this is a cadence mannerism, not an anacrusis because the melodic line is broken by a rest after the repeated pitches of measure 12.

Ex. 5-3. Bartok: *Mikrokosmos*, No. 128.

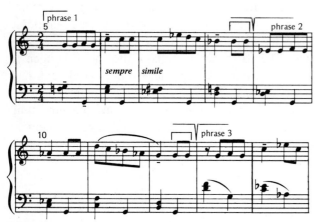

The interesting thing about cadences is that their degree of repose is as much dependent on what succeeds as on what is preceding and immediate. In Ex. 5-4 Bartok has used a distinctive motive to literally ''announce'' each one of a succession of phrases, and the effect of this motive on each preceding cadence is to strengthen its sound of repose. Also at measure 56 there is a sudden change of dynamics, tempo, and orchestral timbre, which further delineates the structural articulation at the cadence point.

Ex. 5-4. Bartok: Violin Concerto No. 2, I.

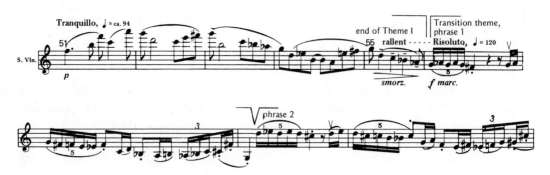

At all structural levels change of any kind is a formal delineator, and the cadence of a phrase can be strengthened or even retroactively created by a change in the following phrase. Changes in the direction of a melodic line are common between successive phrases, and other kinds of change can affect the accompaniment, the texture, and so forth. Ex. 5-4 showed a sudden change of intensity and tempo in measure 56 which heightened the articulation between sections. In Ex. 5-5 the cadence of the first phrase is created by all the customary means of line, rhythm, and harmony; then suddenly in the succeeding phrase the Alberti bass is omitted, and the texture changes from accompanied melody to imitation. Both acts reinforce the cadence of the first phrase.

Ex. 5-5. Mozart: Sonata in F Major, K. 332, I.

Since the cadence articulates structure at the smallest level and since there are many successive phrases in an entire composition, composers have used several devices to gain both a sense of repose and continuation at the cadence points. If musical motion was halted dramatically at each cadence point, continuity would soon be dissipated and musical energy could not accumulate over longer temporal spans. As with all musical effects, a balance of repose and energy is essential with cadences. Some of the ways of achieving musical repose have been illustrated, and their antithesis is found in the devices of weakened cadences, elided cadences, and melodic extensions, all of which supply musical continuance. Weakened cadences result from the use of cadence chord members other than the root in the outer voices or from placing the final cadence chord or pitch on weaker beats of a measure.

Another common technique for balancing the repose of a cadence with desired motion forward is to let the cadence overlap the beginning of the next phrase, a technique named *elision*. Eliding of phrase extremities often shortens the first phrase, and additional musical energy is generated through the change of length. Ex. 5-6 illustrates the elision of the last phrase of a thematic area with the first phrase of a closing area. The bracketed melodic motive simultaneously concludes one phrase and begins the next one.

Ex. 5-6. Brahms: Piano Quintet in F Minor, Op. 34, II.
(piano part)

Melodic continuation fills in the horizontal space between the cadence point of one phrase and the beginning of the next phrase. In the previous Ex. 5-2 the space between phrase end and phrase beginning is filled with continued arpeggiation of the members of the cadence chord. The same harmony begins the next phrase, and the anacrusis to this phrase simply adds to the continuous melodic motion. Melodic continuation of the cadence melody or harmony is much less common as a "filler," however, than is melodic continuation by way of an anacrusis into the next phrase. The melodic "pick-up" not only fills the temporal space but provides forward impetus as well. The anacrusis to a phrase may range from a single note to a long series of tones like the pattern shown in Ex. 5-7. Note also that in this example the longest cadence pitch is placed on a weaker beat of measure 14 as another means of melodic continuation.

Ex. 5-7. Bartok: Violin Concerto No. 2, I.

Copyright 1941, 1946 by Hawkes & Son (London) Ltd.; Renewed 1968. Reprinted by permission of Boosey & Hawkes, Inc.

The Phrase

As the basic structural unit of musical form, the phrase is the most immediate expression of musical direction. At the structural level of the phrase, the musical objectives may appear to be nothing more than the cadence and the following phrase. Gradually, however, consecutive phrases accumulate and begin to shape the larger structure.

All of the elements of music create the phrase, but to the listener melody and rhythm are generally the most audible characteristics. The internal structure of the phrase line is likely to be in one of three patterns: a series of like motives; a linking of two halves or semiphrases; or a line that does not have internal subdivisions. Exs. 5-8 through 5-12 illustrate these three possibilities.

Ex. 5-8. Beethoven: Sonata in F Minor, Op. 2, No. 1, III.

Internal motivic structure

Ex. 5-9. Stravinsky: Octet for Wind Instruments, II.

Internal semi-phrases

Ex. 5-10. Brahms: Intermezzo Op. 76, No. 4.

Internal semi-phrases in sequence

Ex. 5-11. Mozart: Sonata in F Major, K. 332, I.

Continuous line

Ex. 5-12. Dimitri Shostakovich: 24 Präludien, Op. 34, No. 10.

Continuous line

In traditional compositions basic phrase lengths are likely to be two, four, or eight measures long, depending on the tempo. Various extensions lengthen certain phrases, but symmetry is the prevailing sound of eighteenth and early nineteenth century musical phrasing. Brahms, who was a traditionalist in most matters of musical structure, seems to have made a deliberate effort to break down the barrier of the bar line and the regularity of the phrasing. The excerpt of Ex. 5-13 is only one of numerous examples in the music of Brahms where the phrases are shorter or longer than the common lengths of two, four, or eight measures.

Ex. 5-13. Brahms: Rhapsody, Op. 119, No. 4

It would be interesting to trace composers' increasing exploration of durational elements to discover if there is a parallel with the exploration of tonal resources that was taking place in the late nineteenth century. At any rate, irregular phrasing has become as common in twentieth century music as changing meters and all other exploitation of duration.

Repetition of the Phrase

When a phrase is repeated immediately after it is stated composers have often changed the repetition. Some of the commonly used modifications of a repeated phrase are illustrated in Exs. 5-14 through 5-16. In traditional literature repeated phrases are most likely to be modified through melodic embellishment or change of register, while twentieth century changes in the repeated phrase typically express increased interest in the resources of timbre, duration, and intensity.

Ex. 5-14. Beethoven: Sonata in F Minor, Op. 2, No. 1, III.

Repeated phrase with change of register and some melodic change at the cadence.

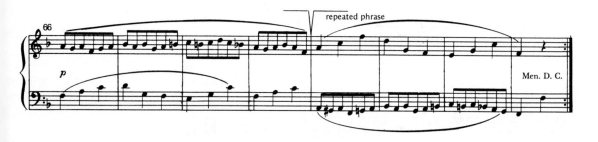

Ex. 5-15. Prokofieff: Symphony No. 5, Op. 100, II.

Repeated phrase with melodic embellishment at the beginning

Ex. 5-16. Prokofieff: Symphony No. 5, Op. 100, I.

Repeated phrase with changes of timbre (orchestration), duration (rhythm and meter), and intensity (dynamics)

Extensions of the Phrase

In many compositions the phrasing will create a general pattern of regularity through commonly used phrase lengths, and phrases that are shorter or longer than expected will be aurally distinctive. Shortened phrases may be inherently so, or they may be the result of elided cadences. Lengthened phrases may also be inherently so, but more often the lengthened phrase has been extended by one or more of several techniques. Any of the melodic or harmonic components of a phrase can be repeated; any of the melodic components of a phrase can be used sequentially or imitatively. These devices used at any point in a phrase may extend it beyond the common phrase length of the composition.

Before examining the use of extension techniques, several things need to be noted. The terms *repetition, sequence,* and *imitation* are fairly specific in meaning and distinction. All three terms describe successive recurrence of a musical idea. Repetition, however, implies that essentially the same pitches are still present in the restatement, regardless of modifications, while sequence implies transposition of the essential pitch contour. In a homophonic texture, repetition and sequence are usually effected in the melody line, wherever it is placed, although sequence can be a harmonic transposition as well as a melodic one. By fundamental definition imitation suggests two or more melodic lines in a statement-answer arrangement and implies a more polyphonic texture. Repetition and sequence are particularly common techniques for extending a phrase, but they are just as frequently used to form phrases that are not extended. For instance, Exs. 5-2, 5-8 and 5-10 illustrate regular four-measure phrases formed almost completely by internal sequence, and Ex. 5-6 begins with repeated measures although the phrase is a regular length. Only if a phrase is longer than most of the surrounding phrases is it considered extended.

By far the most frequent device for phrase extension, repetition can be applied to the following elements of the phrase:

1. Introduction figures at the beginning
2. Any motive or melodic fragment
3. Either half of the phrase
4. Any chord within the phrase or at the cadence

Imitation and sequence are most often internal phrase extensions, although sequence can be used with a final melodic fragment to form a modulatory bridge into the next phrase.

In Ex. 5-17 the phrase is extended by repetition at both the beginning and the end. The repeated accompaniment figure that initiates the phrase is also instrumental in outlining the cadence harmonies and their repetition. In this example the melodic line of the cadence is modified when the cadence chords are repeated.

Ex. 5-17. Prokofieff: Symphony No. 5, Op. 100, II.

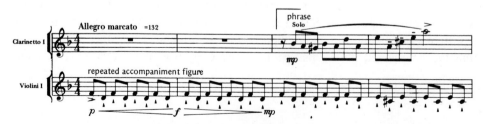

The entire phrase of Ex. 5-18 grows out of repetition and sequence of a single motive. The internal phrase structure is so integrated that no appearance of the motive sounds "extended," and the asymmetry of motive use provides some energy to a melodic line that halts every measure.

Ex. 5-18. Brahms: Piano Quintet in F Minor, Op. 34, I.

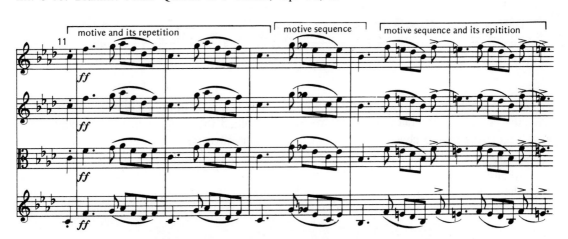

The next use of repetition extends the first half of the phrase so that finally the phrase length is doubled. Used near the beginning, repetition of a half phrase will have the sound of interrupting the impetus of the phrase toward the cadence.

Ex. 5-19. Beethoven: Sonata in C Minor, Op. 10, No. 1, I.

Repetition of the last half of a phrase has a quite different aural effect than does repetition of the first half. When well used this technique seems to stretch out the motion of the phrase, and the cadence in Ex. 5-20 is immediately weakened in order not to impede the flow. The origin of the repeated line is more visual than aural as it is partially concealed in an inner voice.

Ex. 5-20. Schumann: *Album for the Young*, Op. 68, No. 19.

Extension by repeating or prolonging a harmony within the phrase is always in the context of the harmonic rhythm. For example, if there has been in a particular passage a harmonic change every measure or half measure, a chord that is repeated or prolonged for two or more measures within the phrase is likely to disturb the balance of the phrase and to lengthen it. The phrase of Ex. 5-21 is first extended by sequence, then by a prolonged supertonic chord in measures 165-166.

Ex. 5-21. Mendelssohn: Violin Concerto in E Minor, Op. 64, I.

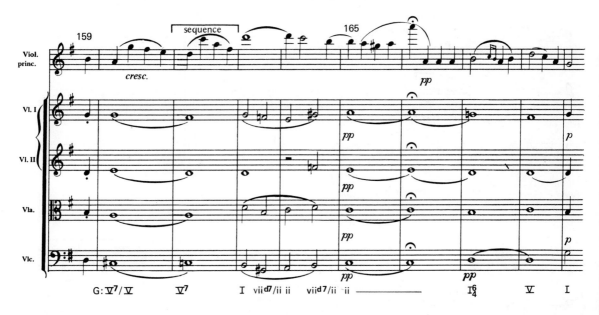

The next two examples illustrate phrases that are extended by imitation. In the phrase of Ex. 5-22 the imitation is of a free canonic type, and the phrase is only slightly lengthened because of the closeness of imitative entry. Ex. 5-23 first uses a dialogue between strings and piano, and the imitative entries grow closer until finally the ensemble is performing identical lines in mid-measure 85.

Ex. 5-22. Kennan: 2 Preludes, No. 2.

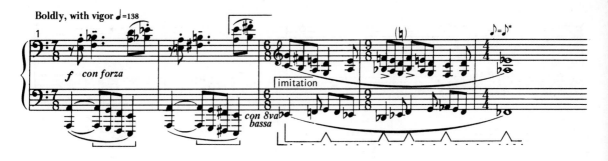

Ex. 5-23. Brahms: Piano Quintet in F Minor, Op. 34, I.

Cadence evasion can be even more diverting than the cadence evasion of Ex. 5-23, and the temporal span needed to return to the original cadence objective may lengthen the phrase without benefit of any other extension technique. In such instances the phrase is considered extended by the act of cadence evasion.

Much of phrase extension takes place at or around the cadence, and several other means of cadence extension are illustrated in the next examples. In measure 6 of Ex. 5-24 the cadence melody is harmonized with the E minor accompaniment figure. When the melodic fragment is repeated in the next measure, the supporting harmony changes to the chord that will accompany the next phrase, thus acting as a link between phrases.

Ex. 5-24. Shostakovich: String Quartet No. 3, Op. 73, II.

A similar effect of linking occurs in Ex. 5-25, but here the cadence line is sequentially stated with a new harmonization that leads to the key of the next phrase.

Ex. 5-25. Brahms: Rhapsody, Op. 119, No. 4.

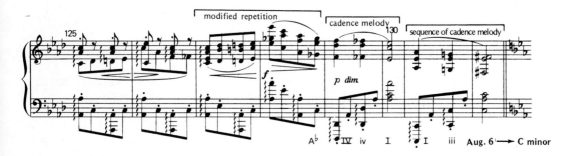

Ex. 5-26 appropriately closes the discussion of cadence extensions by illustrating the addition of the plagal cadence after the phrase has ended.

Ex. 5-26. Chopin: Nocturne, Op. 37, No. 1.

The Period, Double Period, and Phrase Group

Aural analysis of Ex. 5-27 would reveal a ternary structure with Parts A, B and A¹ as marked on the score. Four-bar phrasing is articulated by the rests, and the internal structure of each part is extremely regular. In analysis terms it is customary to designate the internal structure of a single part by a single term that identifies the small formal unit. Part B is only a phrase. Part A¹ is formed of two phrases that are very similar in sound but whose cadential objectives differ. The second phrase completes the idea begun by the first phrase, and the small unit term for the contents of Part A¹ is a *parallel period*. The four phrases of the first part are balanced in almost the same manner as the two phrases of the last part. There is a difference of tonal objective in the departure sound at the end of Part A and the return sound at the end of Part A¹, and the size of Part A is double that of Part A¹. Despite the similarity of halves, the contents of Part A are not a repeated period for the same reason that Part A¹ is not a repeated phrase: essential differences in the cadences at the midpoint and at the end. The four phrases of Part A form a *parallel double period*, and the ternary form represents three different small formal units of graduated size: phrase, parallel period, and parallel double period.

Ex. 5-27. Beethoven: String Quartet, Op. 18, No. 2, IV.

Ex. 5-27. (Continued)

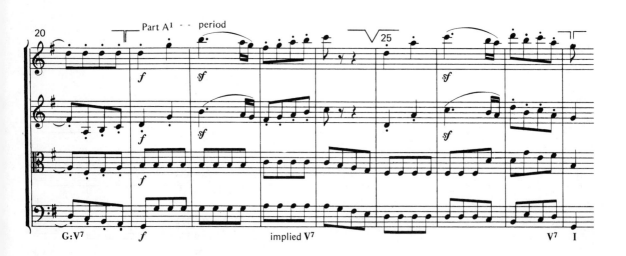

Additional examples of periods and double periods follow to increase familiarity with the terms and the musical meaning of the terms. Ex. 5-28 illustrates a parallel period whose two phrases are three measures each, whose melodic contours and rhythmic patterns are similar, and whose cadences differ. The customary names for the first and second phrases of the period are shown on the score.

Ex. 5-28. Hindemith: *Ludus Tonalis*, Interludium in F.

Sequence forms the two halves of the period in the next example, and repetition as a technique of phrase extension continues the musical motion well past the usual length of a single period. Sequence, repetition, imitation and the special devices of cadence extension are useful to extend any phrase of the basic small formal units. Ex. 5-29 illustrates the use of repetition to extend the second phrase in two different ways. Notice the very light cadence effect in measures 7 and 8 at the end of the consequent phrase, and the expansion of the repeated cadence formula into an extended harmonic form and finally a more terminating melodic sound.

Ex. 5-29. Beethoven: Sonata in F Minor, Op. 2, No. 1, III.

The decision to use a particular phrase length in the analysis of a certain composition should be based on more than the tempo, although tempo is an important factor. Ex. 5-30 is performed in one-beat measures, but rather deliberately so. If there was some sound of greater repose in measure 5, the tempo would not preclude phrases of four bars. However, the rhythmic pattern of this measure is precisely as it has been for three preceding measures, and the ♩ ♪ 𝄾 notation indicates that the eighth note is not an anacrusis to a next phrase. Phrasing of eight measures is indicated here by the musical elements. Ex. 5-30 also illustrates a period whose two phrases are in contrast to one another by direction, duration, and timbre, and the term *contrasting period* is sometimes used to describe the dissimilarity of successive phrases that are held together in this instance by the larger structure.

Ex. 5-30. Prokofieff: Violin Concerto No. 2, Op. 63, III.

(Violin and piano score) Copyright 1947 by the International Music Co. Reprinted
by permission.

Any of the phrases of the small formal units can be repeated, as can any of the
total units. Ex. 5-31 illustrates a period and its embellished repetition that is cut a bit
short at the end by a two-measure elision into a next section. The repeated period constitutes the entire second theme of a much larger form. When a theme is a single part
form (Part A), as it often is in larger works, repetition of the small formal unit that
constitutes the part is an effective technique to emphasize and expand the musical
idea.

Ex. 5-31. Beethoven: Sonata in C minor, Op. 10, No. 1.

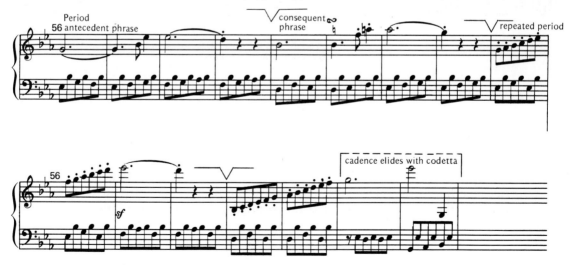

The contrasting double period of Ex. 5-32 has a delightful sound of statement, departure, and return in miniature. The rhythmic symmetry of the first two phrases relates them to one another; the irregular grouping of rhythmic patterns in the third phrase is sufficient change to create an aura of departure; and the regular patterns of the last phrase restore the balance as the line descends with a sound of return. If only this much of the composition is heard the four phrases have an effect of ABA¹ or ABC. However, the following section of the work puts the excerpt of Ex. 5-32 in the smaller perspective of a contrasting double period that forms a single part.

Ex. 5-32. Bartok: Concerto for Orchestra, II.

Copyright 1946 by Hawkes & Son (London) Ltd.; Renewed 1973. Reprinted by permission of Boosey & Hawkes, Inc.

One other small formal unit results from various combinations of phrases. Generally there are three, five, or six phrases in a *phrase group*, and there are a number of ways that the phrases can be grouped and related to one another. In Ex. 5-33 the three phrases could be marked "a b c" to denote that each of them has a certain distinction of melodic line. Cohesion of the three into a formal unit is the result of the similar rhythmic pattern in the first and last phrases and the larger formal structure of a following Part B.

Ex. 5-33. Hindemith: Piano Sonata No. 2, III.

■ Assignment 1 - *Aural and visual analysis of form*

The following musical excerpts will each be an example of a phrase, a period, a double period, or a phrase group, with any of the extensions discussed. There is a certain amount of frustration in formal analysis of a brief excerpt, and it would be desirable to hear the entire work from which the excerpt is taken. As an alternative the excerpt can be played with piano, and, in some instances, the melodic line sung or played will provide enough aural background to analyze the excerpt.

First determine the small formal unit. Your analysis can be checked against the referred analyzed model or formal diagram that appears elsewhere in the book. In deciding on the basic unit of the excerpt, remember several things:

1. The indicated meter and tempo will have considerable bearing on the phrase lengths.

2. If you hear two dissimilar phrases, the small formal unit will be a period. If you hear two similar phrases, the options are that it is a repeated phrase or a parallel single period. Comparing the cadential objective of each phrase will be the decisive factor. The same analysis problem doubled could be a repeated period or a double period. The decision still rests essentially on the similar or dissimilar weight of the midpoint and final cadence. As an example of interpreting combinations of melodic lines and cadences the following diagrams represent interpretations of illustrative combinations of melodic lines and phrases.

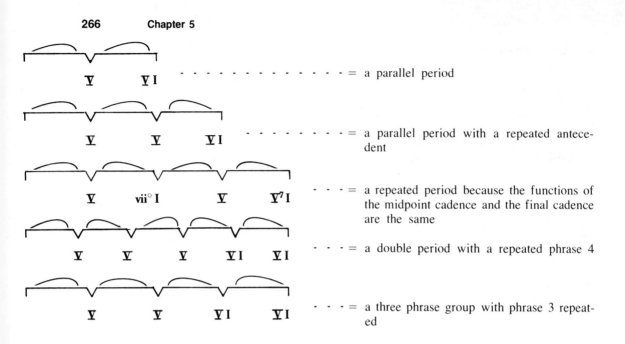

= a parallel period

= a parallel period with a repeated antecedent

- - = a repeated period because the functions of the midpoint cadence and the final cadence are the same

- - = a double period with a repeated phrase 4

- - = a three phrase group with phrase 3 repeated

Musical Excerpts

Ex. 5-34. Bartok: Violin Concerto No. 2, I.
(See Appendix formal diagram for Ex. 8-13)

Ex. 5-35. Beethoven: Sonata in A Major, Op. 2, No. 2, IV.

(See Appendix formal diagram for Ex. 7-10)

Ex. 5-35. (Continued)

Ex. 5-36. Beethoven: Sonata in D Major, Op. 28, I.

(See Appendix formal diagram for Ex. 8-15)

Ex. 5-37. Brahms: Piano Quintet in F Minor, Op. 34, I.

(See Appendix formal diagram for Ex. 8-17)

Ex. 5-38. Hindemith: Piano Sonata No. 2, III.

(See Appendix formal diagram for Ex. 7-15)

Ex. 5-38. (Continued)

Ex. 5-39. Mozart: Sonata in F, K.533/494, III.

(See Appendix formal diagram for Ex. 7-16)

Ex. 5-40. Schubert: String Quartet in D Minor, III.

(See Appendix formal diagram for Ex. 6-23)

Ex. 5-40. (Continued)

■ Assignment 2 - Aural analysis of content

Use the recorded compositions for assignment 1 of Chapter 4 and analyze the small formal units and extensions within each part. If possible do this analysis without using the musical indices.

6 ▪ combination of part forms: ternary design

With the combination of two or more part forms as the basis for a complete work or movement, there begins to emerge a distinction between those composite part forms that are sectional and those that are continuous. The distinction will never be total, but it will rest on the degree to which the sectional or continuous characteristics are present. As a generalization the sectional work will have more full stops and less transition material than the continuous work. A comparison of Exs. 6-1 and 6-12 will reveal both these distinctions. The full stops of Ex. 6-1 occur in Song Form I after the first Part A and the codetta, and in Song Form II after Part C and its recurrence. Performed with repeat marks and the *da capo* the total number of full stops in Ex. 6-1 will equal ten. The full stops of Ex. 6-12 occur in Theme I at the end of Part A, again at the same place when Theme I recurs, and finally at the end of the work—three full stops. As a further distinction Ex. 6-1 has no transition or retransition passages as compared to the fifteen measures of such material in Ex. 6-12.

Song Form with Trio

Two song forms (part forms) combined into one work of a sectional nature are traditionally called *song form with trio*. The structure is so arranged that the first part form recurs immediately after the second one, thus forming a large ternary design. Synonomous terms for the design are *Minuet with Trio* and *Scherzo with Trio*.

Formal incorporation of two small and somewhat dissimilar compositions into one work probably has its historical roots in the *da capo* vocal and choral forms. Other influences come from the Baroque practice of pairing consecutive dance movements in an instrumental suite, with directions to repeat the first dance after the second. The "trio" derives from the Baroque practice of thinning the texture of a second dance to three instruments, a practice that became extinct while the term remained extant. Throughout the latter part of the eighteenth century and most of the nineteenth century the song form with trio often appears as a third movement in a four movement work.

Other examples are found in single works, usually for piano, or as a piece in a set of pieces.

The traditional pattern of the song form with trio is quite stereotyped: it is sectional; at least one of its song forms is binary or ternary; the trio (second song form) is usually delineated by a change of key signature but not of meter signature; and the return of the first song form is often not written out but is indicated by a *da capo* mark at the end of the trio. As a model Ex. 6-1 illustrates many of the typical features of the eighteenth and nineteenth century song form with trio. The work is very sectional, but the close tonal relation between the two song forms and within each of them permits a logical flow of the music despite the full stops followed by a change of key. Each of the song forms is a small ternary design, with the neighbor tone figure serving to relate internal parts and the two song forms. There is, however, a distinction in the incessant rhythmic pattern of the trio that sets it apart from the minuet as a separate song form. More often than not the song form and its trio will have no overt relationship other than a common meter and proximity.

Another typical feature of Ex. 6-1 is the sign at the end of the trio. Even though the ''senza replica'' (without repeats) had not been stated with the *da capo* indication, it is a traditional performance practice to play the first song form the second time without any of its repeats.

Ex. 6-1. Beethoven: Sonata in B♭ Major, Op. 22, III.

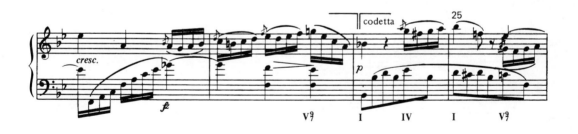

Ex. 6-1. (Continued)

Although Ex. 6-1 clearly represents a sectional type of combined part form (song form with trio), other expectations need to be noted.

Tonality

The expectations about key relationships in the traditional song form with trio differ somewhat with different composers, but overwhelmingly the tonal relationships are parallel modes or closely related keys. Haydn, in his early use of the song form with trio, showed a preference for moving from a major key to the parallel minor key and back again. Examples of this tonal plan are present in many of the minuet movements of his piano sonatas. Other common tonal plans are shown below with certain composers cited as showing some preference for particular schemes:

Song form I	Song form II	Examples
major tonic	V, IV or vi keys	
minor tonic	VI key	Beethoven: Sonatas, Op. 10, No. 2, II; Op. 14, No. 1, II; Op. 27, No. 1, II. Schubert: Sonata in C Minor, Op. posth., III.
major or minor tonic	same key	Beethoven: Symphonies Nos. 1 and 8, III. Schuman: Carnaval, Op. 9, No. 9; Album for the Young, Op. 68, No. 11.

The surprising feature of late romantic examples of song form with trio is the continued close relationship of the tonal schemes in the midst of much use of chromatic harmony. Chopin and Brahms both wrote a number of their shorter piano works in this sectional form, but only two examples of really unusual tonal relation can be cited: Chopin, Mazurka, Op. 17, No. 3, A♭ major to E major; Brahms, Ballade, Op. 118, No. 3, G minor to B major. Tonality as a delineator of form has lost much of its impact in the twentieth century, and the other parameters of music have become more important in this respect.

Formal Content

At least one of the song forms is binary or ternary, and, if the one-part form is used, it is more often the basis for the second song form that the first. For example, if a series of parts produced the aural effect of ABCBA, one might have difficulty determining whether the work was a five-part form or a song form of one part with a trio of three parts. Distinctions in style will be the decisive factor.

Style Relationships

One of the most distinguishing features of this combined sectional form is the difference in style that usually exists between the two song forms. When performed in full Ex. 6-2 illustrates the pattern previously described: ABCBA. The stylistic contrast between Part A and Parts B and C distinguishes the one-part form (Part A) from the next three parts (Parts BCB); the stylistic likeness of Parts B and C cause them to adhere into a small ternary design. The actual formal pattern when the whole work is heard is as follows: Song form I, Part A; Song form II, Parts BCB; Song form I, Part A. Although not shown in Ex. 6-2, the written out return of the first song form is given greater importance by the addition of a two section coda. The first section of the coda is in the style of the partially embellished return of Part A, and the second section is in the style of Part A as it was initially stated. By means of a coda a better balance is achieved in the work.

Ex. 6-2. Beethoven: Eleven Bagatelles, Op. 119, No. 1.

A comparable problem can exist when the second song form is only one part, and the solution again lies in the style similarity or contrast. Two other of Beethoven's Bagatelles will form diagrammatic patterns that are identical: ABACAABABA codetta. Parts A, B, and C of Ex. 6-3 are so similar, and Parts A and C are particularly so, that the total aural effect will be that of a seven-part form with repeats and a codetta.

Ex. 6-3. Beethoven: Seven Bagatelles, Op. 33, No. 6.

In Ex. 6-4 there is an abrupt and pronounced stylistic change at measure 16 when Part C is stated. This disturbance of the congruence formed by Parts A, B, and A will result in the following pattern: Song form I, Parts ABA; Song form II, Part C; Song form I, Parts AABABA; codetta.

Ex. 6-4. Beethoven: Seven Bagatelles, Op. 33, No. 4.

Auxiliary Members

There is no apparent reason why composers occasionally chose to follow the trio with a retransition to the *da capo*. In sectional works such as the song form with trio, the ear of the listener is already conditioned to full pauses followed by a style change by the time the trio ends. Nevertheless, retransitions do appear in this location, and they serve the usual purposes of transitions and retransitions: to aurally prepare the listener for tonality and/or style change. As can be seen by the beginning fragment of Part A. Ex. 6-5, the composer has made no effort in the retransition to bridge the style change to the forthcoming *da capo* but has instead created a sound of anticipation with the evaded cadences and the final cadence on the dominant. There is no separation by a terminating cadence between the end of the trio and the beginning of the retransition, which strengthens the continuous effect and the aural anticipation. Indeed, in the process of dissolution,[1] it is not possible to determine exactly where statement ceases and the act of retransition begins. The change of tonality from the D minor of the trio to the D major of the menuetto is accomplished through the mutual dominant chord.

Ex. 6-5. Mozart: String Quartet in D Major, K. 499, II.

1. Dissolution is the process in music whereby the purpose (e.g., statement) of a musical passage changes to a different purpose (e.g., transition) without the interruption of strong cadence articulation.

Ex. 6-5. (Continued)

evaded cadence and retransition

The retransition illustrated by Ex. 6-6 serves two musical purposes simultaneously: the final cadence of the trio is repeated to form a small extension and it also uses the style of the Scherzo to anticipate its return. The four bars are named retransition rather than codetta since this seems to describe more accurately the primary musical purpose, but there is no question about the concluding sound of the passage.[2] Both song forms are in B♭ major, but there is a considerable style distinction between them which is aurally bridged by measures 64-68.

Ex. 6-6. Beethoven: String Quartet in B♭ Major, Op. 18, No. 6, III.

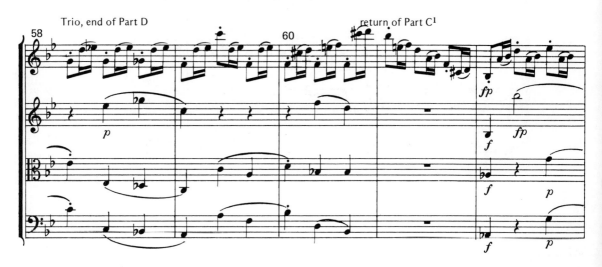

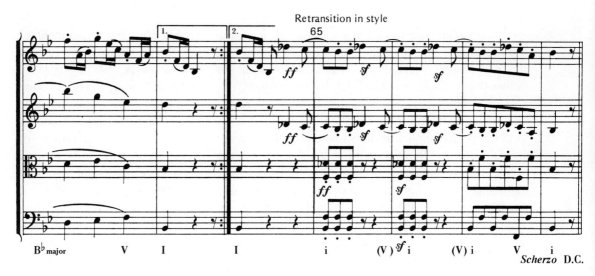

2. Perhaps someone should coin amalgamated terms such as "codition" or "transetta." The potential is infinite.

Ex. 6-6. (Continued)

It is rather rare to find the addition of a codetta or coda after the restatement of the first song form. So often a codetta is an integral part of the first song form that the *da capo* assures a closing section at the end of the work also. Ex. 6-7 illustrates a composition whose written form is in a pattern of song form I, song form II, song form I, codetta. The only difference between the first song form and its recurrence is the omission of the final tonic chord before the codetta. A first and second ending could have accomplished the same effect, but, as any performer knows, the turning of pages in the middle of a continuous passage is not desirable. So the first song form is written again without any changes until the end. The coda is composed of two sections: the first one in the style of the first song form with subdominant implications at the beginning, and the second one acting as an extended cadence in a style that is distinct from either of the preceding song forms. Through the elements of range, dynamics, and rhythmic activity the climax of musical intensity is actually reached in the coda, and the musical intensity is never completely dissipated as the work ends. This example is part of a set of pieces that is performed consecutively, and, since the next piece in the set begins at a much lower level of musical energy, the ending of this work provides contrast.

Ex. 6-7. Schumann: *Kreisleriana*, Op. 16, No. 3.

Code, section 1

Ex. 6-7. (Continued)

Introductions are not particularly common to the combined part forms. When an introduction occurs, its content and length are comparable to that of an introduction that might precede a single part form. An example can be seen in the Chopin Mazurka, Op. 50, No. 2 where eight measures of dominant harmony introduce the characteristic mazurka rhythm.

A new term *link* has been used in Ex. 6-21 of the diagrams in the appendix, the musical pattern of which is shown in Ex. 6-8. The meaning of the term is admittedly less explicit than the meaning of the term *transition*, but a link can be considered as any bridging material between phrases of a part or parts of a theme. Thus it is not leading to a different formal area in the sense of a transition. In Ex. 6-8 (and Ex. 6-21) the aural effect of the link is to introduce another restatement of the much repeated phrase of Part A. The material of the link is derived from the short introduction at the beginning of the work, and, with each use of the link, the accompaniment pattern of Part A is anticipated.

Ex. 6-8. Prokofieff: Symphony No. 5, II.

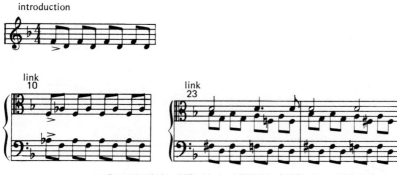

Modification of the **da capo**

When the recurrence of the first song form is written out it seems to have been for the purpose of adding a new codetta or coda, as in Ex. 6-7, or as a means of modifying the restated material. Ex. 6-9 illustrates the influence of variation techniques on other forms. The structural pattern of the entire work is shown below with the variants of the parts indicated by superscripts:

Song form I	Song form II	Song form I	Song form II	Song form I
$\|$: A :$|$$|$: B :$|$	$\|$: C :$\|$ retransition	AA^1BB^1	$\|$: C^1 :$\|$ retransition	AA^2BB^2

This work demonstrates such an amazing blending of typical classical variants and transformations of a more advanced sort that the entire work is presented in Ex. 6-9. Parts A[1] and B[1] employ typical classic variants of scalar passages and nonharmonic tones, with the original melodic contour still serving as a melodic framework. The variant technique of Part C[1] is more typically that of the nineteenth century where a single characteristic sound is abstracted from the original source and used throughout. This often effects considerable change in the original melodic contour, as it does here. The changes of Part A[2] essentially grow out of chromatic nonharmonicism, but the melodic contour of the original Part A is still apparent. The changes in Part B[2] seem to unfold in the manner of true transformation, and the original melodic contour is perhaps more concealed here than in any previous variant.

Ex. 6-9. Haydn: Sonata in E Major (Peters No. 40), III.

Song form II, Part C

25
retransition

30

Song form I, Part A

Part A¹   40

Ex. 6-9. (Continued)

Ex. 6-9. (Continued)

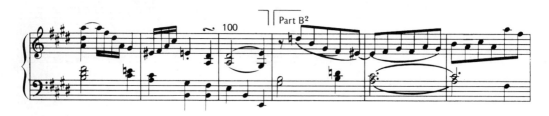

A quite different modification of the recurring first song form is illustrated in Ex. 6-10. The first song form is a binary pattern that is repeated immediately with a new accompaniment and a thicker texture for Part A¹. Part B remains unchanged with each appearance. In the written *da capo* the texture of Part A² is further thickened, as is that of the restated codetta. Changes in texture and also in timbre are techniques that are particularly useful when restating ideas in a chamber or orchestral work.

Ex. 6-10. Brahms: Intermezzo, Op. 117, No. 3.

One additional model will illustrate a twentieth century use of the song form with trio. Ex. 6-11 has many of the characteristic effects of the traditional song form with trio. Both Song forms I and II come to a full stop before continuing on. The tonal relationship of Parts B to Part A is that of dominant to tonic, and the style of each part is closely related by beginning intervallic and rhythmic patterns. Song form II derives more of its material from Song form I than is usual in a traditional song form with trio, but distinction is gained from a new accompaniment pattern, a switching of voices, a different dynamic level and different accentual placement of the melody line.

Determining the phrase structure can present a problem unless one listens for the means of articulation that are characteristic of this work. The cadence of measure 4 is elided and is set off by the longer note and rest which both end and begin a phrase. As an articulative element, duration is here reinforced by the downward leap comparable to the beginning interval. Hemiola halts the motion of the second phrase of Part A. In Part B the first cadence is articulated by duration, a mirror of the characteristic beginning interval, and a shift of the bass ostinato pattern. Similar techniques delineate the remainder of the small structure, with the additional factor of greater vertical consonance at the cadence points.

The retransitions are characterized by an instability that results from the restatement of the bracketed motive on different beats and with different temporal spans. This irregularity is more pronounced because it is surrounded by a texture of a regularly recurring bass ostinato.

The primary distinction between this work and a more traditional song form with trio is the tonality of the restated first song form. Traditionally a restatement occurs in the beginning key of the work, regardless of any other modifications. In twentieth century works tonality simply cannot be relied on to delineate musical form as it did in preceding centuries.

Ex. 6-11. Hindemith: *Ludus Tonalis*, Interludium in C#.

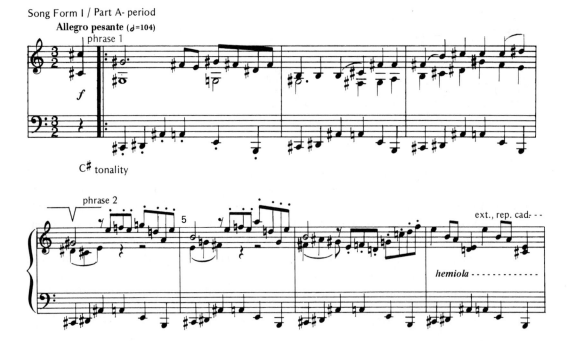

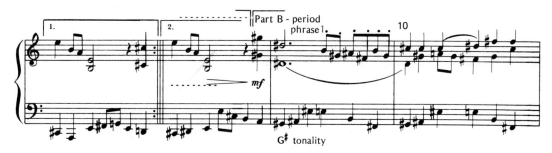

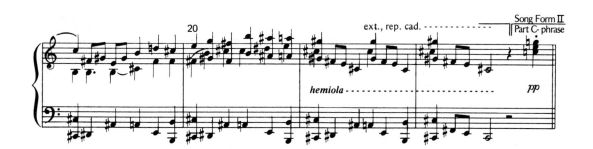

Ex. 6-11. (Continued)

C tonality

Aᵇ tonality

B tonality

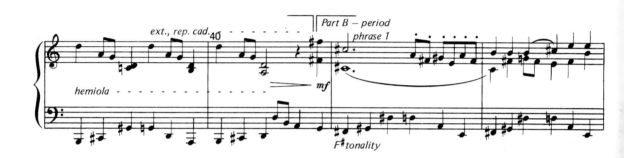

Ex. 6-11. (Continued)

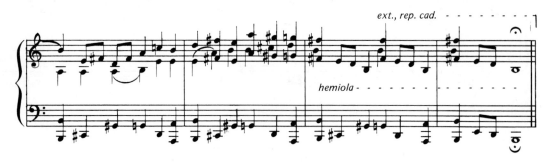

Large Continuous Ternary Form

The effect of tempo on a musical structure may have more impact than we realize. Since the sectional song form with trio is often marked with a moderate to fast tempo, the accumulation of musical energy can maintain the continuity of the work despite numerous sectional pauses. Conversely a work in slower tempo might lose the continuity of musical thought if full stops are frequent. For one thing, the pause is likely to be longer in a slow tempo than in a fast tempo. Another factor might be the extent of the listener's musical memory. These are speculative thoughts. Nevertheless, composers have been inclined to avoid sectionalization when the large ternary form is the basis of a slow movement.

Ex. 6-12 represents a more continuous, large ternary structure than the song form with trio, although the formal diagram of each will appear very similar. As was discussed earlier in this chapter, a number of factors contribute to the difference in effect between Ex. 6-12 and 6-1. This work has only three full stops, and its themes (part forms)[3] are linked by a transition and a retransition respectively. The tonality of the two themes is in third relationship, and a transition of one measure bridges the tonal difference. A two-section retransition of fourteen measures is used to return to the first theme. These circumstances illustrate some important characteristics of transitions and

3. It is a fairly common practice to identify the part forms of a large continuous ternary structure as *themes* rather than *song forms*. This is no doubt a derivative term from the rondo designation sometimes given to this form. One can adjust to the different terms by recognizing that *part forms, song forms,* and *themes* are synonomous terms, and that any distinction in usage is simply the result of traditional vocabulary.

retransitions on which certain aural expectations can be based. First, the length of transition areas is completely unpredictable. Second, the act of bridging tonal and/or style differences can be done in one section or can be divided into two sections that may serve somewhat different musical purposes. Measures 37-41 of the retransition give the effect of departure by modulating to the temporary key of B♭ major. Measure 42 begins as a restatement of Theme I that is interrupted after the third measure to progress through two measures where the musical energy is suddenly increased by dynamics and canonic imitation. In measure 47 the dynamic level suddenly lowers, the texture thins, and the line descends through a diminished seventh chord arpeggiation that ends on V⁷/V in the key of Theme I. Modulation, sequence, fragmented lines, and abrupt tension and release - these all contribute to the aural instability so common to transition areas.

When Ex. 6-12 is heard, similarities to the sectional song form with trio can be noted. Theme I is a ternary form; the arpeggiated bass of Theme II creates a style distinction although both themes share the appoggiatura figure appearing in measures 8 and 28. As a contrast to the song form with trio, Ex. 6-12 has no repetitions of either theme, the work is comparatively continuous in sound, and there is an increase in the amount of material that is not expository.

Ex. 6-12. Beethoven: Sonata in E♭ major, Op. 7, II.

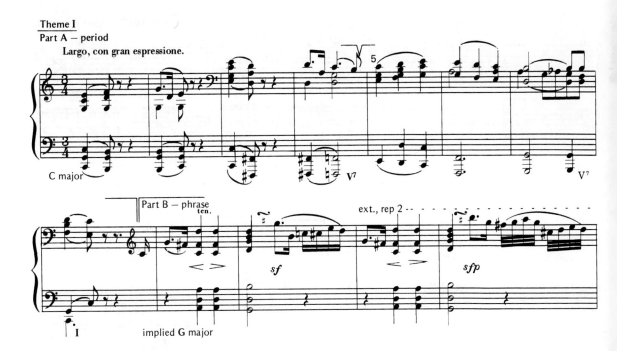

Ex. 6-12. (Continued)

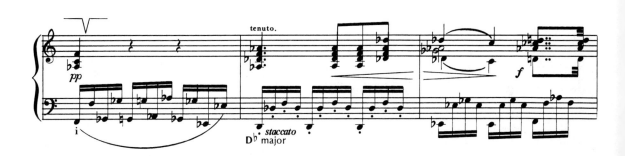

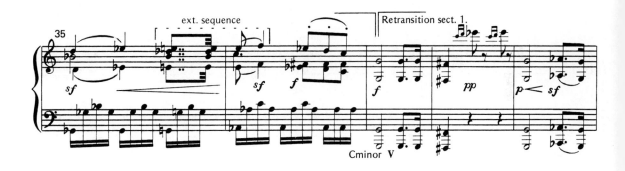

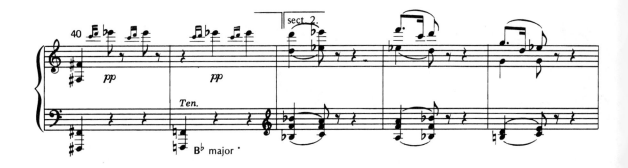

Ex. 6-12. (Continued)

Ex. 6-12. (Continued)

■   **Assignment 1 -** *Aural analysis of form.*

Each ensuing chapter will continue to present larger forms, which, in turn, many contain many more themes (song forms) than are presently contained in the large ternary form. From this chapter forward, the appendix diagrams will consistently indicate consecutive parts within each theme as AB, ABA, ABC, and so on, rather than attempting to designate different letters for the parts of each next theme. For example, a large ternary form may appear thus:

Th. I (or S.F.I)   Th. II (or S.F.II)

Part A ① Part B ② Part A¹ ①   Part A ③ Part B ④ Part A¹ ③

The numbers of the musical indices will clarify a difference of melodic ideas within themes, and it is believed that the visual impact will be more clear.

Musical Indices

Ex. 6-13. Bartok: Concerto for Orchestra, II.
Appendix page—567

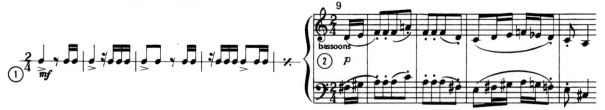

Ex. 6-14. Beethoven: Sonata in F Minor, Op. 2, No. 1, III.
Appendix page—568

Ex. 6-15. Brahms: String Quintet in G Major, Op. 111, III.
Appendix page—569

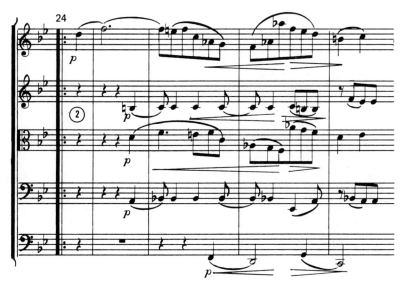

Ex. 6-15. (Continued)

Ex. 6-16. Brahms: Ballade, Op. 118, No. 3.
    Appendix page—571

Several ideas in this work are reused for a second musical purpose. For example, a transposition of idea ① interrupts Part A of Theme II and is then followed by Part A again. In this way the interruption acts as a "departure" before a "return."

Extensions are not marked in the formal diagram of the appendix; only a study of the score can reveal the kind of internal motivic extensions that appear in the phrases of a Brahms' work.

Ex. 6-16. (Continued)

Ex. 6-17. Chopin: Mazurka, Op. 7, No. 2.
Appendix page—571

Ex. 6-18. Chopin: Nocturne, Op. 37, No. 1.
  Appendix page—572

This work has characteristics of both the song form with trio and the large continuous ternary form. Almost all the material is expository, which is typical of the song form with trio. Its tempo is slow, however, and the interval sections are linked to one another by continuous sound. This is characteristic of many of the piano works of Chopin.

Index numbers have not been assigned for the transition to Theme II and the retransition to Theme I because each is a single chord. They are shown below, however, with the other musical ideas.

Ex. 6-18. (Continued)

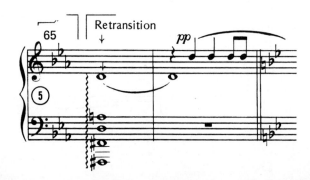

Ex. 6-19. Mozart: Symphony in D Major (Haffner, K.385), III.
Appendix page—573

Ex. 6-20. Prokofieff: Violin Concerto No. 2, Op. 63, II.
Appendix page—574

Counter melody

Ex. 6-21. Prokofieff: Symphony No. 5, Op. 100, II.
Appendix page—575

This work illustrates the means by which a twentieth century composer has extended a combined part form, which is traditionally a rather small form, into a movement whose length is in good proportion with the remainder of this symphonic work. The Prokofieff example should be compared to Ex. 6-13 by Bartok and Ex. 6-24 by Shostakovich in which different means are used to accomplish the same purpose.

Ex. 6-22. Ravel: *Le Tombeau de Couperin*, V.
    Appendix page—577

Impressionist music is essentially tonal, but there are often areas in a work by Ravel or Debussy where analysis in the traditional sense is inappropriate. In the formal diagram of the appendix the tonal areas are indicated, and traditional cadence formulas are shown when they are used. At other cadence points only the pitch name of the chord appears.

Ex. 6-23. Schubert: String Quartet in D Minor, III.
  Appendix page—578

Allegro molto

Ex. 6-23. (Continued)

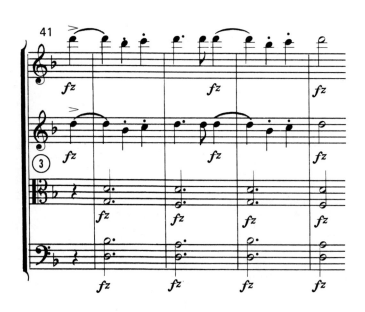

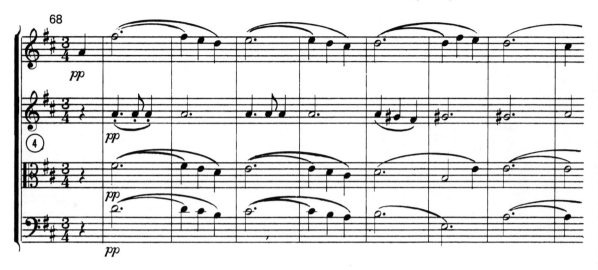

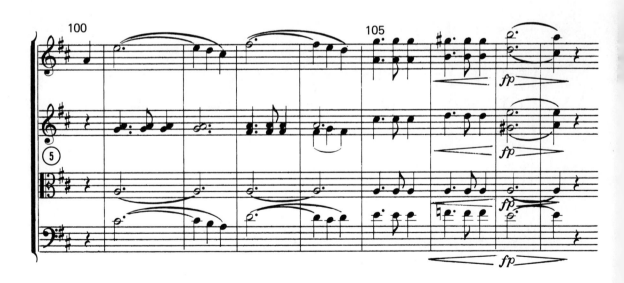

Ex. 6-24. Schumann: *Kreisleriana*, Op. 16, No. 1.
   Appendix page—579

Melodic cadences are less audible in the motor-rhythmic drive of the upper line, and attention should be concentrated on the articulation of the lower voices.

Ex. 6-25. Shostakovich: Symphony No. 5, Op. 47, II.
   Appendix page—580

   This second movement is commonly identified as a Scherzo with trio, despite its continuous sound. The large form is ternary, and the sixth musical idea of the index is first presented as a violin solo accompanied by harp and cello—an orchestral texture that is comparable to the Baroque practice of thinning the texture of a middle section to three instruments.

   Aural analysis of the musical purpose of sequential ideas may be confusing, however, because all the musical ideas sound "thematic" and most of them are regularly phrased. For the purpose of aural analysis certain guidelines are suggested. With the first level of analysis attention should be given to the type of writing that prevails within each melodic area: monophonic, homophonic, polyphonic, or a mixture. A second focus of aural attention can be given to the areas that include one or more musical ideas besides the primary idea. A third focus of aural attention should be the relative stability or instability of the tonality. Those areas that contain mixed textures, several musical ideas, and tonal instability can be identified as transition or retransition passages. The formal diagram of the appendix is changed to fit this consecutive process, and a structural alternative is included.

Ex. 6-25. (Continued)

■ Assignment 2 - *Aural analysis of content*

Diagramming the structure of a musical work is only one of the many ways to begin to understand how a composer has put together the elements of music. If the analysis process ends at this level, the sequence of musical events has been narrated, so to speak, but the reasons for the musical effects of these events are not yet understood.

Ideally, to comprehend the act of creating a musical work is to compose one. Much insight can be gained, however, by seeking to understand musical processes that have been used by very gifted composers.

As you listen again to certain of the compositions of assignment 1, either use the visual aid of the formal diagram or arrange to see both the thematic index and formal diagram. Your attention will then be freed of the "where" to go on to the "why" and the "how."

1. What are the elements of contrast between song forms (themes)?

In all of the compositions of assignment 1, except Ex. 6-17, several of the following contrasting factors are used to distinguish the two song forms:

Pitch   a. The tonality changes to a related key, a parallel key, a foreign key.
            b. Vertical sounds are more dissonant, more consonant.
            c. The melody has more or less accented nonharmonicism.
            d. The melody becomes more disjunct, more conjunct, of higher or lower range, of greater or lesser span.

Duration a. The meter or tempo changes.
            b. The melodic rhythm becomes more regular, more irregular, differently accented.

          c. The accompaniment rhythm becomes more regular, more irregular, changes from triple to duple.

          d. The harmonic rhythm accelerates, slows.

Texture   a. The number of voices (lines) decreases, increases.

          b. The melody becomes legato, accented, staccato.

          c. The accompaniment becomes arpeggiated, chordal, a fundamental bass.

          d. The general texture changes to melody with accompaniment, to an imitative style, to a chordal style.

Timbre   a. The general dynamic level becomes louder, softer.

and   b. Instrumentation changes.

Intensity   c. Melodic doubling thickens, thins.

The preceding listing is not at all comprehensive but is intended only as a guide to these particular compositions.

2. In the compositions where the recurrences of the first song form are written out, what changes have taken place?

An examination of the formal diagrams will reveal any changes in numbers of phrases within a part, of tonality and cadence, of length, or of material restated. Study again only those compositions that have such changes, or that are orchestral and therefore have the possibility of instrumentation changes that would not appear in the formal diagram.

■ Assignment 3. - *Analysis with score*

Each of the examples for further study is a combination of two song forms or themes into a larger ternary structure. In the first group the form as it would be interpreted aurally is indicated by the large ternary structure and the internal parts. For example if Song Form I is scored as the pattern $\|: A :\|: BA^1 :\|$, the first statement would be shown as AABA¹BA¹ and the *da capo* would be shown as ABA¹. Auxiliary members at the beginning and end of the complete work are cited, but internal auxiliary members are not shown. The second group of examples is simply a listing of additional works that form large ternary patterns.

Examples for further study, group 1.

BARBER   Sonata for Piano, Op. 26, II.
(Th.I, ABAB¹ / Th.II, A / Th.I, ABA¹CB¹A²BA / codetta)[4]

BEETHOVEN   Symphony No. 1 in C, Op. 21, III.
(S.F.I, AABA¹BA¹ / S.F.II, AABA¹BA¹ / S.F.I, ABA¹)

BRAHMS   Cello Sonata No. 1 in E Minor, Op. 38, II.
(S.F.I, AABA¹ / S.F.II, AABB / S.F.I, ABA¹)

COPLAND   Third Symphony, II.
(introduction 1-2 / Th.I, ABABA¹ / Th.II, ABA¹ / Th.I ABA / coda 1-2)

HAYDN   String Quartet in d, Op. 76, No. 2, II.
(S.F.I, AABA¹BA¹ / S.F.II, AABA¹BA¹ / S.F.I, ABA¹)

MENDELSSOHN   Violin Concerto in e, Op. 64, II.
(introduction / Th.I, AB / TH.II, ABA¹ / Th.I, A / codetta restatement)

MOZART   String Quartet in D, K.499, II.
(S.F.I AABA¹BA¹ / S.F.II, AABABA / S.F.I ABA¹)

POULENC   Sonata for Flute and Piano, I.
(Th.I, AA¹BA² / Th.II ABA¹ / Th.I, A / coda 1-2)

SCHUBERT   Sonata in E♭, Op. 122, III.
(S.F.I, AABA¹BA¹ / S.F.II, AABA¹BA¹ / S.F.I, ABA¹)

SHOSTAKOVICH   String Quartet No. 3, III
(Th. I, AAB / Th. II, ABA¹ / Th. I, AB / codetta using Th. II A and Th. I A)

Examples for further study, group 2.

BARTOK   Piano Concerto No. 2, II.

            String Quartets, No. I, I; No. 3, I; No. 4, II; No. 5, III; No. 6, II and III.

            Three Rondos, No. 3.

4. For an alternate analysis see Christ et al., *Materials and Structure of Music*, Vol. II, 2nd ed. (Englewood Cliffs, New Jersey: Prentice-Hall, Inc., 1973), p.43.

BEETHOVEN   Bagatelles, Op. 33, No. 4; Op. 119, No. 1; Op. 216, No. 4.

Sonatas, Op. 2, No. 1, II; Op. 2, No. 2, II and III; Op. 2, No. 3, II and III; Op. 7, II and III; Op. 10, No. 2, II; Op. 10, No. 3, II and III; Op. 14, No. 1, II; Op. 26, II and III; Op. 27, No. 1, II; Op. 27, No. 2, II; Op. 28, II and III.

String Quartets, Op. 18, No. 1, III; Op. 18, No. 2, II and III; Op. 18, No. 3, III; Op. 18, No. 4, III; Op. 18, No. 5, II; Op. 18, No. 6, III; Op. 59, No. 2, III; Op. 59, No. 3, III; Op. 74, III.

Symphonies, No. 2 in D, Op. 36, III; No. 3 in E♭, Op. 55, II and III; No. 4 in B♭, Op. 60, III; No. 5 in c, Op. 67, III; No. 6 in F, Op. 68, III; No. 8 in F, Op. 93, III.

BERLIOZ   *Fantastic Symphony*, Op. 14, II, III and IV.

BLOCH   *Poems of the Sea*, I.

BORODIN   Symphony No. 2 in D, II.

BRAHMS   Piano Works, Op. 79, No. 1; Op. 116, No. 3; Op. 116, No. 6; Op. 116, No. 7; Op. 117, No. 3; Op. 118, No. 2; Op. 118, No. 3; Op. 119, No. 2; Op. 119, No. 4.

Sonata in C, Op. 1, III.

Piano Quintet in f, Op. 34, III.

String Quartets, Op. 51, No. 1 in c, III; Op. 51, No. 2 in A, II; Op. 67 in B♭, III.

Symphonies, No. 1 in c, Op. 68, II; No. 3 in F, Op. 90, III.

CHOPIN   Mazurkas, Op. 7, No. 2; Op. 17, No. 1; Op. 17, No. 3; Op. 24, No. 2; Op. 33, No. 2; Op. 33, No. 4; Op. 50, No. 2; Op. 50, No. 3; Op. 56, No. 3; Op. 59, No. 1; Op. 59, No. 3; Op. 63, No. 1; Op. 68, No. 1; Op. 68, No. 2.

Nocturnes, Op. 9, No. 1; Op. 32, No. 2; Op. 48, No. 1; Op. 55, No. 1; Op. 62, No. 1.

DVORAK   Symphony in e, Op. 95, II.

FINE   *Music for Piano*, II.

HAYDN: Sonatas (Peters ed.), No. 1 in E♭, II; No. 2 in e, III; No. 3 in E♭, II; No. 6 in c♯ , III; No. 10 in G, II; No. 11 in G, III; No. 12 in G, II;

No. 13 in E♭, II, No. 14 in F, III; No. 15 in D, II; No. 18 in E, II; No. 20 in D, III; No. 30 in E, III; No. 35 in E♭, III; No. 37 in G, II; No. 40 in E, III.

String Quartets, Op. 74, No. 2, III; Op. 76, No. 2, II; Op. 76, No. 3, III, Op. 77, No. 1, III; Op. 77, No. 2, III.

Symphonies, No. 94 in G, III; No. 99 in E♭, III; No. 100 in G, II and III; No. 101 in D, II and III, No. 103 in E♭, III; No. 104 in D, II and III.

HINDEMITH   Sonata No. 3, II.

MENDELSSOHN   String Quartet, Op. 44, No. 1, II.

MILHAUD   *Scaramouche*, II (Parts A and B combined in the return of Theme I).

MOZART   Serenade for String Orchestra, K.525, III.

Sonatas, K.330 in C, II; K.331 in A, II and III; K.282 in E♭, II; K.136 in B♭, III.

String Quartets, K.421 in d, III; K.428 in E♭, III; K.458 in B♭, III; K.464 in A, II; K.465 in C, III; K.575 in D, III; K.589 in B♭, III; K.590 in D, III.

Symphonies, K.550 in g, III; K.551 in C, III.

PISTON   Symphony No. 4, III.

PROKOFIEFF   Piano Concerto No. 2, Op. 16, II.

SESSIONS   Symphony for Orchestra, II.

SCHUBERT   Sonatas, Op. 147 in B, II; Op. posth. in c, III; Op. posth. in B♭, II; Op. 78 in G, III.

Symphonies, No. 2 in B♭, III; No. 5 in B♭, III.

SCHUMANN   *Carnaval*, Op. 9, No. 9; *Kreisleriana*, Op. 16, Nos. 2, 3, 5, 7, and 8; *Album for the Young*, Op. 68, Nos. 11, 12, and 29.

SHOSTAKOVICH   String Quartet, No. 1, III.

Symphony No. 1, II.

SIBELIUS   Symphony No. 1, III (development of theme I before the trio).

7 ■ larger combinations of part forms

Compositions of larger structural design can be divided into two categories: one in which the material is primarily of statement nature with auxiliary members to introduce, link, or close the statements; and a second category in which the musical materials of the composition are developed or varied as well as stated. Where development does not play an important role, the large structural designs continue to build on a substructure of part forms and auxiliary members, but some one or more factors will exceed the ternary design. Expansion may result from further restatement of themes or from the addition of more themes, and the large form created is either a rondo or a chain of part forms.

The Rondo Principle

The structural principle of the rondo can be understood as an extension of the "statement, departure, return" principle of the large ternary design, with at least one additional departure and return added. The rondo pattern is one of alternating a first theme with two or more contrasting themes or sections. This pattern has already been encountered with the smaller five- and seven-part forms: e.g., ABACA, ABACABA, or ABACADA.

Historically the eighteenth century rondo probably evolved in a line from the medieval vocal *rondeau* through the seventeenth century instrumental *rondeau*. Since that time composers have frequently used the rondo form as the last movement of a three or four movement composition, and, less frequently, as the structure of the slow movement in multimovement works.

Tonality

If a quick survey is made of the tonal relationships found in the traditional rondos of the appendix, it reveals that the tonality continues to be closely related or parallel. The use of parallel modes can lead through keys that are foreign to the beginning tonality of the composition, but the foreign keys are usually brief and transient.

Aside from strengthening the sound of thematic departure and distinction, tonality is used in two other ways in the rondo form. If a second theme recurs again toward the end of a composition, it may be transposed into the key of the first theme so that there is a stronger confirmation of the final tonic key. Exs. 7-10 and 7-11 of the appendix illustrate this scheme. Tonality can also be used in lieu of a third theme, or second departure, as in Ex. 7-17 of the appendix. In this rondo there are only two themes, but the second theme recurs twice, each time in a different key.

Formal Content

Size is one of the major distinctions between the rondo and an alternating five or seven part form. Generally one or more of the themes of a rondo will be in binary or ternary form, and auxiliary areas are often expanded proportionately.

The order of themes will be one of the following illustrative patterns:

Theme I II I II I
Theme I II I III I
Theme I II I III I II I
Theme I II I III I IV I

Composers have frequently treated recurring themes with transposition, abbreviation, variation, or some other change. The continuation of this form into the twentieth century seems to indicate that it is aesthetically successful and also that it is a formal vehicle in which composers can express many different styles.

Style Relationships

The extent of thematic contrast between rondo themes depends very much on the historical period in which a composition was written, and sometimes on the particular composer. As a generalization, classic composers were less intent on expressing their own image through their music, and the themes in a work of the classic period are likely to be quite similar. Moreover, the larger forms were in an evolving state during the eighteenth century, and increasing expertise as well as an increasing sense of composer identity may account for the greater distinction of thematic material in the nineteenth and twentieth century rondos.

The musical elements that create variety or contrast in a composition are the same elements that also create unity. When studying a particular rondo the following categories and their subdivisions may offer an explanation of the manner in which themes are contrasting or complementary to one another. These musical elements will be discussed presently in the context of several compositions.

1. Pitch: tonality; types of chords; melodic contour; melodic range or span; use of nonharmonicism

2. Duration: meter; tempo; melodic rhythm; accompaniment rhythm; harmonic rhythm; temporal length

3. Texture: number of voices; relationship of voices as melody with accompaniment, chordal, contrapuntal, antiphonal; type of accompaniment; use of subsidiary melodies; use of legato, staccato, accent

4. Timbre: use of instrumentation; use of melodic doubling

5. Dynamics: use in gradation or sudden change; use as a complement to the style of melodic writing, range, and instrumentation

Auxiliary Members

In addition to the alternation principle which is basic to the structure, many rondos are also characterized by continuous motion. The internal codetta is therefore rather rare because the nature of a codetta is to deplete musical energy or to effect closure to some degree. An interesting combination of musical purpose can be found in many transition passages which begin as a repetition of the final cadence of the preceding theme, then somehow progress forward without the anticipated closure being effected. Ex. 7-1 illustrates a retransition[1] passage that will ultimately return to a restatement of the first part of Theme I. Part B has ended with a perfect authentic cadence in measures 29 and 30, and the cadence is repeated twice with melodic embellishment in measures 30-34. As the melodic figuration begins for a third time in measure 34, it begins to create a sense of anticipation, partly through listener irritation that such a nondescript pattern should continue to be repeated on identical pitches and partly through the change from an accompanied line to an unaccompanied one. The melodic pattern is used in a rising sequence in measures 35 and 36, and, with the addition of the pitch B♭, the tonic chord of C major becomes the dominant seventh chord of F major. The ultimate purpose of the passage is the return to the key of Part A.

Ex. 7-1. Mozart: Sonata in F Major, K.533/494, III.

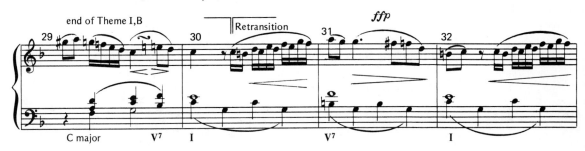

1. Traditionally the term *transition* is used for a passage leading away from Theme I and *retransition* denotes the passage leading to a restatement of Theme I.

Ex. 7-1. (Continued)

A more complex illustration of a passage with dual musical purpose appears in Ex. 7-2. The tempo is *allegro vivace*, and the energy of Theme I can be seen in the last phrase which cadences in measures 30 and 31. This energy is somewhat halted in the next seven measures, which progress harmonically through an evaded cadence and a return to the cadence that ended Theme I. In measures 38-45 the same harmonic progression is repeated with an increase of rhythmic energy. The embellished passage appears to begin a third time in measure 45 but the harmonic objective changes from a cadential extension to a modulation into the second key. The longer note values and the interspersed rests of measures 46-50 anticipate the slower rhythmic style of Theme II.

Ex. 7-2. Schubert: Sonata in A Minor, Op. 143, III.

Examples 7-1 and 7-2 illustrate an analysis problem that increases with the size of the form: that is, the means of distinguishing a codetta from a transition when both musical purposes are achieved within a passage of homogeneous style. One solution lies in the recognition that the location of modulation in a transition passage is unpredictable. If the ultimate purpose of a passage is forward and if the final cadence of the passage is progressive, transition is the more appropriate term for the passage. An alternative is to recognize the sequence of musical functions, determine the relation of musical content to function, and simply note this without the confines of formal terms. For instance, measures 32-38 of Ex. 7-2 are concluding in sound, measures 38-45 somewhat less concluding, and measures 46-50 anticipatory.

An additional facet of transition passages results from the rondo form in which Theme II is restated in the key of the tonic, as follows:

Structure	Th. I	transition	Th. II	Th. I	Th. III	Th. I	transition	Th. II	Th. I
Tonality	C	C → G	G		C	a	C		C

The original modulation purpose of the transition is eliminated, and the composer has several alternatives. The transition restatement can be omitted; or the transition can appear a second time in the expected location but with some changes in tonal direction to maintain the impression of moving toward a new tonality without actually doing so. Ex. 7-3 illustrates the latter technique.

Ex. 7-3. Beethoven: Sonata in E♭ Major, Op. 7, IV.

Ex. 7-3. (Continued)

It will become increasingly interesting to observe the ingenuity of composers to handle the compositional problem illustrated by Ex. 7-3.

Large rondos are frequently concluded with a coda of appropriate proportions. The coda either follows the last restatement of Theme I or it can act as a substitute to replace the final thematic statement. The structures of the two possibilities are illustrated as follows:

Th. I II I III I Coda

Th. I II I III Coda using Th. I material

Ex. 7-4 illustrates the second possibility in which a coda can create a very satisfactory sound of final thematic statement as the material begins to effect closure. This is another instance of a formal area serving two musical purposes. The difference in effect between the initial statement of Theme I and its final statement as coda material is achieved through differences in tempo, accompaniment rhythm, and dynamic levels. Other differences in effect result from the omission of the staccato passages and the energetic rhythmic patterns as the material is restated in the coda. The change of instrumentation allows the melody line to descend to a much lower range than was used in the beginning statement. The whole musical impact of measures 174-186 is of closure, yet the balance of a final restatement of the beginning theme is maintained.

Ex. 7-4. Shostakovich: String Quartet No. 3, Op. 73, II.

Ex. 7-4. (Continued)

Coda, section I

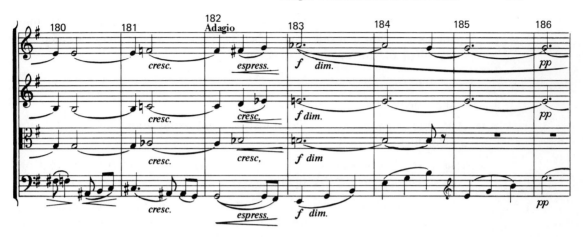

Analysis Models

The following compositions are illustrative of several rondo possibilities, and each one will be briefly discussed. The full scores should be studied with the recorded performance.

Summary of Ex. 7-5

1. Structure and tonality

   Theme I(A♭) II(E♭) I(A♭) III(f) I(A♭) IV(E♭) I(A♭)

2. Formal content

   a. Theme I is a ternary form and Theme III is binary.

   b. The monotony of literal repetition of the rondo theme is relieved by embellishment. Part A of the rondo theme is embellished as it recurs at measures 64, 82, 147, 190, and 210; Part B is embellished as it recurs at measures 72, 132, and 198.

3. Stylistic relationship

   a. Theme II is distinguished from the rondo theme by greater intensity, rhythmic patterns of shorter notes and a characteristic upward leap of a sixth that continues on in the same direction.

b. Themes III and IV are characterized by a relative lack of distinctive rhythmic patterns and, as a result, these themes have more the sound of departure areas than of true thematic material.

4. Auxiliary members.

a. The primary purpose of the transition and retransition areas is to effect modulation.

b. The first transition does, however, anticipate the characteristic interval of a sixth that appears in Theme II.

c. The retransition that begins in measure 110 has an interesting influence on the embellishment of Theme I that follows. In measure 115-116 a rapid arpeggio pattern is introduced. When Part B of Theme I is restated in measure 132 it incorporates the straight arpeggio in sixteenth notes as one of the embellishing features.

d. The brief codetta at measure 155 and the one at the end derive the repeated note figure of sixteenth notes from Themes II, III and IV, in which it appears in various forms.

Ex. 7-5. Haydn: Sonata in A♭ Major (Peters No. 41), III.

Ex. 7-5. (Continued)

Ex. 7-5. (Continued)

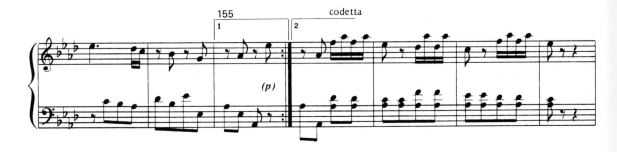

E♭ major

Ex. 7-5. (Continued)

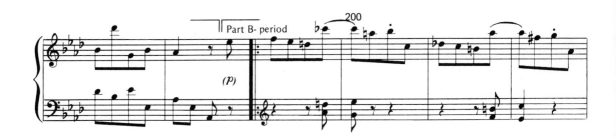

Ex. 7-5. (Continued)

Summary of Ex. 7-6:

1. Structure and tonality

    Theme I(c) II(Ab) I(c) III(C) I(c) II(C) I(c)

2. Formal content

    a. All three themes are initially stated in ternary forms with repeated parts. The three-part structure is less audible in Theme III than it is in the other two forms.

    b. Modification of recurring themes is accomplished by abbreviation and some melodic embellishment. The two embellished areas appear in the second statement of Theme I when each part is repeated. The change of melodic contour is simply an extension of the melodic rhythm of measures 1-2 into the remainder of the melodic line and the accompaniment.

3. Stylistic relationship

    a. The contrast of all themes in this composition is more pronounced than it is in the previous Haydn example, although both works are representative of the classic rondo.

    b. Theme II is distinctive for its legato line, change of accompaniment, and the use of an imitative texture to accompany Part B.

    c. Theme III combines legato and staccato lines, and uses a figure that is derived from the first measure of Theme I. Distinction is given to this theme by the imitative entries at the beginning of Parts A and B and by the use of pedal.

4. Auxiliary members

    a. The transition of measures 110-116 is further illustration of an area with dual purpose. The harmonic progression reiterates the cadence that ended the third statement of Theme I, but there is no final sense of closure in measure 116 because the passage ends on a dominant chord.

    b. The first section of the retransition in measures 137-162 builds the sense of anticipated return by a series of two bar patterns formed of the first two measures of Theme I and a modified inversion of the pattern. The line gradually rises in a sequence as the intensity increases. The second section of the retransition is a prolonged dominant sound that thins at the end to a texture of one instrument on two long notes. Beethoven was such a superb master of the prolonged dominant!

    c. The three sections of the coda form a final ternary pattern by use of material from Theme I in the first and third sections. The second section acts as a departure by introducing a syncopated pattern. The final tonality is major and uses a telescoped figure created from measures 1 and 3 of Theme I.

Ex. 7-6. Beethoven: String Quartet in C Minor, Op. 18, No. 4, IV.

Measures 1-16, Theme I, AABA¹BA¹

Ex. 7-6. (Continued)

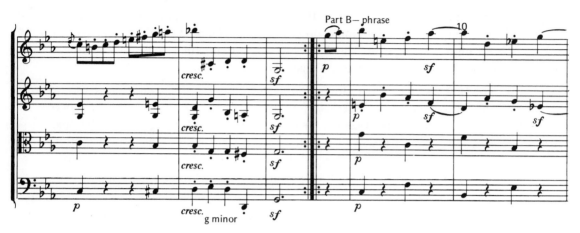

Measures 16-40, Theme II, AABABA

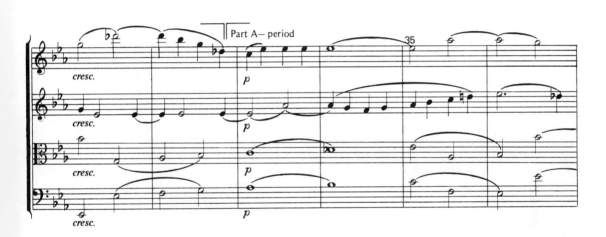

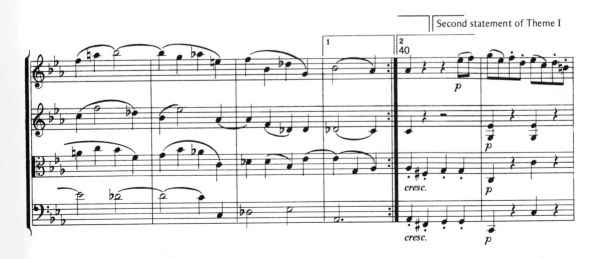

Ex. 7-6. (Continued)

Measures 40-72, second statement of Theme I, AABA¹BA¹

Embellishment of repeated Part A, mm. 49-56

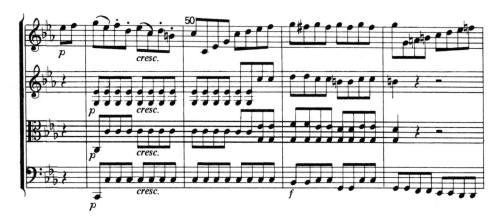

Embellishment of repeated Part B, mm. 65-72

Measures 72-86, Theme III, AABA'BA'

Ex. 7-6. (Continued)

Measure 72-86, Theme III, AABA'BA'

Measures 86-110, third statement of Theme I, AABA'BA'

Measures 110-116, transition

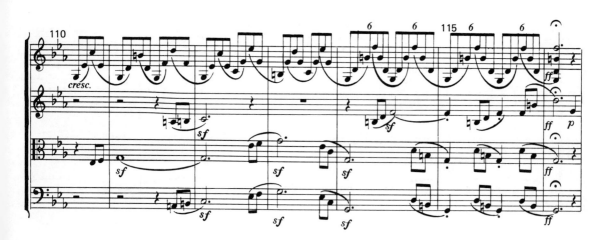

Measures 116-137, abbreviated restatement of Theme II

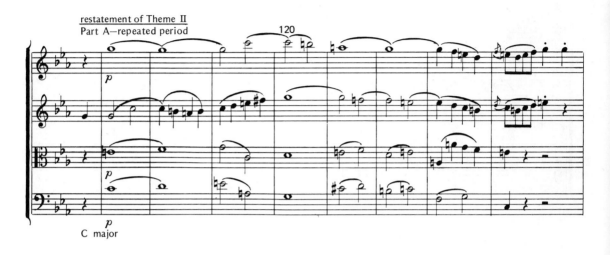

Ex. 7-6. (Continued)

Measures 137-162, retransition

Ex. 7-6. (Continued)

Measures 163-178, last statement of Theme I, ABA[1], prestissimo

Measures 178-217, coda

Summary of Ex. 7-7:

1. Structure and tonality

   Theme I(G d G) II(G C e G) I(a G) II(A C e) I(F♯ B G d G)

2. Formal content

   a. The initial statement of both Theme I and II is ternary.

   b. The second statement of Theme I is abbreviated and, though it begins with the original melodic pitches, there is at least an implication of key change from the substitute harmonies that support the beginning measures. In the final statement of Theme I both melody and harmony are transposed for thirteen measures before the return to the expected key of G major.

   c. The recurrence of Theme II is very concealed by a change of meter, a six bar octave passage that acts as a miniature introduction, and an instability of tonality. When the theme is finally recognizable, it is through the transformed statement of Part B in measure 132.

3. Stylistic relationship

   The real genius of this composition is that the rondo principle can be fashioned with such economy of thematic material. In a typical Brahms manner motives are lengthened into thematic passages and themes are reused with transformation.

   a. Motivic growth begins in Theme I with the derivation of Part B from the motive that ends Part A.

   b. If the melodic line of the first nine measures of Theme II is played with the rhythm and tempo of Theme I, the result will be the first theme with only a few notes added or deleted. The thematic transformation of Theme II is accomplished by changes in tempo, meter, rhythm, accompaniment pattern, and instrumentation. The line becomes staccato, as an appropriate complement to the angularity of the style.

   c. The second part of Theme II is a rhythmic paraphrase of the first five notes of the second part of Theme I. Distinction of sound comes primarily from instrumentation, accents, and the use of pedal tones.

   d. When Theme II is restated at measure 126, Part A is omitted. Part B enters at measure 132, and it is a transformation of the material stated at measure 51. Again the changes are accomplished through meter, rhythm and instrumentation.

4. Auxiliary members

a. The auxiliary area at measure 114 begins as though it will be the second phrase of Theme I, comparable to measure 4. The phrase line does not continue, and the motive is repeated until measure 125. The musical purpose of this passage is not clear. A sense of expectation is created by the repeated motive, and the prominent B major chord begins to sound as a prolonged dominant. The harmonic tension is briefly released by resolution to an E major chord at the end of measure 125. The six measure octave passage that follows uses the triplet motive in a sequence pattern whose tonality is extremely ambivalent. In view of the expectation factors in measures 114-125, this passage has been named a "transition area"; and because measures 126-131 establish the changed tempo and meter, these measures are identified as "introduction measures."

b. The boundaries of the next transition area are not clear, but the musical purpose is. The process of retransition from the second statement of Theme II to the last statement of Theme I begins in measure 180. The melodic line here is a counterpart of measure 87 which, in turn, is a transformation of the triplet figure and resolution notes in measures 4 and 5. Beginning in measure 180, hemiola is used with the pattern, and this begins to slow the rhythmic impetus. The return to a triple meter moves through 9/8 to 3/4. One of the most interesting facets of this retransition passage is the frustration of expectation. The beginning pitch, B, of Theme I is prominently sounded throughout the last six measures before Theme I enters, not on a B, but on A♯.

c. The codetta at measure 233 follows a long cadence extension that uses chords from the parallel mode. The codetta acts simply as a final confirmation of the G major tonality and a final depletion of musical energy.

Ex. 7-7. Brahms: Symphony No. 2 in D Major, Op. 73, III.

Theme I
Part A - period, phrase 2 ext.

Ex. 7-7. (Continued)

Theme II
Part A— phrase, ext.

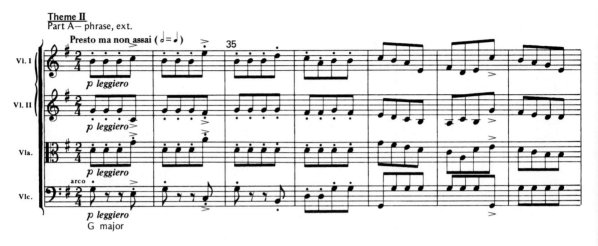

Ex. 7-7. (Continued)

Ex. 7-7. (Continued)

G major

Ex. 7-7. (Continued)

Theme I
Part A - repeated phrase

Ex. 7-7. (Continued)

Ex. 7-7. (Continued)

Ex. 7-7. (Continued)

[like measures 71 — 78]

Ex. 7-7. (Continued)

Ex. 7-7. (Continued)

Theme I
Part A - period, phrase 2 ext.

Ex. 7-7. (Continued)

Ex. 7-7. (Continued)

Ex. 7-7. (Continued)

Summary of Ex. 7-8

1. Tonality

The broad tonal organization is based on a mixture of major and parallel minor modes with a type of axis arrangement between tonalities. The following scheme shows beginning tonal motion of a tritone with the ultimate tonality settling half way between.

measure	1	34	64	83	129	163	171	197	212	244	270
tonal center	B♭/b♭	E/e	f	B♭/b♭	g/G	B	f♯/F♯	A	B♭/b♭	G/g	g

measure	278	293	302	311	338	347–403
tonal center	D	G/g	G	a	B♭	G/g

2. Structure and formal content

A structural sequence of themes would not truly represent the order of musical events. With the third statement of Theme I a subsidiary thematic idea begins to gain increasing importance until it literally replaces the first theme as the alternating or rondo theme. In order to represent this more clearly, melodic index numbers have been placed on the score excerpts, and the structural plan will show the order of formal functions and melodic ideas. The shift from Theme I to the second part of Theme III as the final rondo theme is an interesting modification of the rondo principle. It can also be observed that Theme I does not return after each other theme although it does recur four times. This is not particularly a twentieth century modification of the rondo principle, as an examination of Mozart's Sonata, K.331, III, will reveal.

```
measure           1--17--------------- 34--64----------- 83--99
formal function  Th. I,  A    B       Th. II, A    B    Th. I,  A    B
melodic idea           ①   ②              ③   ④           ①   ②
```

```
        129--163-174--197-205 ----------------- 212---225-----------231
Th. III,  A    B   A¹    B    retransition    Th. I,  A    substitute for B   fragment of
          ⑤    ⑥   ⑤    ⑥    ⑤                      ①    ⑦                    ⑥
```

```
        244--261---------------------270---------278
Th. II,   A                        Th. II,  B    Th. III,  B   or retransition
          ③    ⑥ as counter melody        ④            ⑥
```

```
        293---------302-------311 --------- 323--338
Th. I,   A         Th. III, B  Th. I, B    Th. III, A   Coda
         ①             ⑥          ②            ⑤       ⑥
```

3. Stylistic relationships and auxiliary members

This is a composition of dissimilar ideas in juxtaposition. Contrast is initiated at the onset by the second phrase of the first theme which furnishes contrast to the phrase before and after. Perhaps this is aural announcement that the dissimilarities of the following ideas will not be smoothly bridged. There is relatively little transition material. At measures 30, and again at measures 60 and 238, four bar passages act as section articulation points rather than transition areas. Generally changes of tonality are accomplished before the end of a thematic passage, and the only modulatory transition area lies between the Theme III and a restatement of Theme I.

The movement ends very appropriately with the particular one of the themes that has the most potential for rapid and virtuosic writing.

Ex. 7-8. Prokofieff: Violin Concerto No. 2, Op. 63, III. (violin and piano score)

It is recommended that the reader become familiarized with the sound of the thematic ideas before studying the full score with recording.

Measures I-82, Theme I, II, retransition

Ex. 7-8. (Continued)

Ex. 7-8. (Continued)

Measures 83-129, second statement of Theme I, AB

Measures 129-211, Theme III, ABA¹B retransition

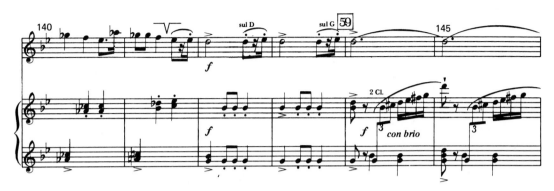

Ex. 7-8. (Continued)

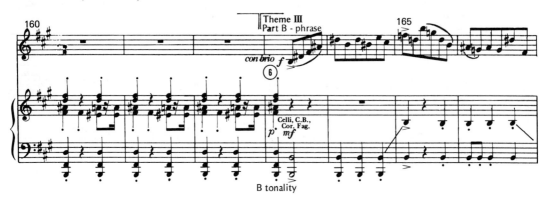

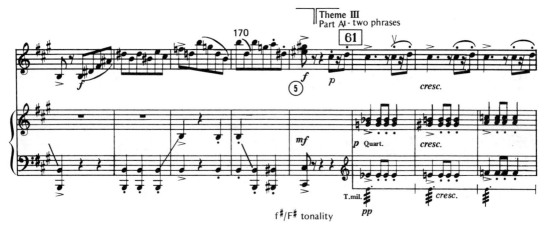

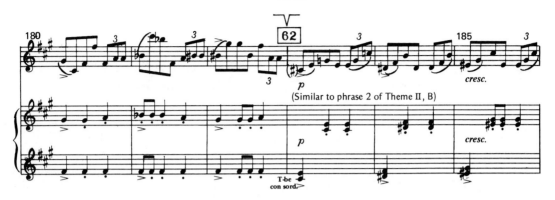

(Similar to phrase 2 of Theme II, B)

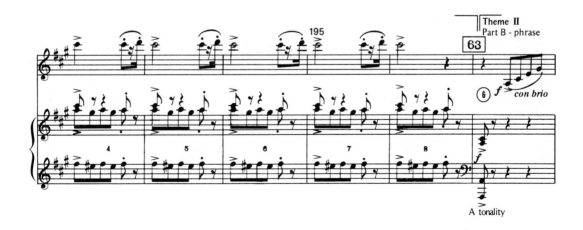

A tonality

Ex. 7-8. (Continued)

Measures 212-237, Theme I, A and substitution for B

Ex. 7-8. (Continued)

Published in 1941 by International Music Co., N.Y. Used by permission of the publisher.

Measures 238-269, sectional articulation and Theme II, A

Measures 270-278, Theme II, B

Measures 278-293, Theme III, B, or retransition

Measures 293-302, Theme I, A

Measures 302-311, Theme III, A

Measures 311-323, Theme I, B

Measures 323-338, Theme III, B

Measures 338-403, Coda

Chain of Part Forms

A series of part forms can be organized without the rondo principle of alternation, and some of the structural patterns are illustrated as follows:

Theme   I   II   III   I

Theme   I   II   III   IV   I

Theme   I   II   III   II   I

The third movement of the Prokofieff Violin Concerto, No. 2 could be considered as a hybrid form between the chain of part forms and the rondo, except that frequent recurrence of a beginning theme at any point in the composition will create at least a rondo effect.

Tonality, formal content, stylistic relationships, and the use of auxiliary members are treated in the chain of part forms just as they are in the rondo. The pattern of

Theme I II III II I forms the visual design of an arch. The aural impression will not be quite that symmetrical, however, because the composition in this form will probably end with the last sounds of a first theme rather than with the first sounds. The arch form has held aesthetic interest for several nineteenth and twentieth century composers, notably Brahms and Bartok. Several examples of the chain of part forms are listed in assignments 1 and 2.

Assignment 1 - *Aural analysis of form*

Before selecting the excerpts for analysis consider some of the ways in which the following sequence of musical ideas can be interpreted in the rondo form:

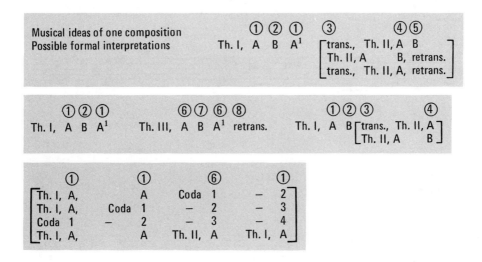

Musical Indices

Ex. 7-9. Bartok: Piano Concerto No. 2, III.
   Appendix page—582

Several unusual features are present in this example of a twentieth century rondo form. With the exception of the first theme, all of the musical ideas are taken from the first movement of the concerto, and they are rhythmically transformed to create the contrasting themes. The departures from Theme I increasingly take the form of a section whose melodic idea is not stated in phrases and parts but is presented in a contrapuntal texture of motivic fragments. Actually each departure, or contrasting theme, is composed of a single melodic idea, but the length and complexity of the movement is far more extensive than that of a large part form.

Ex. 7-9. (Continued)

Ex. 7-10. Beethoven: Sonata in A Major, Op. 2, No. 2, IV.
Appendix page—583

Ex. 7-11. Beethoven: Sonata in E♭ Major, Op. 7, IV.
Appendix page—585

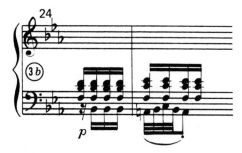

Ex. 7-11. (Continued)

Ex. 7-12. Brahms: Rhapsody, Op. 119, No. 4.
Appendix page—586

In this composition it will suffice to aurally identify the number of phrases without locating precisely where each phrase ends. The first two musical ideas of the index illustrate respectively a phrase of irregular length with a feminine cadence, and a three beat elision of lower voice cadence and upper voice anacrusis. Such phrasing irregularities are typical of the work. In the formal diagram elided phrases are shown where the later phrase begins rather than where the earlier phrase ends.

Ex. 7-12. (Continued)

Ex. 7-13. Chopin: Grande Valse Brillante, Op. 18.
Appendix page—587

Ex. 7-13. (Continued)

Ex. 7-14. Haydn: Sonata in D Major (Peters No. 9), III.
 Appendix page—589

This work represents the facility with which composers of the classic period used variation techniques to modify the recurring theme of a classic rondo. Each return of Theme I is varied from the original statement.

Ex. 7-14. (Continued)

Ex. 7-15. Hindemith: Piano Sonata No. 2, III.
Appendix page—590

Ex. 7-15. (Continued)

Ex. 7-16. Mozart: Sonata in F Major, K.533/494, III.
Appendix page—591

In the analysis of a classic composition one is often reminded that musical form in this period was still in an evolving state where tonality was the primary distinguishing element. Selection of musical materials for thematic contrast or for a particular formal purpose seemed not to have been as important to classic composers as it was to become to composers of the nineteenth century. With arpeggios, scale passages, and appoggiatura figures profuse throughout an entire work, stable key areas will denote themes and closing material, and unstable key areas are likely to be transitions or development.

An additional analysis problem of this work is that Mozart often composed his themes with a chain of fairly dissimilar phrases. This is illustrated by the second musical idea of the index which shows the beginning of three consecutive phrases that constitute a single theme. Note the stylistic difference of the second and third phrases.

Ex. 7-16. (Continued)

Ex. 7-16. (Continued)

Ex. 7-17. Schubert: Sonata in A Minor, Op. 143, III.
Appendix page—592

This composition has only two themes, but it exceeds the large ternary form in a number of ways. The primary means of extending the length of the work is through recurrence of the two alternating themes, recurrences that appear in several unexpected keys. There is much auxiliary material, and one auxiliary area in particular contains techniques of development. The work is very typical of Schubert's compositional style, with much use of extended phrases and modulatory passages that include foreign key relationships.

Ex. 7-17. (Continued)

Ex. 7-18. Schumann: String Quartet in A Minor, Op. 41, No. 1, II.
   Appendix page—594

The "scherzo" marking of this movement suggests the use of the term *song form* rather than *theme*. Either term would be appropriate, however, as only tradition separates them.

Scherzo

Ex. 7-18. (Continued)

Ex. 7-19. Shostakovich. String Quartet No. 3, Op. 73, II.
Appendix page—595

Ex. 7-19. (Continued)

Assignment 2. - *Aural analysis of content*

1. Quite often the transition material leading from one theme to another is derived from the preceding theme or anticipates the succeeding theme. In the following excerpts listen from the beginning through Theme II and note the relationship of transition materials to thematic materials. Also describe the musical elements that create contrast between Themes I and II. Use Exs. 7-10, 7-11 and 7-12.

2. Select several compositions that you have studied well. Listen again to each of them without musical index or formal diagram. Write the complete analysis as you now hear it. If there is time, justify your choice of analysis terms by noting quickly the musical elements and techniques that create the structural purpose.

Assignment 3 - *Analysis with score*

The examples for further study are large combinations of part forms that represent the following structural patterns:

1. Rondos in which the first theme returns after each departure

2. Rondos in which the first theme returns frequently but does not appear after every departure

3. Rondos in which certain of the departure areas are variants or modifications of previously stated themes

4. A chain, or series, of themes in which the rondo principle is lacking

In the first group of examples the auxiliary members at the beginning and end of the composition are cited, as are the parts within each theme. Internal auxiliary members are not indicated. Each work should be analyzed aurally to locate the large structure before the substructure is determined by a study of the score.

Examples for further study, group 1.

BARTOK
Sonata for Piano, III.
(Th. I, AB / Variations of Th. I, A / Th. I, AB^1 / Variation of Th. I, A / Th. I, AB^2 / Variations of Th. I, A / Th. I, AB^3 / codetta)

BEETHOVEN
Sonata in G, Op. 14, No. 2, III.
(Th. I, ABA^1 / Th. II, A / Th. I, ABA^1 / Th. III, ABA^1 / Th. I, ABA^1 / coda)

BRAHMS
Sonata in C, Op. 1, IV.
(Th. I, ABA^1 / Th. II, ABAA^1 / Th. I, A / Th. III, ABA^1/ Th. I, ABA / coda)

DVORAK
Symphony No. 5 in e, III.[2]
(Introduction / Scherzo, ABA ABA / Trio I, ABA / Scherzo, A /

2. On certain recordings of this movement the repetitions of the Scherzo and the second trio are not performed.

Trio II, AABABA / Scherzo, ABA / Trio I, ABA / Scherzo, A /
coda)[2]

PISK   Nocturnal Interlude.[3]
(Th. I, A / Th. II, AB / Th. III, ABA¹ / Th. II, A¹B¹ / Th. I, A
/ codetta)

PISTON   Symphony No. 4, II.
(Th. I, ABA¹ / Th. II, AB— / Th. I, AB¹A¹ / Th. III, AB
$$A^1$$
/ Th. I, A / Th. II, AB— / Th. I, B¹A¹)
$$A^1$$

PROKOFIEFF   Piano Concerto No. 3, Op. 26, III.
(Th. I, A / Th. II, ABA¹ / Th. I, A / Th. III, ABA¹ / Th. I, A /
coda)

SCHUMANN   String Quartet in A, Op. 41, No. 3, IV.
(Th. I, ABA¹ / Th. II, AABA / Th. I, A / Th. III, ABA¹BA¹ /
Th. I, ABA¹ / Th. II, AABA / Th. I, A / Th. III, ABA¹ / Th. I,
A plus coda)

SESSIONS   Symphony No. 1, III.
(Th. I, AB / Th. II, ABC / Th. I, A / Th. III, AB / Th. I, AB /
Th. II, ABC / Th. I, A / coda)

SHOSTAKOVICH   String Quartet No. 4, Op. 83, III.
(Th. I, ABA¹ / Th. II, A / Th. I, A / Th. II, A transposed /
codetta)

Examples for further study, group 2

BARTOK   Concerto for Orchestra, IV.

Three Rondos, No. 1.

BEETHOVEN   Sonatas, Op. 13, III; Op. 22, IV; Op. 28, IV; Op. 49, No. 2, II.

Symphonies, No. 7 in A, Op. 92, III; No. 9 in d, Op. 125, III.

3. Both the score and the recordings are available in an album, *New Music for Piano* with Robert
Helps as pianist, G. Schirmer, Inc., sole selling representative.

BRAHMS   Sonata in f, Op. 5, V.

Symphony No. 1 in c, Op. 68, III.

CHOPIN   Mazurka, Op. 33, No. 4; Waltz, Op. 34, No. 1.

FRANCK   Symphony in d, II.

HAYDN   Sonatas (Peters ed.), No. 2 in e, III; No. 3 in E♭, III; No. 4 in
g, II; No. 5 in C, III; No. 6 in c♯ , II; No. 7 in D, III; No. 20
in D, III; No. 24 in C, II; No. 30 in E, III;

String Quartets, Op. 33, No. 2, IV; Op. 33, No. 6, IV; Op. 76,
No. 4.

MOZART   Serenade for String Orchestra, K.525, II.

Sonatas, K.296 in C, III; K.281 in B♭, III; K.309 in C, III;
K.311 in D, III, K.547a in F, II; K.331 in A, III; K.457 in c, II
and III; K.498a in B♭, IV.

String Quartet, K.428 in E♭, IV.

POULENC   Sonata for Flute and Piano, III.

PROKOFIEFF   Symphony No. 5, Op. 100, IV.

SCHOENBERG   Piano Concerto, Op. 42, IV.

SCHUBERT   Piano Trio No. 1 in B♭, Op. 99, IV.

Sonatas, Op. 53 in D, IV; Op. 164 in a, II.

String Quartet in d, Op. posth., IV.

SCHUMANN   *Kreisleriana*, Op. 16, No. 8.

SCHUMANN   Piano Quintet in E♭, Op. 44, III.

String Quartet, Op. 41, No. 3, III.

SHOSTAKOVICH   String Quartet No. 6, Op. 101, II.

VAUGHAN WILLIAMS London Symphony, II.

8 ■ large forms with development

To create melodies that are striking in some way is a gift that many musicians have. To develop the potential of those melodies by reshaping, elaborating, varying, or combining with other musical ideas is a highly developed craft as well as perhaps an inherent talent. Composer or not, if one considers the act of creating a musical work, common sense indicates that the basic materials of the work must be limited for the sake of the listener. Continuous presentation of new musical ideas will ultimately overwhelm the listener's capacity to organize sound into coherent patterns, and aural chaos will then prevail.

Traditionally the most successful structural means for expanding limited musical materials into compositions of considerable scope were the combinations of part forms with the large ternary or rondo principle, the variation form, and the sonata allegro form. These forms were used in most of traditional instrumental literature, and while their use has declined appreciably in twentieth century compositions, a certain number of composers of this century continue to find the structures useful.

The most important instrumental form to evolve in the music of the western culture was the sonata allegro form of the eighteenth century. This form had its roots in several earlier forms, and research suggests that the Baroque rounded binary structure was an important influence. Mature works of Haydn and Mozart are representative of the fully evolved sonata form, and the universality of this form can be confirmed by the countless examples found in traditional literature of the eighteenth and nineteenth centuries. Almost without exception the sonata allegro is the structure used for the first movement of a multimovement solo sonata, chamber work, or symphony. An adaptation of the structure is the basis of the first movement of the classic concerto. Last movements are frequently in the same structure although one finds a number of last movements that combine characteristics of both the sonata allegro and the rondo forms: by name, sonata rondos or rondos with development.

The Sonata Allegro Principle

The best way to understand the sonata allegro principle is to analyze a number of compositions whose materials are presented in the sonata allegro design. At the level

427

of verbal description this design can be discussed in fairly simplistic terms that will allow for the flexibility found in actual practice. The large form is divided into three sections: the first is the exposition in which the selected musical materials are stated successively; the development section follows, and here the stated materials of the exposition are reshaped, elaborated, varied, or combined; the recapitulation section concludes the composition by restating the exposition materials with the probable addition of a coda at the end. Using the following schematic design as a basis, certain expectations about the content can be summarized.

Ex. 8-1. The general design of a traditional sonata allegro form.

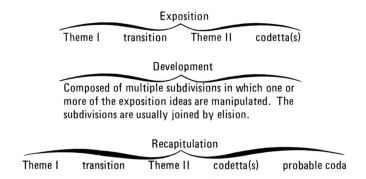

Exposition

Theme I   transition   Theme II   codetta(s)

Development

Composed of multiple subdivisions in which one or
more of the exposition ideas are manipulated. The
subdivisions are usually joined by elision.

Recapitulation

Theme I   transition   Theme II   codetta(s)   probable coda

Tonality

In the classical sonata allegro design tonality was perhaps more important to the delineation of the form than was the distinctiveness of thematic materials. The following tonal pattern crystallized in the sonata allegro of the eighteenth century, and later traditional composers continued to use the pattern with only occasional modifications.

Exposition	Theme I transition Theme II codetta(s)
	first key second key ⟶
Development	additional keys, and areas of rapid key change or tonal ambiguity
Recapitulation	Theme I transition Theme II codetta(s) optional coda
	first key first key ⟶

The recapitulation of all materials in a single key strengthens the "return" effect and so it appears to be aesthetically sound. It does, however, present certain problems that composers dealt with in a variety of ways.

The first problem lies in the recapitulated transition. In the exposition one of the musical purposes of the transition is to bridge the tonality difference. In the recapitulation the need for a modulation from Theme I to Theme II has been eliminated, and the composer can also eliminate the transition, as is done in Ex. 8-7, or he can modify the transition in some way so that it still gives an effect of progressing to a new tonal area.[1] Ex. 8-2 illustrates a technique that was sometimes used by Haydn and Mozart. This transition is essentially nonmodulatory, but tonal progression is left open to two alternatives by the cadence in measures 21-22. The cadential implication at this point is either a G major vii°/V to V or a D major vii° to I. In the exposition Theme II is stated in D major at measure 23; in the recapitulation the identical transition passage is used, but this time it leads to a statement of Theme II transposed into G major at measure 90.

Ex. 8-2. Mozart: Sonata in G major, K.283, I.

----

1. This compositional problem also existed in certain of the large rondo forms, as discussed in Chapter 7 under "auxiliary members."

Ex. 8-2. (Continued)

Another way of treating the problem of the recapitulated transition is illustrated in Ex. 8-3. When the transition recurs in the recapitulation, the modulatory portion of it is essentially deleted, and what remains in measures 202-213 begins and ends as the exposition version did. The similarity of aural effect between the two passages is further increased with the use of diminished seventh chords to weaken tonal stability.

Ex. 8-3. Brahms: String Quartet Op. 51, No. 2, I.

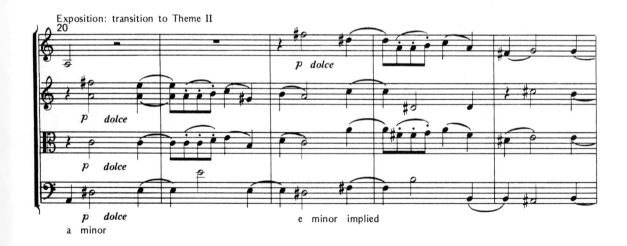

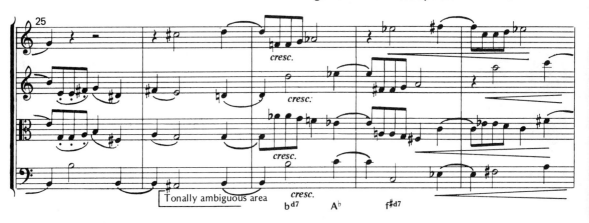

Ex. 8-3. (Continued)

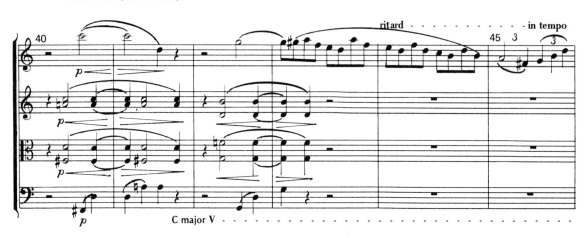

Recapitulation: transition to Theme II.

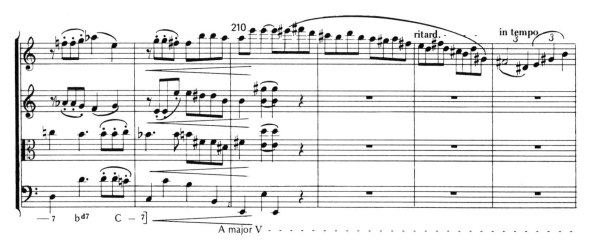

Some of the other tonal patterns that are likely to be found in recapitulated transitions are as follows:

1. Transposition of the beginning of the transition to a second key so that there will be a modulation back to the restatement of Theme II in the first key.

2. Modulation to a second key at the end of the restated Theme I so that the transition must effect a modulation back to the first key.

3. Restatement of the beginning of Theme II in a key other than the first key so that the transition will progress through a modulation.

Composers have made certain other exceptions to the practice of complete "tonic" recapitulation, as illustrated by several of the examples in the chapter. In the first movement of Brahms' String Quartet in A Minor (Ex. 8-9) and of Mendelssohn's Violin Concerto in E Minor (Ex. 8-20) the second theme of each is stated in a major key in the exposition. When these themes recur in their recapitulations they appear respectively in A major and E major rather than in the parallel minor modes of Themes I. When there is an unexpected tonality in the recapitulation of a traditional work, however, it is generally temporary, and the composition ends in the beginning tonality.

Twentieth century composers who have used the sonata allegro form have done so with the greater tonal freedom that generally prevails in compositions of this century. It is interesting to note, however, that in the recapitulation section of a number of twentieth century sonata forms Theme I will recur in the first tonality and the composition will end in this tonality. Several compositions in assignment 1 will illustrate this apparent link with tradition.

One of the characteristic features of the development section is the greater accumulation and more rapid fluctuation of musical tension. Concentration of tension is partially achieved through rapid changes in tonality and by areas of tonal ambiguity, both of which are typical of development sections. The tonalities of the development section also contribute to the contrast of this section to the exposition and the recapitulation. The tonic key is generally avoided, and development tonalities become increasingly more remote from the tonic key as composers of the nineteenth and early twentieth centuries explored new tonal resources.

Formal Content and Auxiliary Members

The number of themes in the exposition is variable, but there are usually only two themes of major importance. In the sonata allegro form, where the emphasis is on development of materials, the themes are likely to be shorter than the themes in a rondo, where the emphasis is on statement of materials. Quite often the first theme of a sonata form is one part only, and more of the exposition is devoted to the second theme and the closing ideas.

The exposition of a classical sonata allegro was traditionally marked for repetition, perhaps to emphasize the thematic materials so that they would continue to be recognizable when developed in the middle section. Later composers omitted this practice of the repeated exposition although many nineteenth and twentieth century sonata forms have retained the double bar as a visual sign that the exposition has ended.

The ending of the exposition is one of the features unique to the sonata form. Other large forms will often end with a coda of multiple sections, which is the equivalent of a series of codettas, but internal codettas are singular. In the sonata form of the eighteenth and nineteenth centuries it is common practice for the exposition to end with two or more codettas that may derive materials from either of the major themes. Rather frequently the first of several codettas will contain the kind of rhythmic energy commonly associated with transitions, a characteristic which tends to accentuate the closing quality of the following codetta. A term that is traditional to the analysis of a sonata form is the term ''closing theme.'' One often sees the abbreviation of the term in edited piano sonatas. A closing theme serves essentially the same purpose as any other extension area after the second theme. It can be distinguished from an adjacent codetta by a more thematic content and a tendency to fall into phrases rather than partial phrases. The distinction is not always clear, however, and it is a term to be used very sparingly.

Another auxiliary member that may appear at the end of the exposition is a transition leading to the development. This member will be found in sonata allegro examples where the development begins in a tonality different than the tonality of the second theme and its codettas.

The potential formal content of the exposition can now be extended beyond that shown in Ex. 8-1 to include the following factors:

Exposition

Theme I	transition	Theme II	Codetta 1	Codetta 2 (closing theme)	transition
usually one part	one or more sections	one or more parts			leads to the development

Whatever the formal content of the exposition, the recapitulation of a traditional sonata form is likely to restate all the same materials in the same order. This affords a very practical basis for identifying any additional material at the end of the recapitulation as a coda, regardless of length or content. In practice, composers from Beethoven on exploited the potential of a final coda so that it often became a fourth large division of the overall form, comparable in scope to the exposition, development, and recapitulation.

The Development Section

The truly unique feature of the sonata allegro form is the development section. A great deal has been written about the development section as an area of dramatic conflict that is finally resolved in the recapitulation. This description may be a bit fanciful, but there is indeed much that is exciting and dramatic in a really fine development section. Musical activity increases, areas of tension and release fluctuate more rapidly, and the whole effect provides a foil to the two outer sections.

The materials for the development section are drawn from any part of the exposition. In one composition, only major thematic materials will be developed; in another work by the same composer a fragment of extension material at the end of the exposition may be the primary source of the entire development section. When listening to the exposition of a sonata form it is virtually impossible to predict which materials will be developed. Herein lies part of the fascination of the form: its vast potential for direction. Occasionally the beginning material of a development section is referred to by the editorial marking of "M.T.," meaning middle or new theme. Such areas can usually be traced to an exposition source that has been transformed. Ex. 8-4 illustrates one such situation.

Ex. 8-4. Mozart: Sonata in G Major, K. 283, I.

Although the composer's choice of materials for development cannot be anticipated, there is a certain predictability about the manner in which certain materials might be developed. Fragmentation is an extremely important development technique, but not all musical material lends itself well to this treatment. The long continuous phrase lines of themes from certain compositions of the Romantic period are occasionally incompatible with the technique of fragmentation, and, if such themes are selected as source material, the development sections of these works may include a great deal of writing that is regularly phrased and of a statement nature. It is possible, however, for a composer to use the technique of fragmentation in a setting of phrased developmental writing, and Ex. 8-5 illustrates this combination. There is such a pervasive lyric quality to the first movement of the Mendelssohn Violin Concerto in E Minor that it is customary to identify even the transition as the "transition theme," and very appropriately the development section continues in the style of thematic statement with symmetrical phrases. The first section of the development begins with a phrase that is simply a transposition of the first phrase of the transition theme. This is followed by two phrases that are fashioned from the beginning transition motive used first in sequence, then in repetition. Thus far a motive has been fragmented from the transition theme, transformed, and set in motion. Section 2 of the development will also present a series of consecutive and regular phrases. Each phrase is created by a fragment of the transition theme, transformed with rhythmic diminution and set into a long virtuosic line that is combined with the first motive (fragment) of Theme I. Regular phrasing continues through most of the development.

Ex. 8-5. Mendelssohn: Violin Concerto in E Minor, Op. 64, I.

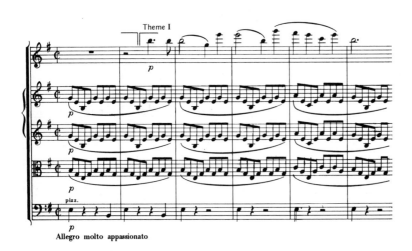

A different effect from fragmentation appears in the development of Beethoven's Sonata in D Major. The total development is very concentrated, and Theme I provides most of the material. In measure 167 of Ex. 8-6 the first section of the development begins with a transposed statement of the first phrase of Theme I. The phrase is repeated with an embellishing figure derived from the transition, but before the embellished repetition ends, the bass suddenly increases in rhythmic motion at measure 183 to begin a second section of the development. Such elision of sections is common within a development and is one of the techniques for maintaining or increasing musical tension and continuous forward motion. The eight bar fragment of measure 183-190 is restated with the voices switched, thus creating imitation and invertible counterpoint for eight more measures until the motive is fragmented further in measure 199. Imitation, or dialogue, continues in two bar fragments into a sequential passage at measure 207. The forward motion is somewhat halted at measure 219 with a one bar fragment and its inversion sounding over a repeated bass note. Description of the passages in Ex. 8-6 serves only the purpose of identifying the sources and development techniques; the effect of the gradual accumulation and concentration of musical energy needs to be heard to be fully appreciated.

Ex. 8-6. Beethoven: Sonata in D Major, Op. 28, I.

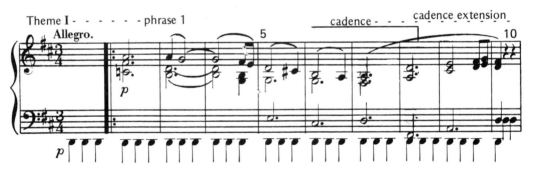

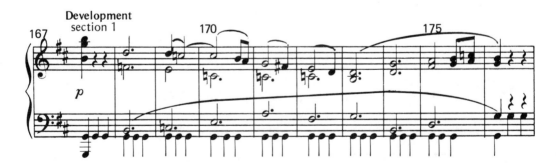

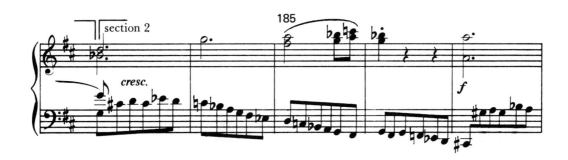

Ex. 8-6. (Continued)

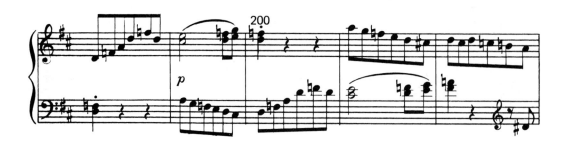

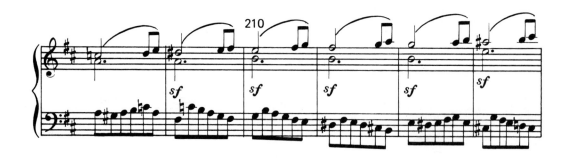

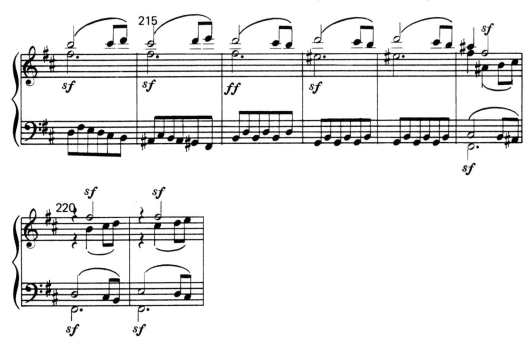

A list of the most common musical activities that take place in the development section would include the following:

1. Source material is derived from any of the exposition material. The derived sources are generally fragments, and they may be treated with variation, transformation, or the fugal techniques of inversion, augmentation, diminution, and occasionally retrograde.

2. The fugal techniques of imitation, stretto, canonic writing, sequence and dialogue are, in fact, an excellent source for passages of musical energy.

3. Of particular value is the developmental technique of combining ideas horizontally or vertically.

4. The development section is subdivided according to materials used and/or techniques of manipulating the materials. Changes in rhythmic activity, texture, timbre, or intensity can also delineate sub-sections. The actual delineation point is often elided to avoid any lessening of musical energy.

5. Tonality in development sections is less stable than it is in the exposition or the recapitulation.

6. In some manner the last section of the development will anticipate the recapitulation. Often this is done tonally through a long dominant chord, possibly reinforced by a pedal.

Analysis Models

In analyzing a traditional sonata allegro form we can assume that all or most of the exposition materials will be restated in the same succession in the recapitulation. A thorough study of the exposition and the recapitulation will better prepare the ear and the eye for a study of the development section. A useful analysis practice is to study the score of the exposition as the recapitulation is heard. If the listener has familiarized himself with exposition materials, this practice will reveal almost immediately any changes that occur in the recapitulation. The scores of Exs. 8-7, 8-8 and 8-9 include only the expositions, developments, and codas. When the recapitulation begins, the score of the exposition can be followed. Any changes in the recapitulation are marked with an asterisk and noted beside the exposition score. Development sources and techniques are similarly noted by each section of the development and the coda.

Ex. 8-7 is representative of Haydn's use of the sonata form in the keyboard sonata. The work precedes by several years the composition of the Opus 33 string quartets in which both polyphonic and homophonic elements appeared in the development sections. The development in this keyboard sonata is composed primarily of the homophonic techniques prevalent in the idiomatic keyboard works of the time.

Ex. 8-7. Haydn: Sonata in F Major (Peters No. 21), I.

Changes in the recapitulation:

*In m.96 Theme I ends with a half cadence, and the transition is completely omitted.

*Theme II is restated in F major.

*New phrases 2 and 3 are formed respectively from motives in m.21 and mm. 12-13.

*A fourth phrase is added; it resembles phrase 3.

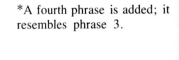

Ex. 8-7. (Continued)

Changes in the recapitulation:

*Codettas 1 and 2 are transposed into F major to complete the tonic transposition of the second key group.

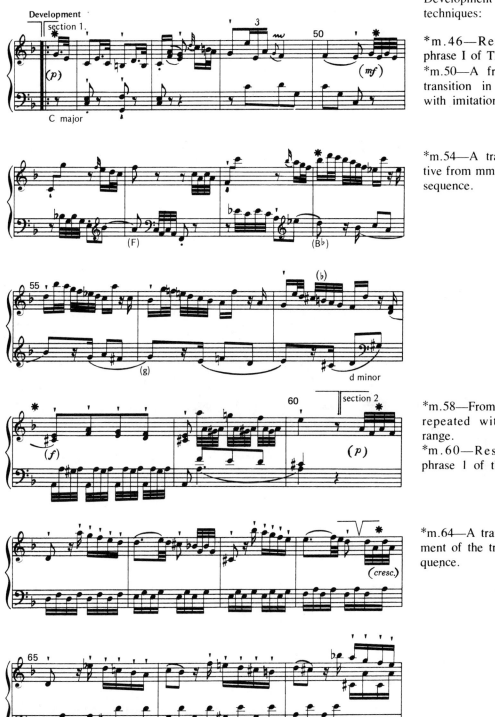

Development sources and techniques:

*m.46—Restatement of phrase I of Theme I.
*m.50—A fragment of the transition in sequence and with imitation.

*m.54—A transformed motive from mm. 2-3 is used in sequence.

*m.58—From mm. 44-45; repeated with change of range.
*m.60—Restatement of phrase I of the transition.

*m.64—A transformed fragment of the transition in sequence.

Ex. 8-7. (Continued)

Development sources and techniques:

*m.68—A fragment from mm. 6-7 in sequence.

*m.77—A short phrase formed of the materials in mm. 33-34 and mm. 44-45; restated sequentially at m. 80.

Development sources and techniques:

*m.83—An inverted fragment of Theme I, repeated.
*m.85.—Recapitulation (see exposition score and margin notes).

Ex. 8-8. Beethoven: String Quartet, Op. 59, No. 1, I.

Changes in the recapitulation:

*A change of mode to F minor leads ultimately to D♭ major.

Ex. 8-8. (Continued)

Changes in the recapitulation:

*_____*A nine bar sequence passage substitutes for the cadential extension and the following codetta. Note that the codetta material appeared at the end of the development.

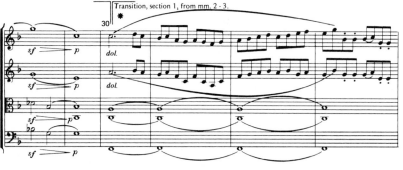

*Transposed to Db major.

*Dialogue with the motive of m. 37 substitutes for this passage and modulates to C major.

Changes in the recapitulation:

*Transposed to C major (or
V of F major).

*Transposed to F major.

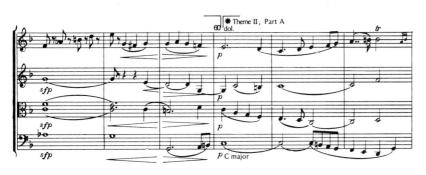

Ex. 8-8. (Continued)

*Transposed to F major.

*Transposed to F major.

*A rising sequence with the motive of mm. 94-95 substitutes for this passage, which remains in F major. This passage acts as a transition to the coda (see coda score).

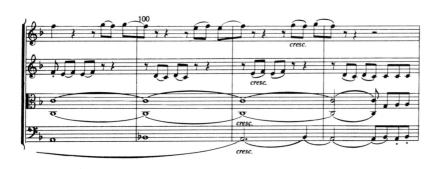

Ex. 8-8. (Continued)

Development sources and techniques:

*m.103—A restatement of mm. 1-4.

*m.107—The motive of m. 94 is used in a series of imitative entries.

*m.111—A transposition of mm. 1-4 with change of registration and instrumentation.

*m.114—The cello uses the arpeggiated line of mm. 79-80. This is imitated with a free inversion in the next measure, a motive that is vertically combined with the viola imitation of the previous four bars. The imitative entries continue to grow closer until the instruments enter in stretto at m. 122.

Development sources and techniques:

*m.125—A motive from mm. 2-3 descends sequentially in an overlapping pattern.

*m.129—The motive of mm. 2-3 is expanded intervallically. The four-bar sequence line is restated twice, and a partial third time before the climax of the octave passage.

Ex. 8-8. (Continued)

Development sources and techniques:

*m.144—The passage of mm. 85-90 is used here to suddenly deplete the musical energy as it did in the exposition.

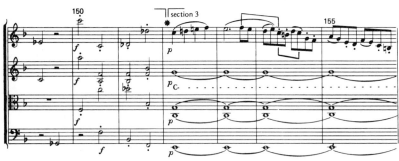

*m.152—The passage begins with a less angular contour of mm. 1-4 that contributes to the relative repose. The figure of mm. 2-3 extends into transformed figures to form a four-bar line. As the line is compressed, the harmonic rhythm accelerates.

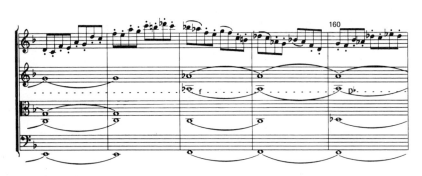

Development sources and techniques:

*m.168—Mm. 1-2 are the basis of a series of imitative entries, some of which are inverted.

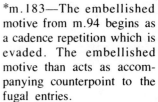

*m.183—The embellished motive from m.94 begins as a cadence repetition which is evaded. The embellished motive than acts as accompanying counterpoint to the fugal entries.

*m.185—The subject of the fugal exposition seems to be new material except for the two bracketed motives from Theme I. Note the tonal relation of the first four entries.

Ex. 8-8. (Continued)

Development sources and techniques:

*m.203—The subject of the fugal exposition is fragmented, and the motive is used in sequence.

Development sources and techniques:

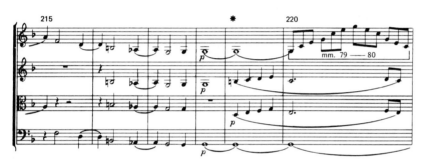

*m.219—The passage begins with a cadential sound. The motive of mm. 1-2 (or mm. 92-95) is combined with fragments from other sources, as noted on the score.

*m.224—The motive of violin I is derived from m.73. The original source of the motive, however, is mm. 2-3. The vertical combination is actually done with two motives of Theme I. Each of the motives is used in a continuous texture of dialogue until m. 236.

Ex. 8-8. (Continued)

Development sources and techniques:

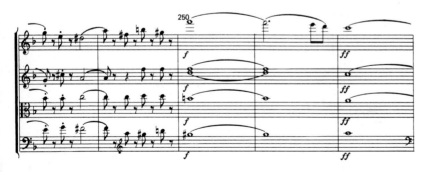

*m.242—The materials of the codetta following Theme I now create an effect of anticipation rather than closure. A progression of unresolved diminished seventh chords begins in m. 245, and the momentary tonal ambiguity heightens the anticipation effect.

Development sources and techniques:

*m.254—The last motive of the developmemt elides with the beginning of the recapitulation (see exposition score and margin notes).

The coda uses many of the same techniques as the development, yet the total effect is decidedly concluding. Stable tonality, limited harmonic progression, a slower harmonic rhythm, and much use of harmonic pedals contribute to the effect of closure.

Ex. 8-8. (Continued)

Ex. 8-9. Brahms: String Quartet, Op. 51, No. 2, I.

Changes in the recapitulation:

*The accompanying triplet figure grows out of one of the canonic lines that ends the development. Violin II takes the triplet figure, and the viola continues with a line established by the other canonic pair at the end of the development.

Changes in the recapitulation:

*The modulation is deflected, and the passage continues in free transposition (see Ex. 8-3).

*Mm. 30-42 are omitted.

*Transposed to A major.

Ex. 8-9. (Continued)

Changes in the recapitulation:

*Transposed to A major.

Ex. 8-9. (Continued)

Changes in the recapitulation:

*Transposed to A minor.

*Transposed to A major.

*Transposed to A major.

Changes in the recapitulation:

*The change here is one of increased intensity through dynamic level, range, and direction. This can be seen on the score at m.372 prior to the score of the coda (see coda score).

*Omitted.

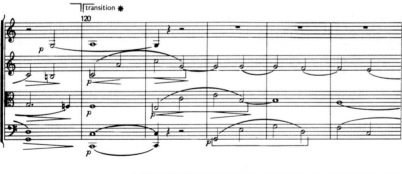

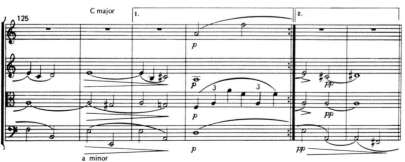

Ex. 8-9. (Continued)

Development sources and technique:

*m.129—The beginning of Theme 1 in imitation.
*m.133—A fragment from m.3 used in dialogue with its inversion. The dialogue descends sequentially.

*m.137—The fragment of m.3 is augmented and gradually transformed by intervallic change.

*m.147—The inner voices move in mirrored stretto, the outer voices in stretto. The horizontal lines are formed by combined fragments, as shown on the score; vertical combination also results.

Development sources and techniques:

*m.151—Sequence of four preceding measures.

*m.155—Sequence of two preceding measures. The motive of mm. 107-108 grows into a chromatic transformation that builds to a climax at m.160.

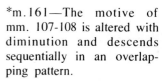

*m.161—The motive of mm. 107-108 is altered with diminution and descends sequentially in an overlapping pattern.

*m.165—Theme I and mm. 104-106 of the closing theme are combined vertically. Mm. 4-5 in the cello become gradually more augmented.

Ex. 8-9. (Continued)

Development sources and techniques:

*m.176—With the beginning fragment of Theme I, violin I and the viola form a mirror canon. Violin II moves canonically with the cello in a motive that appears to be the embellished and inverted motive that ends section 3 of the development (Violin I, mm. 172-175).

*m.183—Recapitulation (see exposition score and margin notes).

Development   sources   and
techniques:

*m.278—Canonic writing
that extends the previous exposition mm. 110-111.

*m.283—Canonic entries
that extend the previous exposition mm. 112-113.

*m.289—Mm.20-21 in the
lower strings combine horizontally with mm.1-3 in violin I and continue through a
triplet extension of the line.

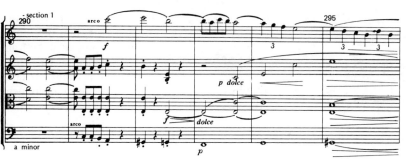

*m.297—This begins as a
repetition of the preceding 8
mm. Violin I, however,
moves to a higher and more
dramatic range, and is extended more elaborately in
descent.

Ex. 8-9. (Continued)

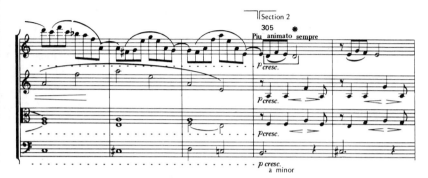

Development sources and techniques:

*m.305—The figure in violin I is a rhythmic transformation of mm.3 that extends into a four-bar phrase.

*m.309—As part of the accumulating musical tension, the four-bar phrase is repeated in a higher octave range.

*m.312—The transformed contour of the beginning motive is present in both upper instruments. The transformation in violin I is taken by the two inner instruments at mm.315-320 accompanied by the cello in a figure resembling the beginning accompaniment.

*m.321—The last set of canonic entries include two entries that are a retrograde of the beginning motive.

The Sonata Allegro Form in the Twentieth Century

The sonata form may well have reached the final stage of its evolution in the first half of this century. Twentieth century composers who have continued to use the sonata allegro principle have worked within the same large framework as that used by eighteenth and nineteenth century composers. Some of the internal structural changes have evolved from changes that began in the nineteenth century, such as the greater flexibility in tonal relations. A certain degree of tonal focus is essential to form, so tonality as a structural articulator has not been abandoned but it has been greatly de-emphasized. Pitch (that is, melody, tonality, and harmonic progression) has become simply one of the elements that can make structure audible and coherent, and the other elements of rhythm, texture, timbre, and dynamics have become very important articulators of form. Another twentieth century structural change that has its roots in nineteenth century practices is a tendency to replace the codetta at the end of the exposition with a genuine closing theme that is equal in importance to preceding themes.

The recapitulation of the twentieth century sonata form has been particularly affected by two general characteristics of contemporary composition: the process of continuous development and the avoidance of literal repetition. In the process of continuous development, techniques for manipulating thematic fragments in the middle section may continue to be used with the full themes when they are recapitulated. For example, if a fragment of a theme is inverted in the development section, that same theme may be inverted when it is fully recapitulated; or if fragments of two themes are developed together, the recapitulation version of the two themes may be in vertical or horizontal combination. The tendency of twentieth century composers to avoid literal repetition often results in an abbreviated recapitulation or a recapitulation in which the order of themes is changed. In nineteenth century literature there are some isolated examples of abbreviated recapitulations, such as the omission of Theme I in the first movements of the Chopin Sonata in B♭ Minor and Sonata in B Minor. In the works of nineteenth century composers who were using the sonata form extensively, however, the recapitulation was likely to be expanded rather than abbreviated.

Expectation about twentieth century sonata forms must be based, then, on the knowledge that internal structure may be modified in any number of ways within the large framework of exposition, development, and recapitulation.

Ex. 8-10 illustrates a twentieth century sonata form that combines both traditional and contemporary characteristics. Structurally the work is quite traditional, with a recapitulation that restates most of the exposition material and with a coda that stylistically balances the development section. The continuous motive development is typically twentieth century in character.

Ex. 8-10. Barber: Sonata for Piano, Op. 26, I.

Characteristic sounds of Theme I are the bracketed rhythmic motive and the chromatic line in "turning" patterns.

Elements that contribute to the thematic stability are the use of repeated patterns, regular phrasing, and a bass pattern that outlines a first inversion major-minor seventh sound.

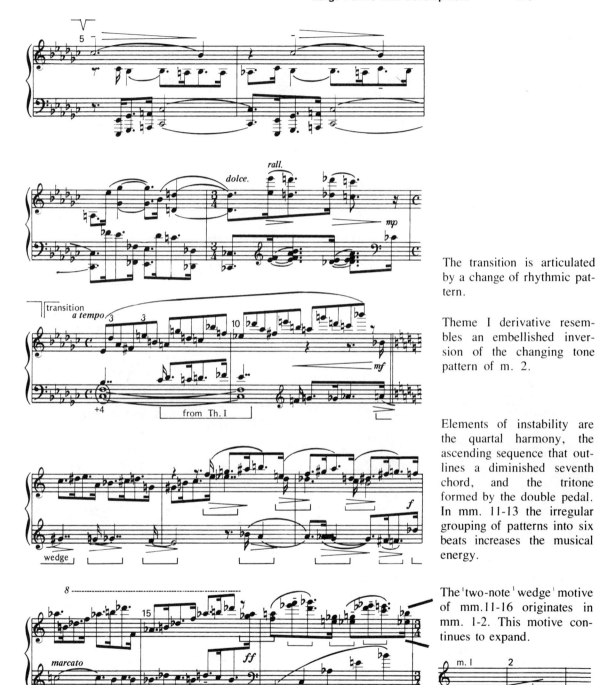

The transition is articulated by a change of rhythmic pattern.

Theme I derivative resembles an embellished inversion of the changing tone pattern of m. 2.

Elements of instability are the quartal harmony, the ascending sequence that outlines a diminished seventh chord, and the tritone formed by the double pedal. In mm. 11-13 the irregular grouping of patterns into six beats increases the musical energy.

The 'two-note' 'wedge' motive of mm.11-16 originates in mm. 1-2. This motive continues to expand.

Ex. 8-10. (Continued)

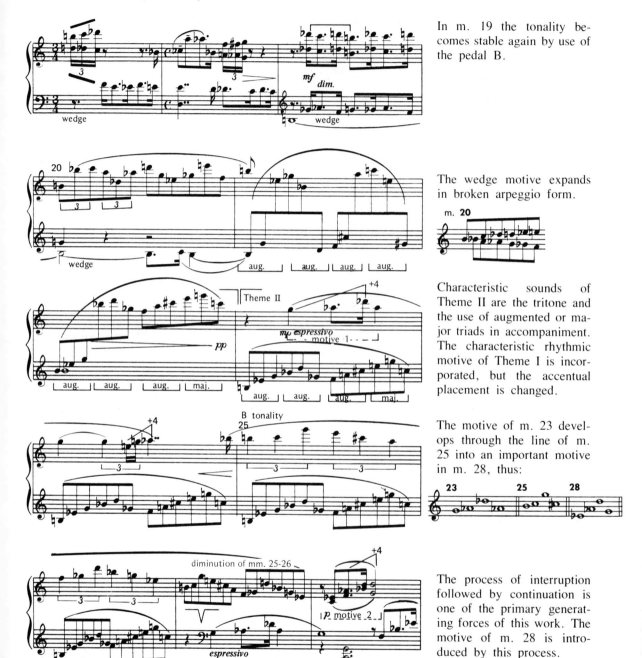

In m. 19 the tonality becomes stable again by use of the pedal B.

The wedge motive expands in broken arpeggio form.

m. **20**

Characteristic sounds of Theme II are the tritone and the use of augmented or major triads in accompaniment. The characteristic rhythmic motive of Theme I is incorporated, but the accentual placement is changed.

The motive of m. 23 develops through the line of m. 25 into an important motive in m. 28, thus:

23   25   28

The process of interruption followed by continuation is one of the primary generating forces of this work. The motive of m. 28 is introduced by this process.

The phrase extension at m. 32 develops as an embellished "turning" figure, and thus is related to m. 2.

A new rhythmic pattern articulates the section that begins at m. 35. The materials of mm. 35-50 form a closing section, but within the passage different musical purposes are achieved. The musical effect of the tritone chord of mm. 35 and 38 leading to the *stringendo* is one of motion. Each of the chromatic wedge patterns ends on a major seventh, which further contributes to the unresolved or unstable, effect.

Ex. 8-10. (Continued)

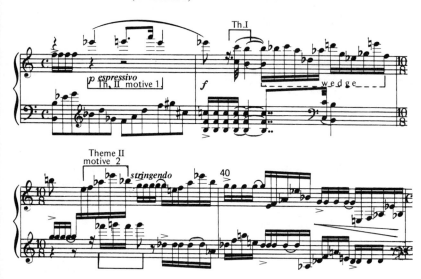

The relative stability of mm. 41-44 results from the concealment of the tritone and from its resolution in alternating chords. Also, repetition of patterns contributes to an aural effect of stability.

The aural effect of anticipation is created in mm. 45-50 by the interruption process and its cessation.

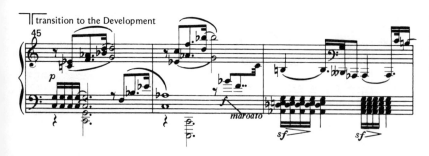

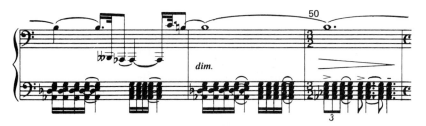

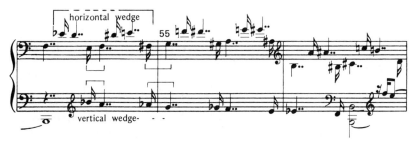

Section 1 of the development is based entirely on the materials of Theme I. The section begins as a restatement of phrase 1 that is extended through a dialogue of horizontal and vertical wedge motives. The rhythmic activity begins to accelerate in m. 57 through a separation of the three lines and a thickening of the texture in the next measures. The activity reaches a climax in measure 60 with the phrase presented again with its simultaneous inversion - a development of the wedge motive. Imitation by a double wedge a fourth below increases the vertical dissonance. Dissipation of the energy begins with the descending dialogue at m. 62.

Ex. 8-10. (Continued)

The phrase that began in m. 66 is interrupted with the retrograde rhythmic pattern initiated in m. 60. Throughout the composition developed forms of a motive are introduced inconspicuously prior to their more extensive and audible use.

The energy of the articulation rhythm at m. 71 is kept at a low level by the rest preceding and the melodic extension following.

Section 2 develops the transition rhythm and the second motive of Theme II. A neighbor tone is added to the transition rhythm in m. 76. This increases the melodic impetus of the accompaniment, which now takes the form of an ostinato. The climax of the section is achieved through gradual extension of register and thickening of texture.

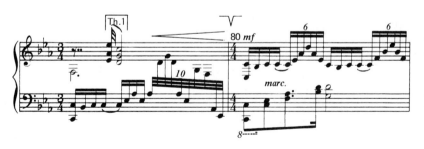

Quartal structures are used vertically with the motive of Theme I in mm. 79 and 83, and horizontally in the arpeggiated line that extends higher and higher.

Ex. 8-10. (Continued)

An interesting feature is the use of pedal to support the increasing musical tension. Pedal is the particular non-harmonic tone of the traditional period that continues to exert a dissonant effect in twentieth century writing.

At m. 86 where the musical energy might begin to dissipate, a *stringendo* marking furnishes continued impetus into section 3.

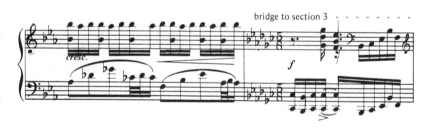

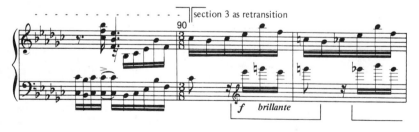

The material of section 3 comes from m. 39, and the lower voice motive furnishes a further example of extensive and audible use of an idea that was introduced inconspicuously at some prior point.

The effect of the retransition is to establish the tonality of the recapitulation and to furnish a stylistic foil to Theme I. One of the many excellent features of this composition is a fine sense of timing in the preparation for a next passage. Although the material of this section is sparse and repetitious, the rhythmic drive to the recapitulation is wonderfully well timed.

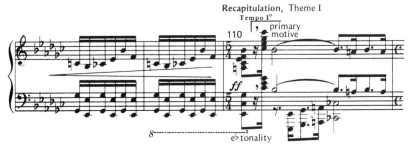

Changes in the recapitulation:

Theme I is restated with a thicker texture and the more intense impact of a leap in the primary motive.

Ex. 8-10. (Continued)   Changes in the recapitulation:

✳ *Mm. 14-15 of the exposition are omitted, and the following material is transposed
a minor third higher.

Changes in the recapitulation:

*M. 22 of the exposition is omitted. This was the measure that linked the arpeggio line of the transition to the accompaniment pattern of Theme II.

Ex. 8-10. (Continued)

Changes in the recapitulation:

* This interval was a major sixth in the exposition. Its contraction to a perfect fifth here changes the interval of transposition for the following material to a perfect fourth higher instead of a minor third higher.

*Mm. 35-38 are omitted, and the material is again transposed a minor third higher.

Changes in the recapitulation:

*Mm. 45-47 are omitted. The preceding omission and this one contribute to the gradual lowering of the musical energy. Each of the omitted areas acted in a transition capacity.

*M. 148 substitutes for mm. 49-50. The circled notes act as double leading tones to the forthcoming tonality, thus:

Ex. 8-10. (Continued)

Changes in the recapitulation:

*Mm. 151-158 of the coda are comparable to the second section of the development, with several exceptions that are influential in distinguishing the respective purpose of each area. First, the material of the coda is transposed to the tonic tonality.

*The second arpeggiation of m. 156 is simply a repetition of the first one, rather than an extended version as it was in m. 81.

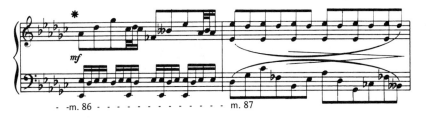

- -m. 86 - - - - - - - - - - - - m. 87

*Mm. 82-85 are omitted. These were the measures of greatest musical tension in section 2 of the development. In the measure that matches m. 86 of the development, the stringendo is omitted, and in the following measure the neighbor tone pattern is rhythmically augmented. This is the last of the motives that emerge from an inconspicuous position to one of prominence. From m. 159 to m. 164, the further augmented neighbor tone forms a motive, above which reminiscent fragments from the exposition appear as noted.

Ex. 8-10. (Continued)

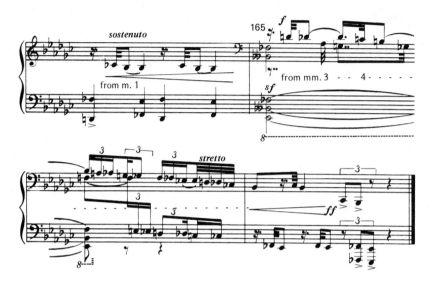

Structural Modifications of the Sonata Allegro Principle

Because of its flexibility the sonata principle has also been used with certain traditional modifications. Some of the modifications affect the length and proportions of the structure. Other modifications are related respectively to the performing medium or to the location of the sonata form in a multimovement work.

The Slow Introduction

Length and proportion are modified in the numerous symphonies and overtures in which the allegro section of the first movement is preceded by a fairly lengthy and slow introduction. Because of the usually slow tempo, the actual duration of an introduction will be somewhat greater than the number of measures seems to indicate.

This combination presents an interesting phenomenon of a beginning section that may or may not have an overt relationship with the allegro section to which it is linked. There is no particular pattern for the contents of an introduction. Often it will be divided into sections according to the material presented. There may be anticipation of musical ideas that will appear in the allegro, although this particular feature is not common until the late nineteenth century. The introduction can create aural and psychological preparation for the allegro by acting as a foil to an abrupt and rapid first theme.

More specifically the slow introduction to the symphonies of Haydn, Mozart, and Beethoven are generally not anticipatory of the material in the allegro. Of the late symphonies of Haydn, only three are without slow introduction: Nos. 87, 89, and 95. Mozart began a number of symphonies with introductions, for example, the Symphonies in C Major, K. 425, in D Major, K.508, and in E♭ Major, K.543. Four of the Beethoven symphonies are introduced with a slow section preceding the allegro: namely, the first, second, fourth, and seventh. An interesting example of a slow introduction to a chamber work is found in Beethoven's String Quartet, Op. 59, No. 3. By a progression of chromatic harmonies the tonal objective is completely concealed. The introduction begins and ends on a diminished seventh chord, and the progressions within are equally ambiguous. The aural suspense gives a fine illustration of the psychological impact that can be created by an introduction.

A notable nineteenth century illustration is the introduction that begins the Symphony No. 1 of Brahms. The introduction divides into four subsections by virtue of the materials. and there is much foreshadowing of the Allegro theme. Several twentieth century composers have written symphonic or chamber works with introductions whose materials will appear later in the sonata form. Some examples are the Sonata for Two Pianos and Percussion and the Concerto for Orchestra by Bartok; Hindemith's Symphony, *Mathis der Maler* and Vaughan Williams' Symphony No. 4 provide additional examples. In the introduction to Sibelius' Symphony No. 1 a rather haunting melody is presented by the clarinets accompanied only by timpani. There seems to be no resemblance between this melody and the materials of the first movement allegro. A certain cyclic effect is created, however, when the same introductory melody, now harmonized and orchestrated, precedes the fourth movement. A more extensive use of an introductory melody appears in the Bartok Sixth String Quartet. The beginning unaccompanied viola solo is marked *mesto*, and this mournful theme is followed by a second introductory section with full quartet. Very little direct relationship exists between the introductory solo and ensuing sonata allegro, although if the work is heard often, one begins to detect subtle thematic ties. Very directly, however, the *mesto* theme introduces the second and third movements. The cyclic effect is rounded out by the use of the *mesto* theme and Themes I and II of the first movement as integral components of the fourth movement.

The character and purposes of the lengthy, slow introduction seem to have been affected by evolutionary change as were other sections of the sonata form.

The Sonatina

Length and proportion are modified conversely in the sonatina. The diminutive meaning of the name is reflected either by a lightness and brevity of style or by a diminution of size. The latter definition is more accepted, and the sonatina can be explained as a sonata allegro form in which the development complex is replaced by a short retransition that is usually a single section. In traditional compositions the slow movement of a three or four movement work may use the sonatina form. The relative absence of this structure in multimovement works of the twentieth century can perhaps be attributed to the penchant of contemporary composers for continuous development. A number of compositions have been listed in assignment 3 under the heading *Sonatina*, and it can be noted that almost all of them come from traditional literature.

The Classical Concerto Form

Musical form is a complex of contrasts that range from the primary contrast of sound and silence through contrasts afforded by all elements of music. The concerto form adds the dimension of contrast between performing media. In the concerto grosso of the Baroque period the element of contrast was provided by a group of solo performers in conjunction with the orchestra. As composers of the eighteenth century turned to the sonata and symphony forms, and to the sonata allegro structure in particular, the solo classical concerto evolved almost inevitably.

The solo concerto is a medium that has universally delighted performers and listeners. In the best sense it represents a cooperative effort of composer, soloist, conductor, and orchestra. The regular plan of the classical concerto is three movements: fast, slow, fast. Most commonly the first movement is in sonata allegro form, but it is sonata form with a modification that is unique to the classical concerto. The orchestra first presents an exposition of materials in the tonic key, and this is followed by a second exposition featuring the soloist accompanied by orchestra. In the solo exposition the tonal plan adheres to the expected plan of two keys, but the material presented will include new musical ideas that better exploit the virtuosic possibilities of the solo instrument. Some of the thematic and auxiliary materials of the orchestral exposition will be restated in the second exposition but the order of these materials may change. The development and recapitulation sections are respectively a working out and restatement of ideas by soloist and orchestra in cooperation.

A further modification of the sonata form occurs toward the end of the concerto recapitulation, approximately where the coda would begin in the regular structural pattern. The orchestra sounds a cadential tonic six-four chord and the soloist presents an unaccompanied cadenza. Until the concertos of Beethoven, performers were at liberty to improvise their own cadenzas with all the virtuosity that they possessed. When the soloist was not also a composer this practice inevitably led to a dazzling display of mediocre musical material that was often unrelated to the rest of the movement. Consequently, Beethoven and his successors wrote the cadenza as an integral and related section of the total form. The solo cadenza traditionally ended with a trill on the dominant chord as a signal for the conductor to bring in the orchestra, and the movement was finished with dispatch. The following schematic plan represents the formal events and the tonality of the classical concerto:

Orchestral exposition	Presentation of thematic and auxiliary materials. First key ———————————————————————————————→
Solo exposition	Presentation of some new thematic and auxiliary materials as well as some of the materials from the orchestral exposition. First key ——————————————————→ second key ——————→
Development	A cooperative working out of materials from either exposition, with much figuration and passage work for the soloist. Additional keys; more rapid key change.
Recapitulation	A cooperative restatement of materials, more often comparable to the solo exposition in the sequence of materials. The solo cadenza occurs just before the final one or two codettas of the orchestra. First Key ———————————————————————————————→

The first movement of Mozart's Piano Concerto in B♭, K.595 illustrates the profusion of thematic materials that is so typical of the classical concerto. A first step in understanding the structure of the composition is to hear it several times and to note large sections and the order of musical events.

Ex. 8-11. Mozart: Piano Concerto in B♭ Major, K.595, I.

Ex. 8-11. (Continued)

The characteristic that can be noted from the following sequence of musical events (by index number) is that the materials and the order of materials differ from one exposition to the next.

Order of materials:

Orchestral exposition	1	2	3	4	5	6	7			
Solo exposition	1	8	9	10	2	3	4	11	12	5
Development	1	1	1	1						
Recapitulation	1	8	9	10	2	3	4	11	5	6
cadenza	4	2	1	1						
final codettas	12	7								

When concluding the analysis of the work, special attention needs to be given to the tonality and the apparent musical purpose of a passage. With such profusion of materials and with much of it figural, any real distinction of thematic and auxiliary materials lies in the musical purpose of a passage. A more detailed formal analysis of the first movement of the Mozart Piano Concerto in B♭, K.595, follows in Ex. 8-12. Most of the thematic writing is one-part with much figural extension.

Ex. 8-12. Formal diagram of Mozart's *Piano Concerto in B♭*, *K.595*, I.

Orchestral exposition, mm. 1-73, entirely in B♭ major

Theme (1)   cadential ext.   Theme, Part A (2)   Part B (3)
3 phrases   2 phrases, ext.   rep. phrase, ext.

codetta (4)   transition (5)   Closing Theme (6)   codetta (7)
                   implies modulation   rep. phrase, ext.

Solo exposition, mm. 74-183

Theme (1)   cadential ext.   transition (8)   Theme (9)
3 phrases   3 phrases, ext.
B♭ major   B♭:V   f minor

transition (10)   Theme, Part A (2)   Part B (3)
f minor to F major   2 phrases, ext.   rep. phrase, ext.

codetta (4) codetta (11)   codetta (12)   transition (5)
                                                           F major to b minor

Development, mm. 184-235

section 1 mm. 184-196   section 2, mm. 196-210
  (1)   dialogue between   transposed restate-   (1) imitation— — — — — — —
phrase and ext. b minor   ment C major   (8) added in piano
                                             E♭ major (e♭ and ambiguous tonality)

section 3, mm. 210-224
combined; each in   ⎡ (10) derivative in piano; ⎤
in sequence   ⎣ (1 ext) in orchestra   ⎦
g minor (rapid key change)

section 3, cont.   retransition, mm. 224-235
combined; each in   ⎡ (8) derivative in piano ⎤   (1) fragment repeated with
imitation and seq.   ⎣ (1) derivatives in orchestra ⎦ harmonic changes
E♭ major (rapid key change)   g minor   B♭ major

Recapitulation, mm. 235-362, entirely in B♭ major except for the B♭ minor of (9)

Mm. 235-238 are a restatement of the solo exposition materials through codetta (11) . The recapitulation then continues as follows:

transition (5)   Closing Theme (6)   cadenza, 4 sections   codettas (12) and (7)
implies   (4) (2) (1 ext) (1)
modulation   ends on I$^6_4$ ends on V tr ∼

Composers of the eighteenth and early nineteenth centuries struggled with the first movement plan of the classical concerto because it continued as a rather unnatural combination of concerto grosso and classical symphony elements. Credit for the solution must be given to Mendelssohn, who was essentially a traditionalist. In the first movement of his Violin Concerto in E Minor the solo violin begins with the orchestra in a single combined exposition that follows the plan of the sonata form. The result was so successful that it has continued as the concerto plan into the twentieth century. A comparison of the first movements of the violin concertos of Mendelssohn (Ex. 8-19) and Bartok (Ex. 8-13) with the Mozart concerto will represent at least the major changes since the classical concerto.

The Rondo with Development

The last movement of a multimovement work has never crystallized into one particular form, as has the first movement. Composers have variably used the rondo, the variation, or the sonata form to conclude a multimovement composition, and it was inevitable that the great interest in the techniques of the sonata form would exert some influence on the rondo form. Possibly to balance the profound statement of a first movement sonata form, composers occasionally wrote the last movement as a rondo with development. No single structural plan emerged; rather, a number of different schemes appear for the rondo with development, and some of them are illustrated in the following compositions:

Beethoven: Sonata in f, Op. 2, No. 1, IV.
Th. I Th. II Th. III development of Th. I Th. I Th. II Cl. Th.

Brahms: String Quartet, Op. 51, No. 2, IV.
Th. I Th. II Th. I Th. II development of Th. II Th. I Th. II

Schubert: Sonata in a, Op. 42, IV.
Th. I Th. II Th. I development Th. I Th. III Th. I Th. II development Th. I

Sibelius: Symphony No. 4, Op. 63, II
Th. I Th. II development of Th. I Th. III Th. I Cl. Th. Coda that develops

Additional rondos with development are listed in assignment 3.

■ Assignment 1 - *Aural analysis of form*

The following steps are suggested for the analysis of the exposition and recapitulation of sonata allegro examples:

1. Become familiar with the musical excerpts through playing or singing them.

2. Locate and make note of the beginning of each consecutive musical idea in the exposition.

3. Determine the location of the recapitulation, and note the order of the consecutive musical ideas as compared to the order in the exposition.

4. Make some educated guesses based on expectations about the form, then listen again to determine the musical purpose of the exposition ideas: statement, transition, or closing in effect; phrased or fragmented; tonally stable or unstable.

In analyzing the development section, the following preliminary steps are suggested:

1. Determine the number of sections according to the articulating factors of source material, treatment of the source material, or changes in texture, timbre, intensity, or rhythmic activity.

2. Study the musical index to determine the sources used at particular locations. Identify the most prominent development techniques.

Musical Indices

Ex. 8-13. Bartok: Violin Concerto No. 2, I.
Appendix page—596

The concerto uses the cyclic technique of incorporating melodies from one movement into another movement. The last movement of the concerto presents all the important thematic material of the first movement in the same order.

Ex. 8-13. (Continued)

The sixth musical idea contains all twelve tones of the chromatic scale. The idea is not treated as a "row" in serial composition, but the particular quality of a twelve tone melody distinguishes each of the transformations.

Ex. 8-14. Beethoven: Sonata in C Minor, Op. 10, No. 1, I.
Appendix page—599

Note the relationship of musical idea ⑧ to ideas ③ and ⑤.

Ex. 8-14. (Continued)

Ex. 8-15. Beethoven: Sonata in D Major, Op. 28, I.
Appendix page—600

The first musical idea is better interpreted as an extended eight measure phrase. It is suggested that eight measure phrasing be used throughout.

Ex. 8-15. (Continued)

Ex. 8-16. Beethoven: String Quartet, Op. 18, No. 2, IV.
   Appendix page—601

Ex. 8-16. (Continued)

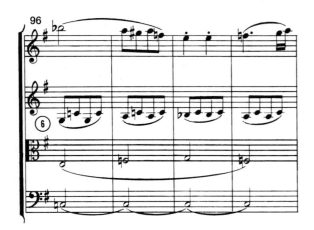

Ex. 8-17. Brahms: Piano Quintet in F Minor, Op. 34, I.
Appendix page—602

    All of the musical ideas have a ''thematic'' sound. Tonal stability or instability will affect the musical purpose of each to a considerable degree.

Ex. 8-17. (Continued)

Ex. 8-17. (Continued)

Ex. 8-18. Haydn: String Quartet, Op. 76, No. 4, I.
Appendix page—604

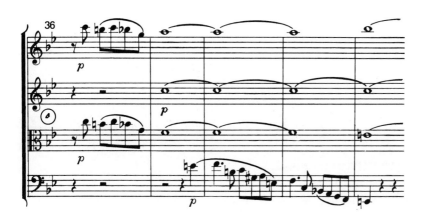

Ex. 8-19. Hindemith: Piano Sonata No. 3, I.
Appendix page—605

Ex. 8-20. Mendelssohn: Violin Concerto in E Minor, Op. 64, I.
Appendix page—606

This concerto represents certain experiments in form. There is no double exposition, the cadenza is placed in an unusual location and the first movement is linked to the second movement by a sustained bassoon tone.

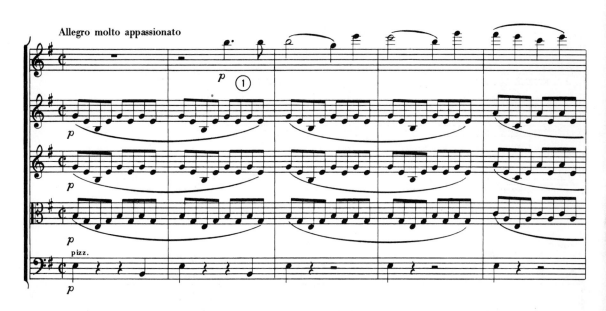

Ex. 8-20. (Continued)

Ex. 8-20. (Continued)

Ex. 8-20. (Continued)

Ex. 8-21. Mozart: Sonata in F Major, K.332, I.
Appendix page—608

Ex. 8-21. (Continued)

Ex. 8-22. Prokofieff: Symphony No. 5, Op. 100, I.
    Appendix page—609

  Motivic fragmentation and manipulation form much of the development. After several hearings it may be useful to mark the motives within each musical idea on the index so that they can be noted in greater detail on the formal diagrams.

Ex. 8-22. (Continued)

Ex. 8-23. Schubert: String Quintet, Op. 163, I.
     Appendix page—611

Ex. 8-23. (Continued)

Ex. 8-23. (Continued)

Ex. 8-24. Shostakovich: Symphony No. 5, Op. 47, I.
Appendix page—613

The composer has used motivic fragmentation and motivic development throughout the entire movement. Exposition themes are created from a limited number of motives that appear in different juxtapositions and that expand into different forms. The development section proper is simply an intensification of the motive manipulation that prevails from the beginning of the work.

Ex. 8-24. (Continued)

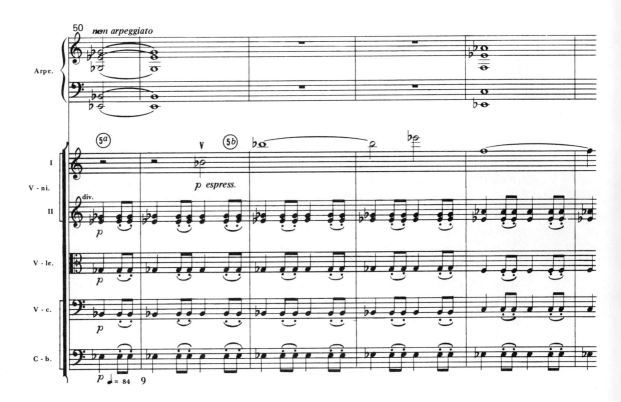

Ex. 8-24. (Continued)

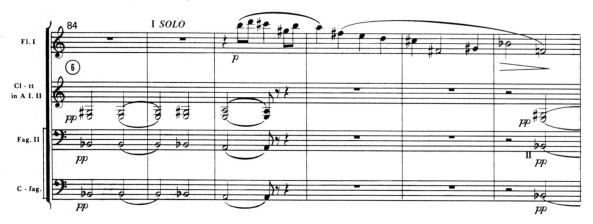

■ **Assignment 2 -** *Aural analysis of content*

    In aural analysis of content it is important to restrict the area of concentration momentarily. This is particularly necessary when analyzing a structure that is as complex as the sonata form. Even the most experienced and knowledgeable of musicians find it difficult to comprehend aurally and intellectually all the musical factors of a composition in a single hearing. The following procedures suggest certain areas of concentration.

a. Select several compositions from the chapter discussion or from assignment 1 that you have thoroughly studied. Listen again to each of them without musical index or formal diagram and write the complete analysis as you now hear it. Using tape deck or cassette go through the composition again, stopping the performance at the end of each formal area so that you can verbalize the reasons for your written analysis. This can be done with other members of the class or with a fellow musician who has not studied the work. Verbalizing intellectual and affective responses often strengthens and clarifies comprehension for the speaker.

b. Listen again to the development sections of the compositions in assignment 1 to determine the musical factors that articulate the subsections. For example, in the Bartok Violin Concerto, Ex. 8-13, the second subsection begins at measure 179. The factors that contribute to the aural articulation are as follows: the solo violin line descends to a low range and a momentary position of subordinance; a slight *ritardando* precedes the section and a return to the tempo begins it; the texture, and coincidentally the timbre, changes with the imitative entries in the string section; the chromatically descending bass line that ends the first subsection reaches its tonal objective at the beginning of the second subsection.

c. Using the formal diagrams as a guide, listen to selected development sections from assignment 1 and jot down or discuss the most obvious development techniques as they occur. For instance, in the String Quintet of Schubert, Ex. 8-23, it is apparent from the formal diagram that codetta materials are combined horizontally and vertically. In addition, imitation occurs in the first subsection, and a complex texture of dialogue, canonic imitation, and sequence begins subsection two.

d. Another interesting area of aural analysis is the determination of climax points. This can be done for an entire movement, since musical tension will increase and decrease throughout, but the more logical area for greatest musical tension is in the development section. An aural determination of the area of greatest musical tension in the development of the Hindemith Piano Sonata No. 3, Ex. 8-19, would place it just before the second subsection. Some of the musical factors that contribute to the accumulating tension are the ascending sequence of the upper voice motives, the changes of motivic length, the increase of dynamic level, the change of bass pattern and the gradual widening of the distance between lines. It is more important to discover the means by which composers have created and dissipated areas of musical tension than it is to determine the single climax point of a composition. This latter determination is quite subjective and will depend in large part on the effect that certain particular musical elements have on a particular listener.

e. Other musical factors for specific aural attention are the means by which composers prepare for the recapitulation, the musical effects and materials found in codettas at the end of the exposition, and the development techniques used in the codas.

■ Assignment 3 - *Analysis with score*

The examples for further study include sonata allegro forms as well as some additional sonatinas and rondos with development. Group 1 of the additional examples shows a skeletal outline of the structure with some measure numbers indicated. Analysis alternatives are not cited although they are possible in a number of instances. Each work should be analyzed aurally to locate the large structure before the substructure is determined by a study of the score.

Examples for further study, group 1

BARTOK   Sonata for Two Pianos and Percussion, I.

Expo. 1   32   84   105
              intro. / Th. I ABA¹, tr. / Th. II, tr., / Th. III

Devel. 133 - 274

Recap. 274   292   332   383
Th. I A¹, tr. / Th. II, tr. / Th. III (fugal) coda

BEETHOVEN   Sonata in C, Op. 2, No. 3, I.

Expo. 1   27
Th. I, tr. 1-2 / Th. II, tr., Th. III, codts. 1-2-3

Devel. 90 - 138

Recap. 139   161   218
Th. I, tr. 1-2 / Th. II, tr., Th. III, codts. 1-2 / coda 1-2-3

BRAHMS   Symphony No. 3 in F, Op. 90, I.

Expo. 3   36
Th. I, tr. Th. / Th. II AB, codts. 1-2, tr.

Devel. 77 - 119

Recap. 120   149   183
Th. I, tr. Th. / II AB, codts. 1-2, tr. / coda

CAZDEN   Sonata Op. 53, No. 3, I.²

Expo. 3   25
Th. I ABA¹ / Th. II ABA¹, codt. (derived from Th. II)

Devel. 47 - 114

Recap. 116   126   143
Codt. (substitute for Th. II) / Th. I AA / coda

HAYDN   String Quartet, Op. 76, No. 2, I.

Expo. 1   14   50
Th. I / Th. II group, quasi-devel. / codt.

Devel. 57 - 98

Recap. 100   126   139
Th. I, cdt. from Th. II group / Th. II / coda

HINDEMITH   Piano Sonata No. 2, I.

Expo. 1   41
Th. I, tr. / Th. II

Devel. 63 - 94

---

2. Both the score and the recording are available in an album *New Music for Piano* with Robert Helps as pianist, G. Schirmer, Inc., sole selling representative.

Recap. 95	117 145

Th. I, canonic tr. / Th. II / coda

MOZART   String Quartet, K. 589 in B♭, I.

Expo. 1   45

Th. I, codt., tr. 1-2 / Th. II, codt.

Devel. 72 - 130

Recap. 131   179

Th. I, codt., tr. 1-2 / Th. II, codt.

SCHUBERT   String Quartet, Op. posth. in d, I.

Expo.

1   61   115

Th. I ABCA¹, tr. / Th. II A, quasi-devel., B, tr. / Cl. Th., codt.

Devel. 141 - 198

Recap.

198   218   272

Th. I A¹, tr. / Th. II A, quasi-devel., B, tr. / Cl. Th., codt. /

299

coda 1-2-3

SIBELIUS   Symphony No. 4, Op. 63, I.

Expo. 1   6   29

intro. / Th. I, tr. / Th. II, codt. 1 (derived from Th. I)-2

Devel. 54 - 88

Recap. 89

Th. II, codt. 1 (derived from Th. I)-2 as coda

STRAVINSKY   Symphony in Three Movements, I.

Expo. 1   31   78

Th. I abc / Th. II AB, tr. / Cl. Th. 1-2

Devel. 148   170 204   267 300 307

sections A   B   A¹ / retr. A   B   A¹

Recap. 335   368   386

Th. II AB / devel. / Th. I caba

VAUGHAN WILLIAMS Symphony No. 4 in f, I.

Expo. 1   49   84

intro / Th. I / Th. II ABA¹, tr.

Devel. 123 - 178

Recap. 179   189   212   228
     intro. / Th. I / Th. II A / coda

Examples for further study, group 2

Sonata Allegro Form

BARBER	Symphony No. 2, I.
BARTOK	Concerto for Orchestra, I and V.
	Music for Strings, Percussion and Celeste, II.
	Piano Concertos, No. 2, I; No. 3, I.
	String Quartets, No. 1, III; No. 2, I; No. 4, I; No. 5, I; No. 6, I.
	Violin Concerto No. 2, III.
BEETHOVEN	Piano Concertos, No. 1 in C, I; No. 2 in B♭, I; No. 4 in G, I; No. 5 in E♭, I.
	Sonatas, Op. 2, No. 1, I; Op. 2, No. 2, I; Op. 7, I; Op. 10, No. 2, I; Op. 10, No. 3, I; Op. 13, I; Op. 14, No. 1, I; Op. 14, No. 2, I; Op. 22, I and II; Op. 27, III; Op. 31, No. 3, I and II; Op. 53, I; Op. 90, I.
	String Quartets, Op. 18, No. 1, I and IV; Op. 18, No. 2, I; Op. 18, No. 3, I and IV; Op. 18, No. 4, II; Op. 18, No. 5, I and IV; Op. 18, No. 6, I; Op. 59, No. 1, II, III and IV; Op. 59, No. 2, I and II; Op. 59, No. 3, I, II and IV; Op. 74, I; Op. 95, I; Op. 130, I; Op. 131, I and VII; Op. 135, I and IV.
	Symphonies, No. I in C, Op. 21, I, II and IV; No. 2 in D, Op. 36, I, II, and IV; No. 3 in E♭, Op. 55, I; No. 4 in B♭, Op. 60, I and IV; No. 5 in c, Op. 67, I and IV; No. 6 in F, Op. 68, I, II, IV and V; No. 7 in A, Op. 92, I and IV; No. 8 in F, Op. 93, I and IV; No. 9 in d, Op. 125, I.
BERLIOZ	Symphonies, *Fantastique*, I; *Harold in Italy*, I.
BORODIN	Symphony No. 2, I and IV.
BRAHMS	Clarinet Quintet, Op. 115, I.

Piano Concertos, No. I in d, I; No. 2 in B♭, I.

Sonatas, Op. 1 in C, I; Op. 5 in f, I.

String Quartets, Op. 51, No. 1, I; Op. 67, I.

String Quintets, Op. 88, I and IV; Op. 111, I and IV.

String Quintet, Op. 36, I.

Symphonies, No. 1 in c, Op. 68, I; No. 2 in D, Op. 73, II and IV; No. 4 in e, Op. 98, I.

Violin Concerto in D, I.

CHOPIN   Sonatas, Op. 35 in b♭, I; Op. 58 in b, I.

COPLAND   Symphony No. 3, IV.

DEBUSSY   String Quartet No. 1, Op. 10, I.

DVORAK   String Quartet, Op. 96, I.

Symphony No. 5 in e, Op. 95, I and IV.

FRANCK   Piano Trio, Op. 1, No. 1, IV.

Piano Quintet in f, I, II and III.

String Quartet in D, IV.

Symphony in d, I and III.

HANSON   Symphony No. 2 (Romantic), I.

HAYDN   Sonatas (Peters ed.), No. 1 in E♭, I and III; No. 2 in e, I; No. 3 in E♭, I; No. 4 in g, I; No. 5 in C, I; No. 6 in c♯, I; No. 7 in D, I; No. 8 in A♭, I and III; No. 9 in D, I and II; No. 12 in G, I; No. 13 in E♭, I; No. 14 in F, I and II; No. 15 in D, I and III; No. 16 in C, I, II and III; No. 17 in G, III; No. 18 in E, I and II; No. 19 in B♭, I and II; No. 20 in D, I; No. 22 in B♭, I; No. 23 in A, III; No. 25 in c, I and III; No. 26 in E♭, I, II and III; No. 27 in B♭, I; No. 30 in E, I; No. 31 in D, I; No. 32 in E♭, I; No. 33 in A, I; No. 34 in F, I and III; No. 35 in E♭, I; No. 36 in A, I; No. 37 in G, IV; No. 39 in b, I and III; No. 40 in E, I; No. 41 in A♭, I; No. 42 in C, I; No. 43 in C, I and III.

String Quartets, Op. 3, No. 5, I and III; Op. 33, No. 2, I; Op. 76, No. 3, I; Op. 76, No. 5, I; Op. 77, No. 1, I and IV; Op. 77, No. 2, I and IV.

Symphonies, No. 88 in G, I; No. 94 in G, I and IV; No. 99 in Eb, I and II; No. 100 in G, I and IV; No. 101 in D, I; No. 104 in D, I and IV.

HINDEMITH	Cello Concerto, I.
	Piano Concerto, I and III.
	Sonata for Two Pianos, II.
	String Quartet, Op. 22, II.
	Symphony, *Mathis der Maler*, I.
HONNEGER	Symphony No. 5, I and III.
MENDELSSOHN	Piano Concerto in g, I.
	String Quartets, Op. 44, No. 1, I; Op. 44, No. 2, I.
	Symphonies, No. 3 in a, I, II and III; No. 4 in A, I and IV; No. 5 in d, I.
MOZART	Piano Concertos, K.414 in A, I; K.453 in G, I; K.459 in F, I; K.467 in C, I; K. 482 in Eb, I.
	Sonatas, K.279 in C, I and III; K.280 in F, I, II and III; K.281 in Bb, I; K.282 in Eb, I; K.283 in G, I, II and III; K.284 in D, I; K.309 in C, I; K.310 in a, I and II; K.311 in D, I; K.330 in C, I and III; K.332 in F, III; K.333 in Bb, I and II; K.457 in c, I; K.498a in Bb, I; K.533/494 in F, I and II; K.547a in F, I; K.576 in D, I.
	String Quartets, K.387 in G, I, II and III; K.421 in d, I; K.428 in Eb, I and II; K.458 in Bb, I and III; K.464 in A, I and IV; K.499 in D, I and IV; K.589 in Bb, I; K.590 in F, I.
	Symphonies, K.385 in D, I, II and IV; K.504 in D, I, II and III; K.508 in D, I, II and III; K.543 in Eb, I and IV; K.550 in g, I, II and IV; K.551 in C, I, II and IV.
	Woodwind Quintet, K.452 in Eb, II.
PISTON	Sonata for Violin and Piano, I and III.
PROKOFIEFF	Piano Concerto No. 3, I.
	Symphonies, Classical, I and IV; No. 5, I and IV; No. 7, I.
	Violin Concerto No. 2, I.

RAVEL	Piano Trio, I.
	String Quartet No. 1, I.
RIMSKY-KORSAKOV	Symphonic Suite, *Scheherazade*, III.
SCHOENBERG	Piano Concerto, Op. 42, I.
SCHUBERT	Piano Quintet, Op. 114 in A, I.
	Piano Trio, Op. 99, No. 1 in B♭, I; Op. 100, No. 2 in E♭, I.
	Sonatas, Op. 42 in a, I; Op. 53 in D, I; Op. 120 in A, I and III; Op. 122 in E♭, I; Op. 143 in a, I; Op. 164 in a, I; Op. posth. in c, I; Op. posth. in A, I; Op. posth. in B♭, I.
	String Quartets, Op. 125, No. 2 in E, I; Op. 168, No. 9 in B♭, I; Op. 168, No. 10 in g, I.
	Symphony No. 2 in B♭, I and IV; No. 5 in B♭, I and IV; No. 6 in C, I and IV; No. 8 (Unfinished) in b, I and II; No. 9 in C, I and IV.
SCHUMANN	Piano Concerto in a, I.
	Piano Quintet, Op. 44 in E♭, I.
	String Quartet, Op. 41, No. 1, I and IV; Op. 41, No. 2, I and IV; Op. 41, No. 3, I.
	Symphonies, No. 1 in B♭, I and IV; No. 3 in E♭, I and V; No. 4 in d, IV.
SHOSTAKOVICH	String Quartets, No. 2, I; No. 3, I; No. 4, IV; No. 5, I; No. 6, I.
	Symphony No. 1, I and IV.
SIBELIUS	Symphony No. 1, I, II and IV; No. 3, I; No. 4, I and IV.
STRAUSS, R.	Symphonic Poem, Op. 120 "Don Juan."
STRAVINSKY	Septet, I.
TSCHAIKOVSKY	Symphony No. 3 in D, I; Symphony No. 4 in f, I; Symphony No. 5 in e, I and IV.
VAUGHAN WILLIAMS	Symphony No. 2 (London), I and II; No. 3, I and IV; No. 4, IV; No. 6, I.

Sonatina: some of the following examples lie between a genuine sonatina and a fully realized sonata form.

BARBER	Piano Sonata, Op. 26, III.
BEETHOVEN	Sonatas, Op. 10, No. 1, II and III; Op. 49, No. 2, I. String Quartet, Op. 18, No. 1, II. Symphony No. 8 in F, II.
BERLIOZ	Symphony, *Harold in Italy*, IV.
BRAHMS	Piano Quintet, Op. 34, IV. Symphony No. 4, II.
HAYDN	Sonatas (Peters ed.), No. 29 in A, I; No. 34 in F, II; No. 42 in C, II.
MENDELSSOHN	String Quartet, Op. 44, No. 1, III. Symphony No. 4 in A, II.
MOZART	Serenade, "Eine Kleine Nachtmusik," I. Symphonies, K.385 in D, II; K.543 in E♭, II. Sonatas, K.332 in F, II; K.281 in B♭, II; K.279 in C, II; K.311 in D, II; K.576 in D, III; K.282 in E♭, III.
RIMSKY-KORSAKOV	Symphonic Suite, *Scheherazade*, II.
SCHUBERT	Sonata, Op. 120 in A, II and III. Symphony No. 9 in C, II.
SHOSTAKOVICH	String Quartets, No. 1, I; No. 5, II; No. 7, I.
SIBELIUS	Symphony No. 2, II.
VAUGHAN WILLIAMS	Symphony No. 4 in f, II.

Rondo with development or sonata rondo:

BEETHOVEN	Sonatas, Op. 27, No. 1, IV; Op. 31, No. 1, III. String Quartets, Op. 59, No. 2, IV; Op. 95, IV; Op. 130, IV; Op. 131, II.

BRAHMS	String Sextet, Op. 18, IV.
	Symphony No. 4 in e, Op. 98, III.
DEBUSSY	String Quartet No. 1, Op. 10, IV.
HAYDN	Symphony No. 88 in G, IV.
MOZART	Sonata K.310 in a, III.
SCHUBERT	Sonatas, Op. posth. in c, IV; Op. posth. in A, IV: Op. posth. in B♭, IV.
	String Quintet, Op. 163, IV.
SHOSTAKOVICH	String Quartets, No. 2, III; No. 3, V; No. 5, III; No. 6, IV.

9 ■ unusual forms

Expectations about the form and content of a composition grow out of knowledge and experience. Such expectations are extremely useful as long as they remain sufficiently flexible to accomodate unusual forms. Composers have explored the possibilities and extended the limits of musical structure just as they have done with all the other parameters of music, and unusual forms appear in the music of any style or period. Certain compositions, such as the first movement of the Mendelssohn Violin Concerto, were unusual in their time, but the innovations were absorbed into the common practices of composers. Other compositions display a formal arrangement that continues to be recognized as unique in the context of period, style, or performing media.

Analysis of a musical work whose materials are organized differently than any of the commonly used forms, or adaptations thereof, is as much a psychological problem as an analytical one. We all tend to perceive and organize musical sounds according to familiar patterns. Uniqueness within established patterns is appreciated; uniqueness of the structural pattern itself can disturb us in much the same way that we are disturbed when we read a literary passage whose words are familiar to us but whose larger meaning cannot be comprehended. A composition may be in a familiar medium, it may move through a succession of musical sounds that introduce, state, bridge, develop, or conclude, and yet the broad structural outline may be puzzling. Understanding at all levels is essential to the sensitive interpretation of a composition, and both attitude and resources may need to be expanded when one analyzes a musical work that is uniquely structured.

Most composers are creative persons as well as craftsmen. When a composer organizes his musical materials into unusual forms, he may do so for a variety of reasons but generally not for the reason of ignorance. Often information about an unusual composition can be found by reading related literature in books and periodicals. The four examples of unusual forms that are presented later in this chapter are from string quartets, and one could seek information about them in any of the books that deal with chamber music[1] as well as in literature about each composer and his works. Music his-

1. Some of the publications devoted exclusively to chamber literature are Cobbett's *Cyclopedic Survey of Chamber Music,* and books by Gleason, Robertson (ed.), and Ulrich.

tory books, annotated anthologies of musical literature and unpublished dissertations often provide critical and analytical information. If the work is multimovement, an analysis of the remaining movements may furnish guidance for the analysis of the unusual movement. The most valuable resource of all is the sound of the composition. If a composition is heard a great many times and if the listener concentrates all his knowledge and analytical skills toward each hearing, the large structural plan of the composition will eventually become clear.

The following four examples represent works written at different points in each composer's career. The quartets of Debussy and Bartok were written before the midpoint of their careers, and the Haydn and Franck quartets were written toward the end of each man's life. Haydn wrote over eighty string quartets, Franck and Debussy each wrote one, and Bartok wrote six. Other differences among the four composers include the degree to which each used the traditional large forms in their total output, but only Debussy showed a marked disinclination to use the large, traditional forms. Each of the following examples, however, is unique in the context of the traditional multimovement string quartet, and the structure of each is presented in diagrammatic form prefaced by brief comments concerning the structure of the entire work.

Haydn's String Quartet, Op. 77, No. 1 is a four movement work in which the first and last movements are traditionally structured in sonata form, and the third movement is the expected minuet with trio. Although the second movement is the unusual form, the other three movements have several uncommon features that complement the uniqueness of the second movement. In the first movement the second theme is not recapitulated; in the third movement the melody of the trio is directly derived from the melody of the minuet; and the last movement is one of Haydn's "monothematic" compositions in which the second theme of the sonata form begins as a transposition of the first theme. Thus the true monothematicism of the adagio movement appears in a large formal plan unified by this common characteristic. The development of a single theme seems unusual until one considers the available means for extending one musical idea to a length appropriate to an internal movement of a multimovement work: the single theme can be repeated with variations or it can be developed. The latter technique is used.

Ex. 9-1. Haydn: String Quartet, Op. 77, No. 1, II.
  (Theme I, development, Theme I, codetta)

Measure	1	8	16	18	21
Formal function	Theme I, 1st period	2nd period	Development, section 1		
Tonality	E♭		b♭		B♭
Comments		Variant of 1st period	Fragmentation. Sources: mm. 1-2; 10;		13, 14, 11.

Measure	30	33	37
Formal function	Section 2		
Tonality		D♭	f
Comments	Begins as a cadence	Fragmentation & sequence Source: mm. 1-2.	

Measure	43	45	47
Formal function	Section 3		
Tonality	D♭		f
Comments	Fragmentation, sequence and free canonic imitation. Sources: mm. 1-2; 9 and 11.		

Measure	55	58	66
Formal function	Theme I, 1st period		2nd period
Tonality	E♭	G♭	E♭
Comments	Original phrase 1; phrase 2 modified.		Same as mm. 9-14.

Measure	72	83
Formal function		Codetta
Tonality		E♭
Comments	Modified by evaded cadence & extension.	Source: mm. 1-2.

The D major String Quartet of Franck is a four movement work employing cyclic techniques. The first movement is the unusual form and represents an amalgamation of a large ternary pattern with a sonata allegro form. The melody of Part A of the binary introduction is used again for a fugato section that appears before the development of the sonata form, and the two parts of the introduction are restated as a final coda. The materials of the sonata allegro are relatively distinct from the materials of the slow introduction, fugato, and coda.

The remaining three movements are respectively a scherzo with trio, a five part slow movement and a final sonata allegro. The only unusual structural features of these three movements are the arrangement of the middle movements as fast-slow rather than the more traditional reverse arrangement and the cyclic element.

Ex. 9-2. Franck: String Quartet in D Major, I.

(Introduction ABA¹B¹   Fugato A   Coda AB)
                        Exposition   Development Recapitulation

Measures	1	15	27	41	57
Formal function	*Introduction,* A		B	A¹	B¹
Primary melodic idea	①		②	①	②
Additional melodic ideas					
Tonality	D	D	A/a	D	D/d
Comments		Possible transition			

Measures	71	74	81
Formal function			*Exposition,* Theme I 3 phr. grp.
Primary melodic idea			③
Additional melodic ideas			
Tonality	D		d
Comments		Anticipates Th. I	

Measures	96	105	113	121	127	131	134
Formal function	Transition, Section 1	Section 2			Section 3		
Primary melodic idea	④	⑤			⑥		
Additional melodic ideas		④					
Tonality	d	d	E♭	a♭	A♭/a♭	B	D
Comments	Anticipates Th. II						

Measures	138	163	173
Formal function	Theme II, 3 phr. grp.	Codetta	*Fugato,* 1st entry
Primary melodic idea	⑦	③ ⑦ ①	①
Additional melodic ideas			
Tonality	F	F	f
Comments	Imitative		Possible Section 1 of development

Measures	179	185	191
Formal function	2nd entry	3rd entry	4th entry
Primary melodic idea	①	①	①
Additional melodic ideas			
Tonality	c	f	c
Comments	Tonal answer		Tonal answer

Ex. 9-2. (Continued)

Measures	197	203	206	209
Formal function	Episode	5th entry	6th entry	7th entry
Primary melodic idea		①	①	①
Additional melodic ideas				
Tonality		b♭	D♭	
Comments	Sequence	Abbrev.	Abbrev.	Abbrev.

Measures	213	218	223	227
Formal function	Transition	*Development,*	section 1	
Primary melodic idea		③	⑤	③
Addition melodic ideas				
Tonality		g		B♭
Comments				

Measures	231	233	237	248	252	256
Formal function			Section 2	Section 3		
Primary melodic idea	⑤		④	⑥		
Additional melodic ideas		③-⑥		④		
Tonality	b♭		f	C/c	E♭/e♭	F♯/f♯
Comments						

Measures	259	271
Formal function	Section 4	Recapitulation, Theme I 3 phr. grp.
Primary melodic idea	⑦	③
Additional melodic ideas		
Tonality	A	d
Comments	Imitation; sequence	

Measures	286	288	290	292
Formal function	Transition Section 1			
Primary melodic idea	④			
Additional melodic ideas				
Tonality	d	D	f♯	F♯
Comments		Tonal digression		

Measures	297	305	313		315	319
Formal function	Section 2				Theme II 3 phr. grp.	
Primary melodic idea	⑤					
Additional melodic ideas						
Tonality	f♯	G			B	D
Comments			Mm. 121-137 replaced by 2 mm.		Imitative	

Ex. 9-2. (Continued)

Measures	340	354	360	367-373
Formal function	*Coda,* A	B		
Primary melodic idea	①	②		
Additional melodic ideas				
Tonality	D	D/d	tonally unstable	D
Comments		Modified		

Each movement of the Debussy String Quartet No. 1 is unusual in a particular way although only the fourth movement seems a complete departure from any of the traditional forms. The first movement is a sonata form whose second theme (measure 39) is not restated in the recapitulation or whose alternate second theme (measure 63) appears immediately before the development and again immediately before the final coda with no intervening codettas. The second movement is the fast inner movement, and it is organized sectionally around one primary motive and its transformation. There is only one melodic departure in this movement. The third movement is slow, and it is shaped in an arch form that can be interpreted either as Themes I II III II I or as Introduction, Themes I II I, Coda.

The work is cyclic and the ''motto theme'' appears in the first, second, and fourth movements. The last movement begins as though it might take the shape of a rondo, but the principle of alternating themes is dissipated after the statement of the third theme.

Ex. 9-3. Debussy: String Quartet No. 1, Op. 10, IV.
(Introduction, Themes I II I III, development, coda)

Measures	1	3		15
Formal function	Introduction, Section 1			Section 2
Primary musical idea	①			③
Additional musical ideas		②		
Tonality	D♭		E	D♭
Comments		Transformation of motto theme		Transformation of motto theme

Measures	31	45	55
Formal function	Theme I, A	B	A^1
Primary musical idea	④	⑤	④
Additional musical ideas			
Tonality	g	Modulatory	
Comments		Suggests motto theme	

Measures	59			90	98	114
Formal function	Theme II			Retransition		Theme I, A
Primary musical idea	⑥			⑥	④	
Additional musical ideas						
Tonality	g	F	b♭	G♭	Modulatory	F
Comments	Derivation of Theme I, A, m. 2				Augmented	

Measures	125		141	
Formal function	Theme III		Theme III cont.	
Primary musical idea	⑦		⑦	
Additional musical ideas	Ostinato from Theme I and II			
Tonality	c♯	E	C	Modulatory
Comments	Augmented transformation of motto theme		Augmented and syncopated transformation of motto theme	

Ex. 9-3. (Continued)

Measures	165	181	216	232	241
Formal function	Transition		Development, Section 1		
Primary musical idea	④	⑦	④	⑥	④
Additional musical ideas	⑦			⑥	⑦
Tonality		C	c	d D	
Comments		Theme III, further augmented		Theme II, augmented	

Measures	252	264	282	289	299
Formal function	Section 2				
Primary musical idea	⑦	④	⑦	⑦	⑦
Additional musical idea		④			
Tonality	G				E G
Comments			Augmented	Augmented	Transformed

Measures	326	355
Formal function	Coda	
Primary musical idea	⑦	
Additional musical ideas	⑥	
Tonality		
Comments		

Stevens has described the second movement of the Bartok String Quartet No. 2 as conveying the impression of a rondo without actually using the structural plan of one, and this impression can be generally assimilated after repeated hearings. The first movement is a sonata allegro that evolves through continuous development of motives, a style of composition that was to become characteristic of Bartok's music. The third, and last, movement is a chain of five sections plus a coda, and the movement exemplifies motivic transformation.

As often happens with a work of Bartok's, committing the structure of the work to paper in diagrammatic form fails to properly represent the motivic growth and interrelationship of motives. The primary theme is characterized by an accompaniment of repeated sonorities which so strongly identify the theme that rather drastic melodic transformations can be aurally accepted. In the broad plan, Theme I, or its transformation, is always followed by one or two variant forms that are related by the same kind of transformation. Transition passages contain the unstable tritone of the introduction idea or they effect a tempo change.

The particular analytical problem in this work is distinguishing among statement, transition, and development.

Ex. 9-4. Bartok, String Quartet No. 2, II.

Measures	1	8	12
Formal function	Introduction motive	Accompaniment	*Theme I*, A
Primary melodic ideas	①	Repeated 8ths	②
Tonality	d	d	
Comments	Ends with a m2 descending above a chord		

Measures	25	49	52	59
Formal function	A variant, ext.	Accompaniment	A^1	A^1 variant
Primary melodic ideas	②	Repeated 8ths	②	②
Tonality				
Comments	Ends with the m2 articulation			

2. Halsey Stevens, *The Life and Music of Bela Bartok* (New York: Oxford University Press, 1964 rev. ed.), p. 181.

Ex. 9-4. (Continued)

Measures	69	77	79
Formal function	Transition 1	Accompaniment	*Theme I,* A^2
Primary melodic ideas	①	Repeated 5ths	②
Tonality	Unstable	d	
Comments	Some inversion; ends with m2	m2 added to accompaniment	

Measures	89	103	108	118
Formal function	A^2 variant	Ext.	Transition 2	
Primary melodic ideas	②	①	①	② and ①
Tonality			Unstable	
Comments				Vertical combination

Measures	139		152	156
Formal function	*Theme II*	Ext.	Accompaniment	*Theme I,* A^3
Primary melodic ideas	③	③	Repeated 8ths	②
Tonality	G B♭		d	
Comments	Uses tritone of ①		m2 added	

Measures	165	173	182
Formal function	A^3 variant 1	A^3 variant 2	Accompaniment
Primary melodic ideas	②	②	Repeated 8ths
Tonality			
Comments			Filled-in 3rd added

Ex. 9-4. (Continued)

Measures	187	195	205
Formal function	A⁴	A⁴ variant	Transition 3
Primary melodic ideas	②	②	①
Tonality			Unstable
Comments		Accompaniment begins to grow into ♪♪♪♪ of ① in tr.	Repeated chords added; tritone filled-in at first; ends with imitation

Measures	234	255	272
Formal function	*Development* Section 1	Section 2	Section 3
Primary melodic ideas	② and ①	①	Repeated chords and ①
Tonality	Unstable		d
Comments	Vertical combination as at m. 119		m2 added before repeated chords and developed into the arpeggiated 3rds of ②

Measures	284	304	312
Formal function	Transition 4	*Theme III*	
Primary melodic ideas	②	④	④
Tonality	d Unstable	E	Unstable
Comments	Anticipates ④	Contains inverted tritone of ①	

Measures	328	338	359
Formal function	Transition 5		*Theme II*
Primary melodic ideas	④	④	③
Tonality	(d) Unstable	(C♯)(B)	Unstable
Comments	Inverted and in imitation	Diminutive, so resembles ♪♪♪♪ of ①	

Ex. 9-4. (Continued)

Measures	380	390	402	414
Formal function	Transition 6	*Theme I*, A^5	A^5 variant 1	A^5 variant 2
Primary melodic ideas	③	②	②	②
Tonality	(B) Unstable	g	F	c♯
Comments				

Measures	425	445	
Formal function	Development of introduction materials		
Primary melodic ideas	①		
Tonality	c♯	Unstable	e♭
Comments	Repeated chords added	Climax point followed by dissolution of energy	

Measures	468	480------------------------559
Formal function	Transition 7	*Coda*
Primary melodic ideas	① , ② and ④	② and ①
Tonality	e♭ as upper leading tone to d	d
Comments	Repeated chords of M7 and A4	Some use of A^4

Comprehension of an unusual form will evolve through the same process of musical and intellectual growth as comprehension of a work that is organized in a more traditional pattern: each returning to the composition will reveal new facets and deepen understanding and appreciation. As a musical composition is known and loved, so is it interpreted to others.

Appendix

The formal diagrams are designed to be as concise as is possible for immediacy of visual impact. To do this has necessitated the use of a certain number of abbreviations, symbols, and combinations of the two.

Abbreviations

cad.	= cadence
ext.	= extended by
ext. imit.	= extended by imitation
ext. rep. 1	= extended by repetition of the preceding one measure
ext. rep. mot.	= extended by repetition of the preceding motive
ext. seq. 2	= extended by sequence of the preceding two measures
phr.	= phrase
rep. phr.	= repetition of the immediately preceding phrase
rep. phr. 1	= repetition of a prior phrase that does not immediately precede
S.F.	= song form
Th.	= theme

Symbols

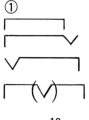

= the index number of a musical idea

= a single phrase that constitutes a part

= a phrase that is a component of a larger unit

= the end of a part

= optional phrase articulation

= a measure indication where cadential elision takes place, or where formal units begin and end in the same measure without elision.

553

Combined Symbols and Abbreviations

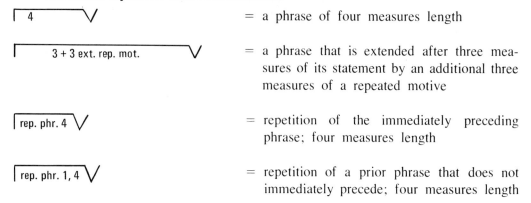

4 ⌄	= a phrase of four measures length
3 + 3 ext. rep. mot. ⌄	= a phrase that is extended after three measures of its statement by an additional three measures of a repeated motive
rep. phr. 4 ⌄	= repetition of the immediately preceding phrase; four measures length
rep. phr. 1, 4 ⌄	= repetition of a prior phrase that does not immediately precede; four measures length

Chord Analysis Symbols

Where shown, the chords of traditional works use standard analysis symbols (inversions are not indicated), with one exception: the chord ninths, elevenths, and thirteenths are shown simply as arabic numbers with no attempt to indicate intervallic quality since this is not essential to the formal analysis. If the quality of dissonance is relevant to any discussion of the musical content of a work, such distinction will appear in context of the discussion. Occasionally in a twentieth century excerpt the pitch name of certain chords, such as cadence chords, will be shown.

Tonality

There has been no effort to distinguish in the diagrams transient keys from more stable keys, but transience of tonality can be determined in many instances by brevity of temporal span. Indeed, many transient keys could have been analyzed as altered chord progressions. Since the diagrams are designed to interpret aural analysis, however, the noting of transient tonalities seems a more faithful representation of the aural effect.

Upper and lower case letters indicate respectively major and minor keys in tonal music. In twentieth century works the same distinction of mode is noted if there is a strong tonal inclination toward major or minor. In works or passages of works where tonality is definitely not major or minor but is still tonally oriented in some way, upper case letters and accidentals are used with the term "tonality" to indicate this. If a tonality is indicated in a diagram, it can be interpreted as continuing until the next tonal indication appears.

Chapter 2: Formal Diagrams

Ex. 2-24. Bartok: Violin Concerto No. 2, II.

Theme	Introduction 1 meas.	Melody 1	Melody 2 ext.
Var. 1	none	same	same
Var. 2	1 meas.	same	same
Var. 3	none	same	same
Var. 4	none	extended	same
Var. 5	none	same	same
Var. 6	none	extended	same
Var. 7	none	same	same

Ex. 2-25. Beethoven: String Quartet, Op. 18, No. 5, III.

Theme	Melody 1	Melody 2	Melody 1
Var. 1-5 Coda	same	same	same

Ex. 2-26. Brahms: Variations and Fugue on a Theme by Handel, Op. 24.

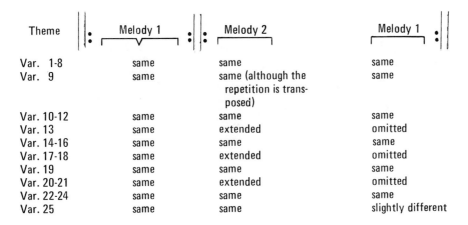

Theme	Melody 1	Melody 2	Melody 1
Var. 1-8	same	same	same
Var. 9	same	same (although the repetition is transposed)	same
Var. 10-12	same	same	same
Var. 13	same	extended	omitted
Var. 14-16	same	same	same
Var. 17-18	same	extended	omitted
Var. 19	same	same	same
Var. 20-21	same	extended	omitted
Var. 22-24	same	same	same
Var. 25	same	same	slightly different

Ex. 2-27. Mozart: Sonata in A Major, K. 331, I.

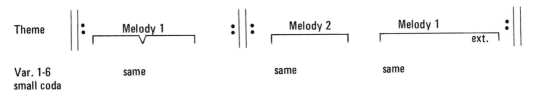

Theme	Melody 1	Melody 2	Melody 1 ext.
Var. 1-6 small coda	same	same	same

Ex. 2-28. Schubert: String Quartet in D Minor, Op. posth., II.

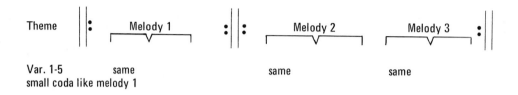

Theme ‖: Melody 1 :‖ ‖: Melody 2 Melody 3 :‖

Var. 1-5   same   same   same
small coda like melody 1

Ex. 2-29. Schumann: Symphonic Etudes, Op. 13.

	Theme Melody 1	Melody 2	Melody 1	
Etude I	same	‖: same	same :‖	
Etude II	‖: extended :‖	‖: extended	extended :‖	
Etude III	‖: same :‖	‖: same	extended :‖	
Etude IV	‖: same :‖	‖: same	same :‖	
Etude V	‖: same :‖	‖: same	same :‖	
Etude VI	‖: same :‖	‖: same	same :‖	
Etude VII	‖: same :‖	‖: extended	extended :‖	
Etude VIII	same	‖: same	same :‖	
Etude IX	extended	‖: extended	same :‖	⎡ addition of an internal closing section. ⎣
Etude X	‖: same :‖	‖: same	same :‖	
Etude XI	‖: extended :‖	same	extended	
Etude XII, finale				

Ex. 2-30. Shostakovich: String Quartet No. 1, II.

Theme   Melody 1

			ext.		
Var. 1	same	same	extended	same	(although the entire melody is transposed)
Var. 2	same	abbreviated	same	extended	(although the mode of the melody changes)
Var. 3	same	same	same	extended	

Chapter 3: Formal Diagrams.

Ex. 3-39. Bach: *Well Tempered Clavier*, Book I, Fugue No. 18.

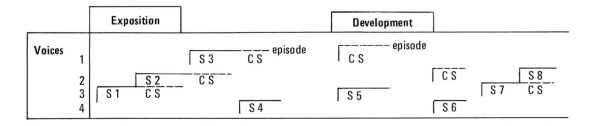

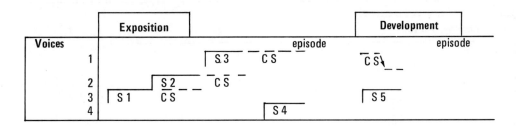

Ex. 3-40. Bach: *Well Tempered Clavier*, Book I. Fugue No. 23.

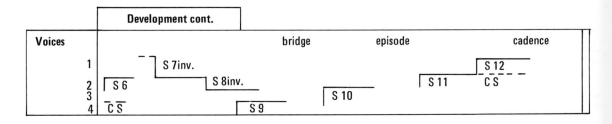

Ex. 3-41. Bach: Two Part Invention No. 5.

Ex. 3-42. Bach: Three Part Invention No. 3.

Ex. 3-43. Hindemith: *Ludus Tonalis*, Fugue No. 9.

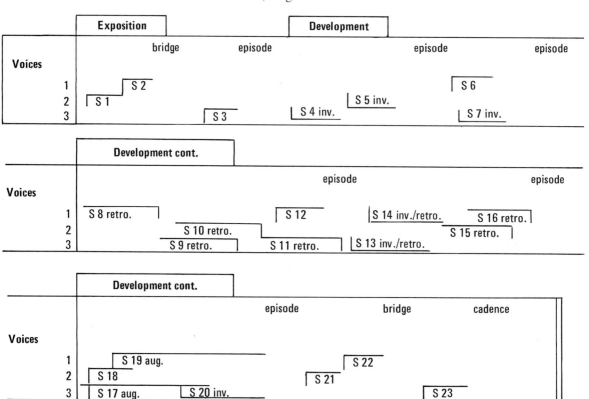

Ex. 3-44. Mendelssohn: 6 Preludes and Fugues, Op. 35, Fugue No. 2.

Exposition			Development		
Voices	bridge	episode	episode	bridge	
1		S 4		S 7	S 8 ext.
2	S 3				
3	S 2	C S	S 6		S 9
4	S 1 C S	C S	S 5		

Development cont.				
Voices	episode	episode bridge	episode	cadence
1		S 11	S 12	S 14 ext.
2			S 13	
3				
4	S 10			

Ex. 3-45. Shostakovich: 24 Preludes and Fugues, Op. 87, Fugue No. 5.

Exposition			Development		
Voices	bridge	episode	episode		
1	S 2	C S	S 4		
2	S 1 C S		C S	C S	S 6 C S
3		S 3		S 5	C S S 7

Development cont.			
Voices	episode	episode	episode
1	C S	S 10 abbrev.	C S
2	S 9		
3	S 8 C S		S 11 abbrev.

Development cont.			
Voices		episode	cadence
1	S 12 ext.	S 14 abbrev. S 17 abbrev.	C S
2	S 13 ext.	S 15 abbrev.	
3		S 16 abbrev.	S 18 ext.

Chapter 4: Formal Diagrams

Ex. 4-28.   Bartok: *Mikrokosmos*, No. 128 (ABA¹)

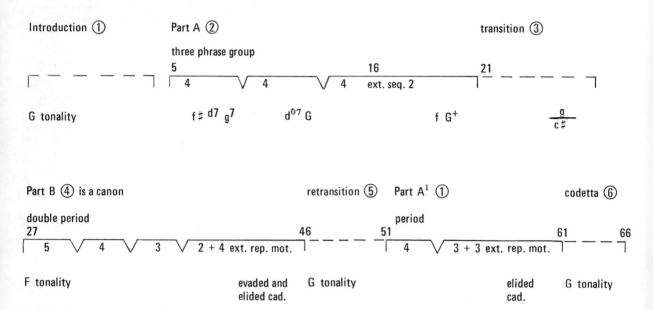

Ex. 4-29.   Beethoven: Eleven Bagatelles, Op. 119, No. 5 (ABA¹)

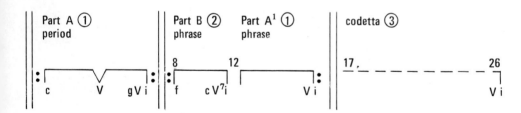

Ex. 4-30.   Brahms: Piano Quintet in F Minor, Op. 34, II. (ABA)

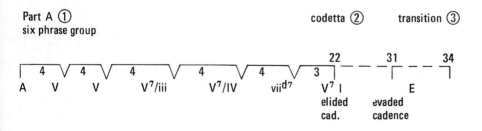

Part B ④
double period

retransition ⑤

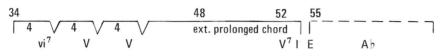

34
4 ∨ 4 ∨ 4 ∨   48   52   55
    vi⁷   V   V   ext. prolonged chord   V⁷ I   E   A♭

Part A ①
six phrase group

75
4 ∨ 4 ∨ rep. phr. 1, 4 ∨ rep. phr. 2, 4 ∨ 4 ∨ 4 ∨ 4 ∨ 2   104
  V⁷   V   V   V   V⁷/iii   V⁷/V   vii^{d7}   V⁷ I
                                                                               elided cad.

Coda, section 1 ⑥   section 2 ⑦

104   117   126
   elided cadence V⁷ I   V⁹ I

Ex. 4-31. Chopin: Mazurka, Op. 7, No. 3. (ABCDA)

Introduction ①   Part A ②   Part B ③
                    repeated period   repeated period

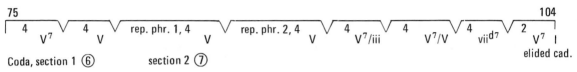

                      9   24
       8   4 ∨ 4 ∨ 4 ∨ 4   4 ∨ 4 ∨ 4 ∨ 4
f   iv i   V   iv i   c V i   f V⁷i   A♭ V⁷ I   f V⁷ I   A♭ V⁷ i

Part C ④
repeated period

40
4 ∨ 4 ∨ 4 ∨ 4
D♭ IV I   A♭ V⁷ I   D♭ V⁷ I   A♭ V⁷ I

Part D ⑤
repeated period

56
4 ∨ 4 ∨ 4 ∨ 4   ext. rep. 1
e♭ V⁷ I   D♭ V⁷ i   e♭ V⁷ I   D♭ V⁷ I

Ex. 4-31. (Continued)

retransition ⑥   introduction ①

74 — — — — — 77 — — — — — 85
┌ — — 3̄ — — ┐ — — 8 — — ┐
            f v

Part A ②
double period

85   105
┌ 4   V 4   V 4   V 4   ext. rep. 2 ext. rep. 2 ext. cad. ┐
  iv i   V   iv i   V⁷ i   V⁷ i   V⁷ i   iv i

Ex. 4-32. Chopin: Mazurka, Op. 41, No. 2. (ABCBA¹)

Part A ①   Part B ②
repeated period   repeated period

                                          17
┌ 4   V 4   V   4   V 4 ┐ ┌ 4   V 4   V 4 V 4 ┐
  e   V⁷i   b II i   V⁷i   b II i   B   V⁹   g♯ V B   V⁹   g♯ V

Part C ③   Part B ②
period   repeated period

33   40
┌ 4   V 4 ┐ ┌ 4   V 4   V 4   V 4 ┐
  B V⁷I   g♯ V⁷i   B   V⁹   g♯ V B   V⁹   g♯ V

Part A¹ ①
period

57   68
┌ 4   V   4   ext. rep. 1   ext. rep. 1   rep. cad. ┐
  e   V⁷i   b II i   b II i

Ex. 4-33. Haydn: Sonata in E♭ Major (Peters No. 32), II. (ABA¹)

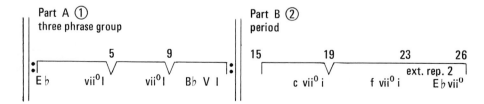

Part A ①   Part B ②
three phrase group   period

            5   9   15   19   23   26
┌   ┐   ┌   ext. rep. 2 ┐
 E♭   vii⁰I   vii⁰I B♭ V I   c vii⁰ i   f vii⁰ i   E♭ vii⁰

Part A¹ ①
three phrase group

vii⁰ I   vii⁰7   ext. seq. 2   V I

26   31   36 38   44

Ex. 4-34. Haydn: String Quartet in E♭ Major, Op. 33, No. 2, III. (ABAB¹A¹)

Part A ①
repeated period

transition ②

Part B ③
period

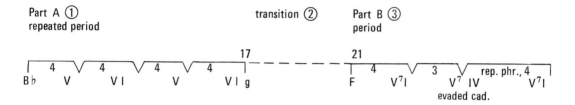

Part A ①
period

Part B¹ ③
three phrase group

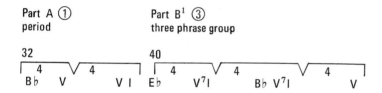

Part A¹ ①
three phrase group

codetta ④

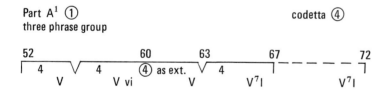

Ex. 4-35. Hindemith: *Ludus Tonalis.* Interludium in F. (ABC A¹C¹C²)

Part A¹ ①
period

Part B ②
period

Part C ③
period

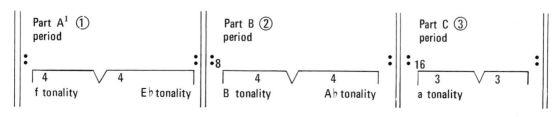

Ex. 4-35. (Continued)

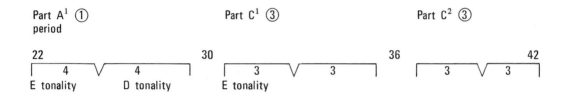

Ex. 4-36. Kabalevsky: 24 Preludes, Op. 38, No. 6. (ABA')

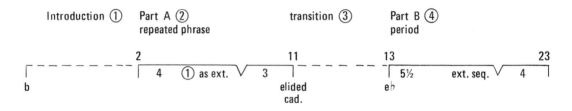

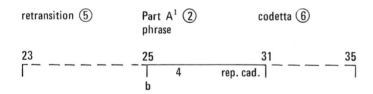

Ex. 4-37. Kennan: 2 Preludes (1951), No. 2. (ABA')

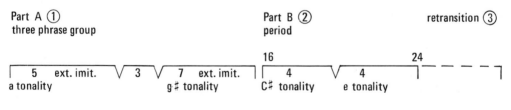

Ex. 4-38. Mozart: Sonata in C Major (K.309), H. (AABABA)

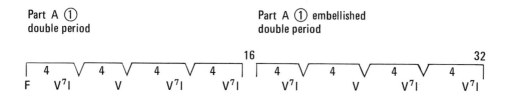

Part A ① double period

Part A ① embellished double period

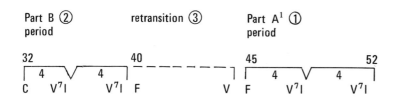

Part B ② period   retransition ③   Part A¹ ① period

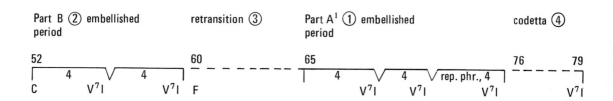

Part B ② embellished period   retransition ③   Part A¹ ① embellished period   codetta ④

Ex. 4-39. Schumann: *Kinderszenen*, Op. 15, No. 2. (ABA¹BA¹)

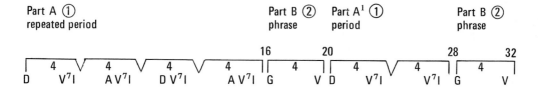

Part A ① repeated period   Part B ② phrase   Part A¹ ① period   Part B ② phrase

Part A¹ ① period

Ex. 4-40. Schumann: *Kinderszenen*, Op. 15, No. 8. (ABA)

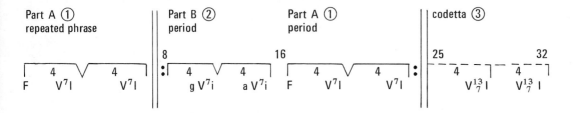

Ex. 4-41. Schumann: *Album for the Young*, Op. 68, No. 7. (AB)

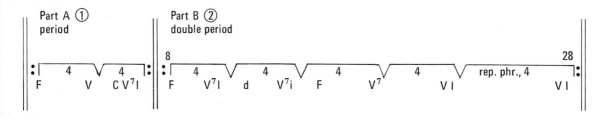

Ex. 4-42. Schumann: *Album for the Young*, Op. 68, No. 19. (AB)

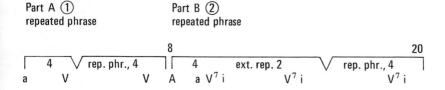

Ex. 4-43. Shostakovich: 24 Präludien, Op. 34, No. 10. (ABA¹)

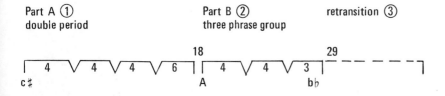

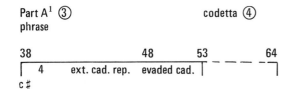

Part A¹ ③   codetta ④
phrase

Chapter 6: Formal Diagrams

Ex. 6-13. Bartok: Concerto for Orchestra, II. (S.F. I II I)

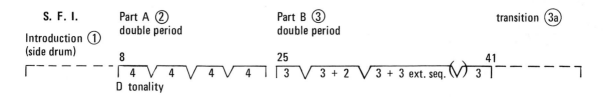

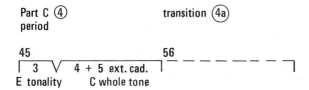

Part C ④   transition ④a
period

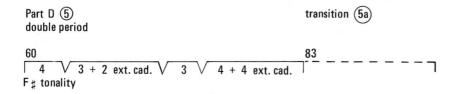

Part D ⑤   transition ⑤a
double period

Part E ⑥   codetta ⑥a
double period

Ex. 6-13. (Continued)

S. F. II (Trio)

Part A ⑦   retransition ⑧
double period

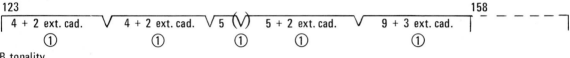

123   158
┌─ 4 + 2 ext. cad.   V 4 + 2 ext. cad. V 5 (V)   5 + 2 ext. cad.   V   9 + 3 ext. cad. ─┐ ┄┄┄┄┄┐
        ①   ①   ①   ①   ①

B tonality

S. F. I

Part A ②   Part B ③   transition ③a
double period   double period

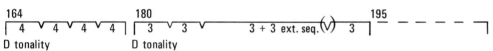

164   180   195
┌─ 4 V 4 V 4 V 4 ─┐ ┌─ 3 V 3 V   3 + 3 ext. seq.(V) 3 ─┐ ┄┄┄┄┄┄┄┐
D tonality   D tonality

Part C ④   transition ④a   Part D ⑤   transition ⑤a
period   period

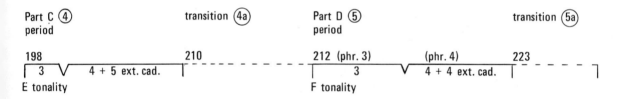

198   210   212 (phr. 3)   (phr. 4)   223
┌─ 3 V   4 + 5 ext. cad. ─┐ ┄┄┄┄┄┄┄┄┄┄┄┄┄┄┄┄   ┌─   3   V 4 + 4 ext. cad. ─┐ ┄┄┄┄┐
E tonality   F tonality

Part E ⑥   codetta ⑥a
three phrase group

228   (phr. 4)   248   263
┌─ 3   V 3 + 7 ext. rep. mot. V 3 + 5 ext. rep. mot. ─┐ ┄┄┄┐
D
─ tonality   D tonality
C

Ex. 6-14. Beethoven: Sonata in F Minor, Op. 2, No. 1, III. (S.F. I II I).

S. F. I (Menuetto)

Part A ①   Part B ②   retransition ③
period   phrase

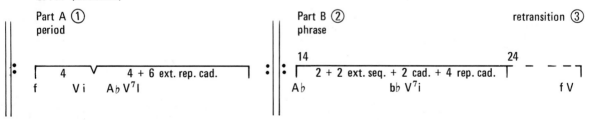

                                                      14   24
╟┃: ┌─ 4   V   4 + 6 ext. rep. cad. ─┐ :┃╟┃: ┌─ 2 + 2 ext. seq. + 2 cad. + 4 rep. cad. ─┐ ┄┄┄┐
    f   V i   A♭ V⁷I   A♭   b♭ V⁷i   f V

Part A¹ ①
phrase

28
┌─────────────────────────────────────┐
│ 2 + 2 imit. + 2 seq. + 2 cad. + 4 rep. cad. │
f V^7 i

S. F. II (Trio)

Part A ④
period

40
┌─────────────────────────────────────┐
│   4   2 + 2 ext. seq. + 2 cad.   │
F V^7I   C V^7I

Part B ⑤   Part A¹ ④
repeated phrase   repeated phrase

50   66   73   Men. D.C.
┌───────────────────────────┐ ┌───────────────────────────────┐
│   4   4 + 7 ext. seq.   │ │   4   rep. phr., 4   │
F V^7I V^7 V^7I V^7I

Ex. 6-15. Brahms: String Quintet in G Major, Op. 111, III. (S.F. I II I).

S. F. I

Part A ①
six phrase group

┌──────────────────────────────────────┐
│ 4   4 (v) 4   4   4 (v) 4 │
g vii^{d7} III   V vii^{d7} III   d V^7I

Part B ②
five phrase group

24
┌──┐
│ 4   4   4   rep. per., 4 + 2   4   14, ext. seq., ext. cad., │
c V^7i b♭ V VI ♯iv^{d7} ♯iv^{d7} g Ger⁶ i_4^6 g rep. cad.   V I

Ex. 6-15. (Continued)

S. F. II (Trio)

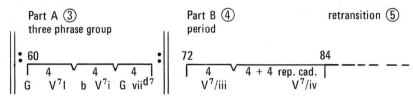

Part A ③   Part B ④   retransition ⑤
three phrase group   period

```
:| 60              4      4      4   |:|  72              4        4 + 4 rep. cad.        84
     G   V⁷I   b  V⁷i  G  viid⁷           V⁷/iii                    V⁷/iv
```

Part A¹ ③
three phrase group

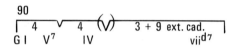

```
90
       4      4    (V)   3 + 9 ext. cad.
  G I  V⁷    IV                  viid⁷
```

S. F. I

Part A ①
six phrase group

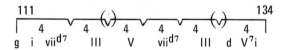

```
111              (V)               (V)        134
    4      4      4      4      4       4
  g  i  viid⁷  III    V   viid⁷  III   d  V⁷i
```

Part B ②
five phrase group

```
134
    4      4      4   rep. phr., 4 + 2      4      14, ext. seq., ext. cad., rep. cad.
  c  V⁷i   bb V VI  ♯ivd⁷        ♯ivd⁷   g  Ger⁶  ⁶₁₄                              V I
```

codetta ⑥

```
170  _ _ _ _  183
  G        ♯ivd⁷ I
```

Ex. 6-16. Brahms: Ballade, Op. 118, No. 3. (Th. I II I)

Th. I

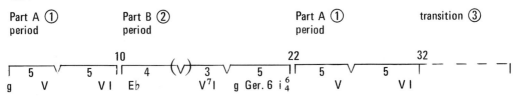

Part A ①   Part B ②   Part A ①   transition ③
period   period   period

Th. II

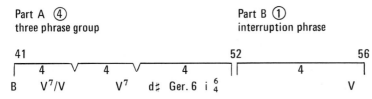

Part A ④   Part B ①
three phrase group   interruption phrase

Part A¹ ④   retransition ⑤
double period

Th. I

Part A ①   Part B ②   Part A ①   codetta ③
period   period   period

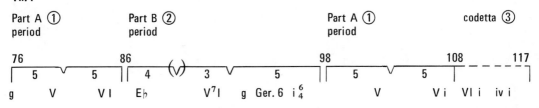

Ex. 6-17. Chopin: Mazurka, Op. 7, No. 2. (S.F. I II I).

S. F. I

Part A ①
double period

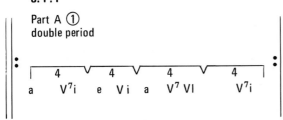

Ex. 6-17. (Continued)

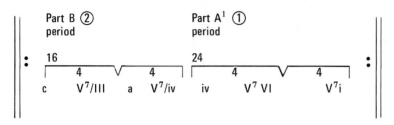

S. F. II

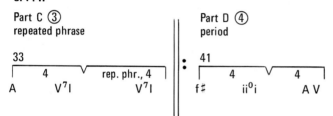

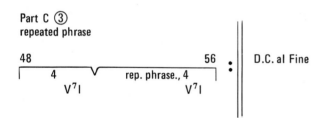

Ex. 6-18. Chopin: Nocturne, Op. 37, No. 1. (Th. I II I).

Th. I

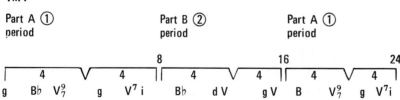

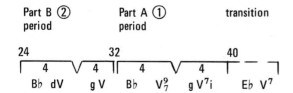

Th. II

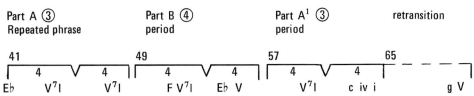

Th. I

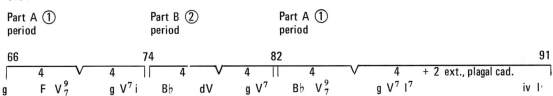

Ex. 6-19. Mozart: Symphony in D Major (Haffner, K.385), III. (S.F. I II I).

S. F. I (Menuetto)

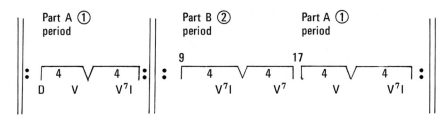

S. F. II (Trio)

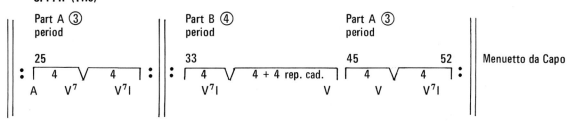

Ex. 6-20. Prokofieff: Violin Concerto No. 2, Op. 63, II. (Th. I II I).

Th. I

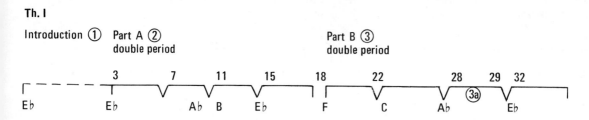

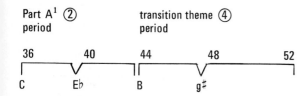

Th. II

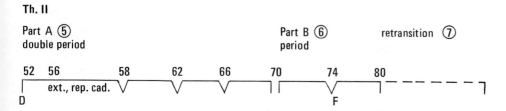

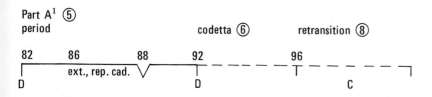

Th. I

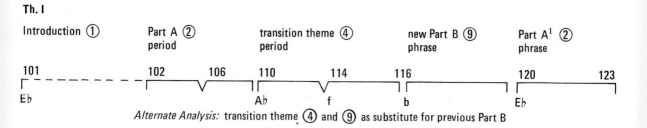

Alternate Analysis: transition theme ④ and ⑨ as substitute for previous Part B

Ex. 6-21. Prokofieff: Symphony No. 5, Op. 100, II. (Th. I II I).

Th. I

Introduction ① Part A ②   link ① A continued ②   link (1-3) ①   ③   ①
            phrase restated with
            some modification

```
        3       7           10      11      14 modified    19      23      27      29      31
 ┌── ── ──┬───────────────┬─── ──┬──────────∨───────────∨───────┬── ── ── ── ── ── ── ──┐
 d               ext. rep. cad.          f                  b
                 F
```

A continued ②   link ① A continued   Transition (1-3)

```
  33          37    41              43      44      48   modified   51
 ┌───────────∨───────────────────┬── ──┬──────────∨────────────┬── ── ── ── ──┐
 b            e     ext. rep. cad.          g                  D
                                                              ─
                                                              d
```

Part B ④   retransition ①
repeated phrase

```
  56          61          65
 ┌───────────∨───────────┬── ── ── ──┐
 E♭
```

Part A¹ ②   link (1-3) A¹ continued ②   phrase   transition ⑤
phrase restated with   phrase   augmented
modification each time   augmented

```
  69          73          78      82      86              90      94              106
 ┌───────────∨───────────┬── ── ──┬─────────────∨──────────────────────┬── ── ──┐
 d           f                   d    ext. rep. mot.        ext. rep. mot.
```

Th. II

Introduction ⑥   Part A ⑦
repeated phrase   three phrase group

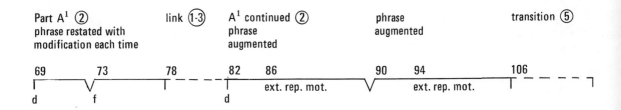

```
  112         116         120     126             130     137             141     150
 ┌───────────∨───────────┤┌──────────────∨──────────────────∨──────────────────┐
 D                       D   ⑦ₐ ext. rep. mot.   ⑦ₐ ext. rep. mot.   ⑦ₐ ext. rep. mot.
```

Ex. 6-21. (Continued)

Part B ⑧
double period

Introduction ⑥
repeated phrase

154   158   162   166   170   174

D   E♭

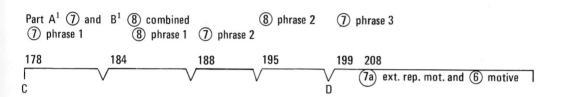

Part A¹ ⑦ and B¹ ⑧ combined   ⑧ phrase 2   ⑦ phrase 3
⑦ phrase 1   ⑧ phrase 1 ⑦ phrase 2

178   184   188   195   199 208

C   D   ⑦ₐ ext. rep. mot. and ⑥ motive

Th. I

Introduction ①

codetta ⑥
repeated phrase

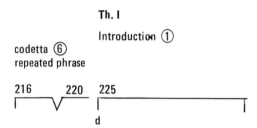

216   220   225

d

Part A ②
phrase restated with
modification each time

link ③   A continued ②

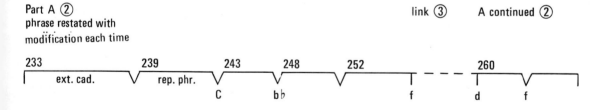

233   239   243   248   252   260

   ext. cad.   rep. phr.
                        C   b♭   f   d   f

Part B ④
repeated phrase

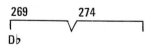

269   274

D♭

Part A¹ ③
phrase restated with
some modification

codetta ④

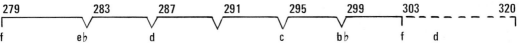

```
279          283      287        291        295        299      303 - - - - - - - 320
|⌐           ⌐V⌐      ⌐V⌐        V          V          V⌐       ⌐⌐                 ⌐|
f              e♭       d                    c          b♭       f    d
```

Ex. 6-22. Ravel: *Le Tombeau de Couperin*, V. (S.F. I II I).

S. F. I

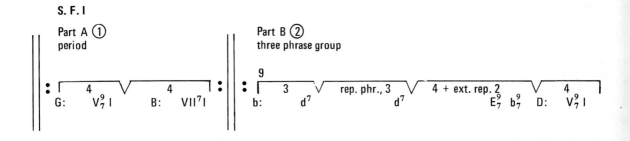

Part A ①
period

Part B ②
three phrase group

```
          4      V      4                      9
‖: |⌐           V      ⌐|  :‖  :‖: |⌐  3      V   rep. phr., 3   V   4 + ext. rep. 2   V   4 ⌐|
    G:  V₇⁹ I        B: VII⁷I         b:     d⁷                 d⁷              E₇⁹ b₇⁹  D:  V₇⁹ I
```

Part A¹ ①
period

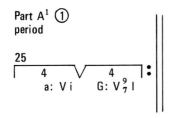

```
25
|⌐    4      V    4  ⌐| :‖
    a: V i   G: V₇⁹ I
```

S. F. II (Musette)

Part A ③
repeated period

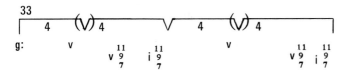

```
33
|⌐   4   (V) 4        V      4   (V) 4   ⌐|
g:       v                           v
              v ⁹(11)  i ⁹(11)            v ⁹(11)  i ⁹(11)
                 ₇        ₇                  ₇        ₇
```

Ex. 6-22. (Continued)

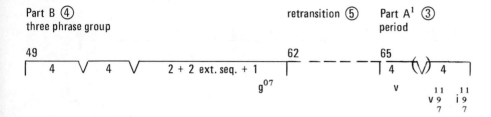

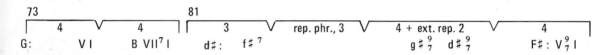

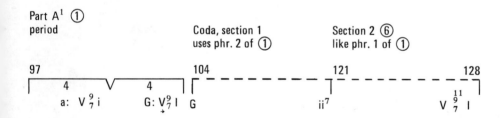

Ex. 6-23. Schubert: String Quartet in D Minor, III. (S.F. I II I).

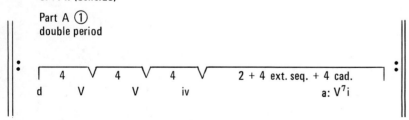

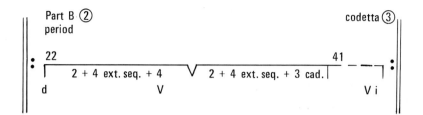

S. F. II (Trio)

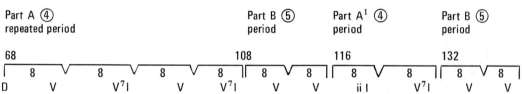

Part A¹ ④
period

148   164
┌─── 8 ──┐ ∨ ┌── 8 ──┐
     ii I   V⁷I

Scherzo D.C.

Ex. 6-24. Schumann: *Kreisleriana*, Op. 16, No. 1. (S.F. I II I)

S. F. I

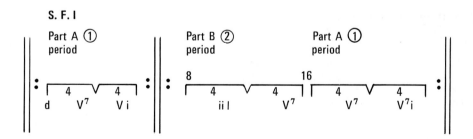

Ex. 6-24. (Continued)

S. F. II

Part A ③   Part B ④   Part A¹ ③
period   period   period

24				32			40		
3	(V)	5		4	V	4		4	V	4
B♭	ii⁰⁷I	F V⁷I		c	V i F	V⁷		V⁷/IV		V I

S. F. I

Part A ①   Part B ②   Part A ①
period   period   period

48		56				67		
4	V	4		4	V	4		4	V	4
d	V⁷	V i		ii⁰i		V⁷		V⁷	V⁷i

Ex. 6-25. Shostakovich: Symphony No. 5, Op. 47, II. (Th. I II I or Th. I II III I II)

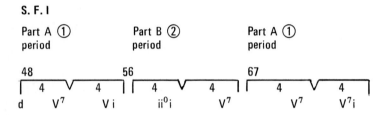

Measure	1	13	21
Texture	monophonic	homophonic	mixture
Primary melodic idea	①	②	③
Additional melodic ideas	none	none	① and ④
Tonality	C	a or C––C	C––g–A––C
Form	Theme I, Part A	Part B	transition
	2 phrases	2 phrases	5-6 phrases
Alternate analysis	Theme I, Part A	Part B	transition

Measure	45	55	64
Texture	homophonic	homophonic	homophonic
Primary melodic idea	④	⑤	④
Additional melodic ideas	none	none	none
Tonality	c	F — — A♭	c
Form	Theme I cont., Part C 3 phrases	Part D 2 phrases	Part C restated 3 phrases
Alternate analysis	Theme II, Part A	Part B	Part A restated

Measure	74	86
Texture	homophonic	homophonic
Primary melodic idea	⑤	⑥
Additional melodic ideas	none	none
Tonality	F — — A♭	C
Form	Theme I cont., Part D restated 2 phrases, ext.	Theme II, Part A 4 phrases, repeated
Alternate analysis	Theme II cont., Part B restated	Theme III, Part A

Measure	118	157-242	242-250
Texture	mixture		homophonic
Primary melodic idea	⑦	① ② ③ ④ ⑤ ④ ⑤	⑥
Additional melodic ideas	⑥ , suggestion of ① and ③	(written D.C. of measures 1-84)	none
Tonality	C — — d♯ — B — — C		A
Form	retransition 3 phrases, repeated	Theme I	codetta 2 phrases
Alternate analysis	retransition	Themes I and II	codetta

Chapter 7: Formal Diagrams

Ex. 7-9. Bartok: Piano Concerto No. 2, III. (Th. I II I III I IV I Coda).

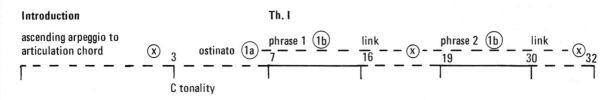

Introduction   **Th. I**

ascending arpeggio to
articulation chord   (x)   3   ostinato (1a)   phrase 1 (1b)   link   (x)   phrase 2 (1b)   link   (x) 32
                                                  7   16   19   30

C tonality

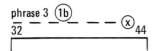

phrase 3 (1b) — — — (x) 44
32

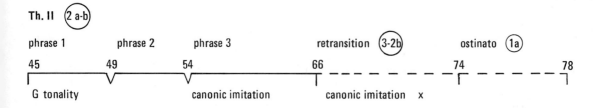

Th. II (2 a-b)

phrase 1   phrase 2   phrase 3   retransition (3-2b)   ostinato (1a)

45   49   54   66   74   78

G tonality   canonic imitation   canonic imitation   x

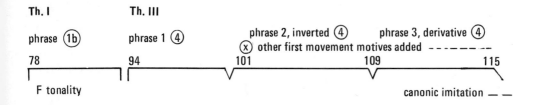

Th. I   **Th. III**

phrase (1b)   phrase 1 (4)   phrase 2, inverted (4)   phrase 3, derivative (4)
                                           (x) other first movement motives added - - - - - -
78   94   101   109   115

F tonality   canonic imitation — —

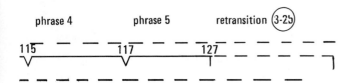

phrase 4   phrase 5   retransition (3-2b)

115   117   127

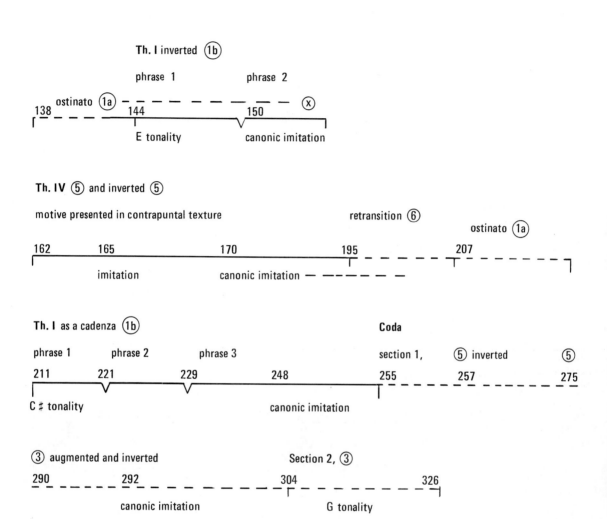

Ex. 7-10. Beethoven: Sonata in A Major, Op. 2, No. 2, IV. (Th. I II I III I II Coda).

Th. I

Part A ① period

Part B ② phrase

Part A¹ ① phrase

transition ③

8

13

16

26

A

E

Ex. 7-10. (Continued)

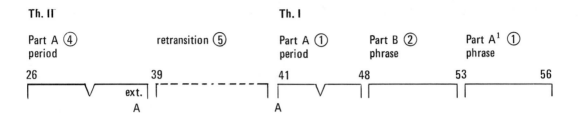

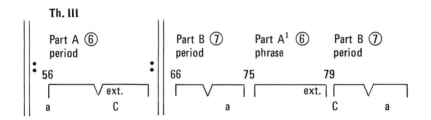

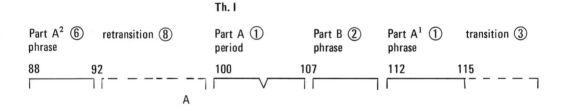

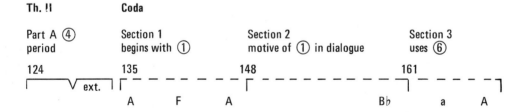

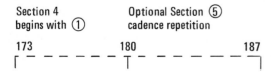

Ex. 7-11. Beethoven: Sonata in Eb Major, Op. 7, IV. (Th. I II I III I II I Coda).

Th. I

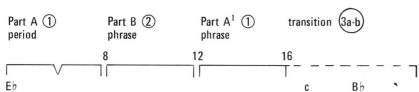

Th. II   **Th. I**

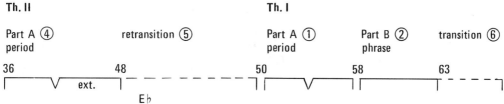

Th. III

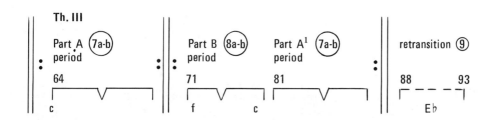

Th. I

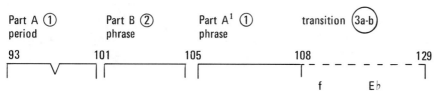

Th. II

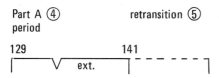

Ex. 7-11. (Continued)

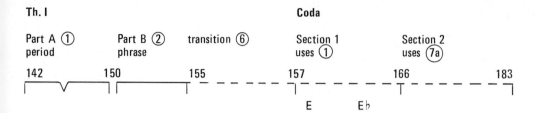

Ex. 7-12. Brahms: Rhapsody, Op. 119, No. 4. (Th. I II III II I Coda).

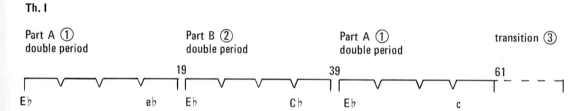

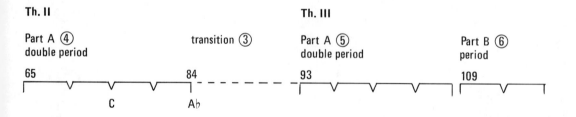

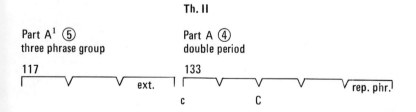

Th. I

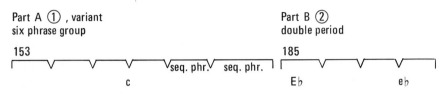

Part A ① , variant
six phrase group

153

c   seq. phr.   seq. phr.

Part B ②
double period

185

E♭   e♭

Coda

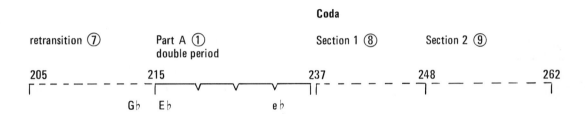

retransition ⑦

205

Part A ①
double period

215

G♭   E♭   e♭

237

Section 1 ⑧

248

Section 2 ⑨

262

Ex. 7-13. Chopin: *Grande Valse Brilliante*, Op. 18. (S.F. I II III IV I)

S. F. I

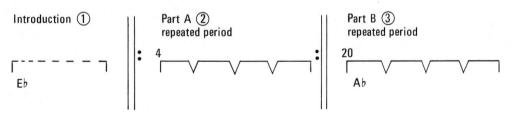

Introduction ①

E♭

Part A ②
repeated period

4

Part B ③
repeated period

20

A♭

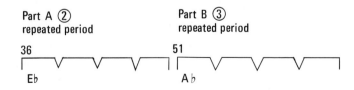

Part A ②
repeated period

36

E♭

Part B ③
repeated period

51

A♭

Ex. 7-13. (Continued)

S. F. II

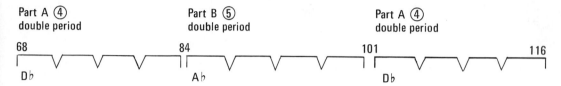

S. F. III

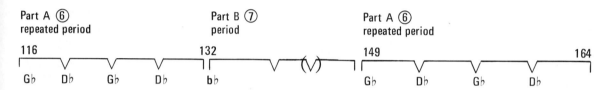

S. F. IV   **S. F. I**

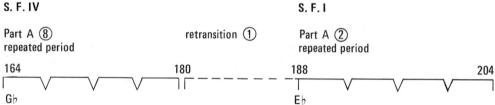

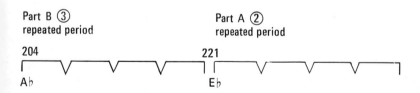

Ex. 7-14. Haydn: Sonata in D Major (Peters No. 9), III. (Th. I II I III I I).

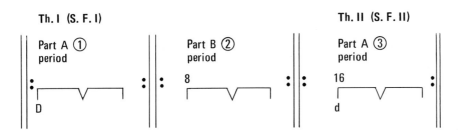

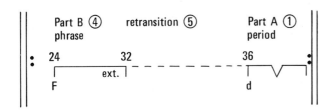

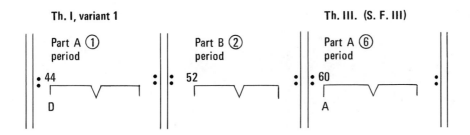

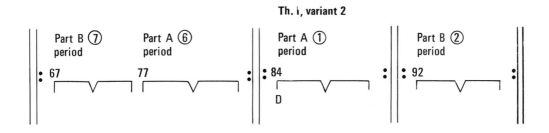

Ex. 7-14. (Continued)

Th. I, variant 3

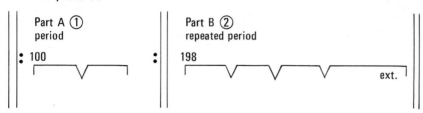

Ex. 7-15. Hindemith: Piano Sonata No. 2, III. (Introduction, Th. I II I III I Codetta).

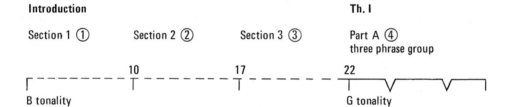

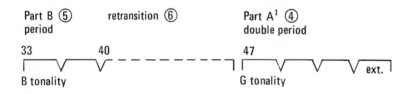

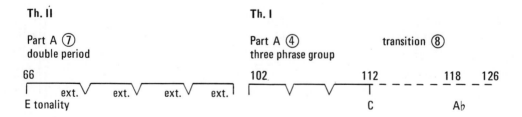

Th. III

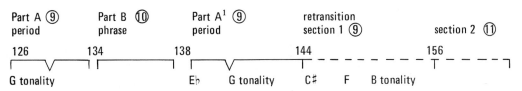

Th. I

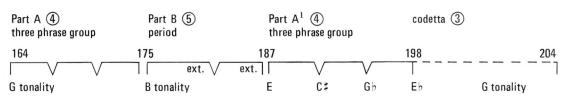

Ex. 7-16. Mozart: Sonata in F Major, K.533/494, III. (Th. I II I III I Coda).

Th. I

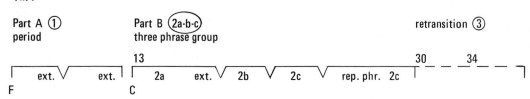

Alternate analysis: Codetta + Retransition

Th. II

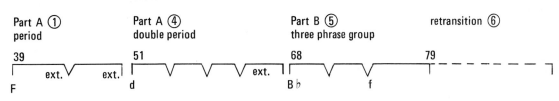

Ex. 7-16. (Continued)

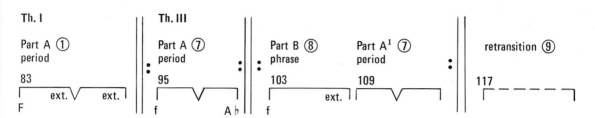

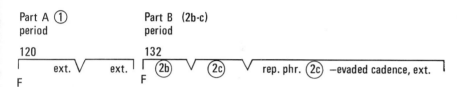

Ex. 7-17. Schubert: Sonata in A minor, Op. 143, III. (Th. I II I   II I   II Codetta)

Th. II

Part A ③
double period

retransition ④

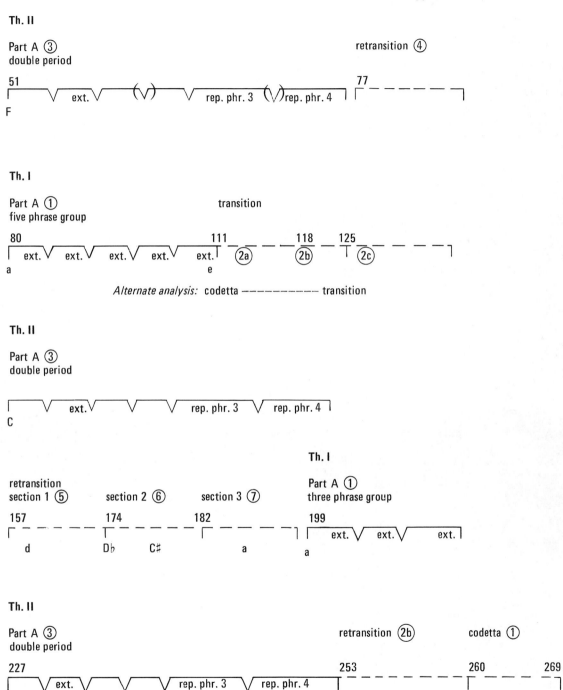

51

F
ext.
(V)
rep. phr. 3
rep. phr. 4
77

Th. I

Part A ①
five phrase group

transition

80

a
ext.
ext.
ext.
ext.
ext.
e
111
②a
118
②b
125
②c

Alternate analysis: codetta — — — — — — — transition

Th. II

Part A ③
double period

C
ext.
rep. phr. 3
rep. phr. 4

retransition
section 1 ⑤

section 2 ⑥

section 3 ⑦

Th. I

Part A ①
three phrase group

157

d
174
D♭   C♯
182
a
199
a
ext.   ext.   ext.

Th. II

Part A ③
double period

retransition ②b

codetta ①

227

A
ext.
rep. phr. 3
rep. phr. 4
253
a
260
269

Ex. 7-18. Schumann: String Quartet in A minor, Op. 41, No. 1, II. (S.F. I II I III I II I).

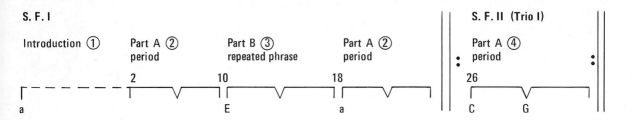

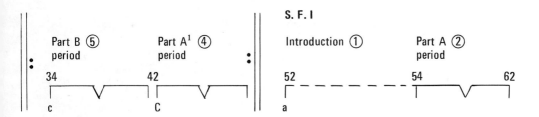

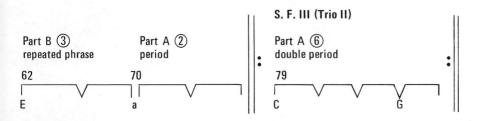

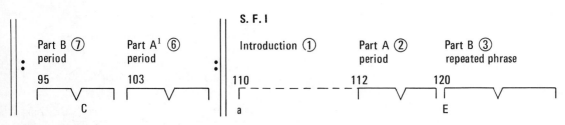

Alternate analysis:

Part B, a double period.

S. F. II

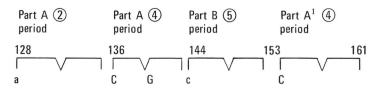

Part A ②   Part A ④   Part B ⑤   Part A¹ ④
period   period   period   period

128   136   144   153   161

a   C   G   c   C

S. F. I

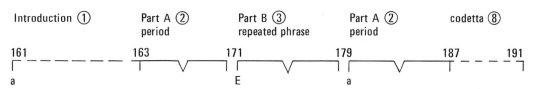

Introduction ①   Part A ②   Part B ③   Part A ②   codetta ⑧
                period   repeated phrase   period

161   163   171   179   187   191

a   E   a

Ex. 7-19. Shostakovich: String Quartet No. 3, Op. 73, II. (Th. I II I II Coda).

Th. I

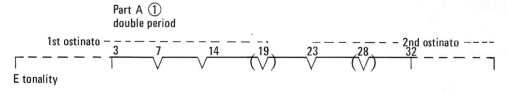

Part A ①
double period

1st ostinato   2nd ostinato
         3   7   14   19   23   28   32

E tonality   (V)   (V)

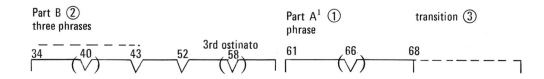

Part B ②   Part A¹ ①   transition ③
three phrases   phrase

                    3rd ostinato
34   40   43   52   58   61   66   68

    (V)   (V)   (V)

Ex. 7-19. (Continued)

Th. II

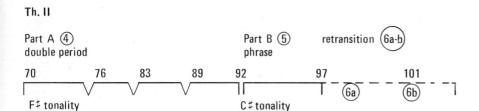

Th. I

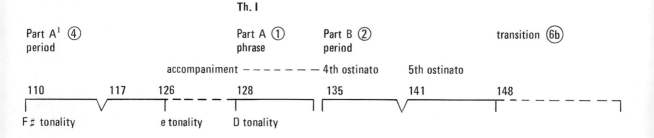

Th. II   **Coda**

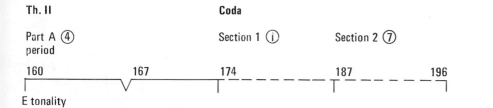

Chapter 8: Formal Diagrams

Ex. 8-13. Bartok: Violin Concerto No. 2, I.

Exposition

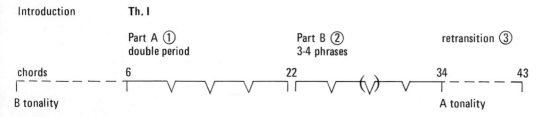

Transition Th. ④

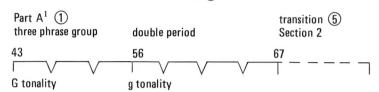

Part A¹ ①
three phrase group   double period

transition ⑤
Section 2

43

56

67

G tonality

g tonality

Th. II   **Closing Th.**

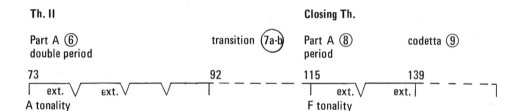

Part A ⑥   transition ⑦a-b   Part A ⑧   codetta ⑨
double period   period

73   92   115   139

ext.   ext.

ext.   ext.

A tonality

F tonality

Development

Sections: 1   2

160   162   164   169   175   179   182   190

Sources: ⑨-②   ① rhythm ⑨-②   ① augmented ⑧   ①   ① rhythm   ①

G tonality   C ♯ tonality

3   4

194   204

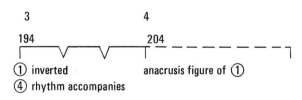

① inverted
④ rhythm accompanies

G tonality

Ex. 8-13. (Continued)

Recapitulation

Th. I

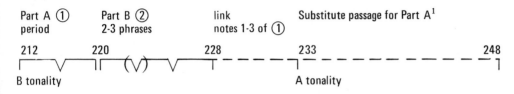

Part A ①   Part B ②   link   Substitute passage for Part A¹
period   2-3 phrases   notes 1-3 of ①

212   220   228   233   248

B tonality   A tonality

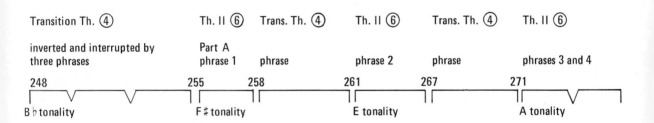

Transition Th. ④   Th. II ⑥   Trans. Th. ④   Th. II ⑥   Trans. Th. ④   Th. II ⑥

inverted and interrupted by   Part A
three phrases   phrase 1   phrase   phrase 2   phrase   phrases 3 and 4

248   255   258   261   267   271

B♭ tonality   F♯ tonality   E tonality   A tonality

transition ⑦a-b   Cadenza   Coda begins like the development.
inverted material   Solo and orchestra ①   Solo   Section 1, ⑨-② and the rhythm of ①

280   203   309   344

D tonality

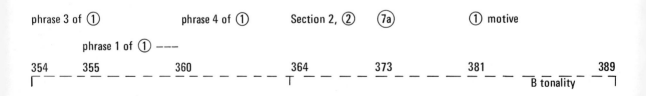

phrase 3 of ①   phrase 4 of ①   Section 2, ②   ⑦a   ① motive

phrase 1 of ① ---

354   355   360   364   373   381   389

B tonality

Ex. 8-14. Beethoven: Sonata in C Minor, Op. 10, No. 1, I.

Exposition

Th. I

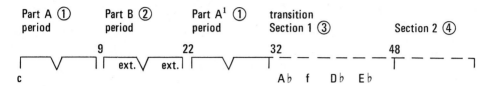

Th. II

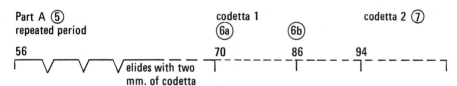

Development

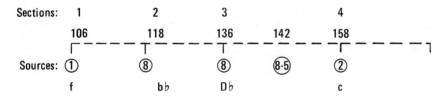

Recapitulation

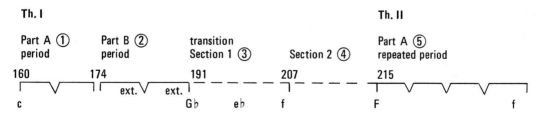

Ex. 8-14. (Continued)

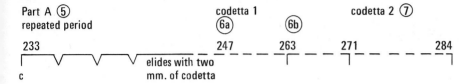

repeated Th. II

Ex. 8-15. Beethoven: Sonata in D Major, Op. 28, I.

Exposition

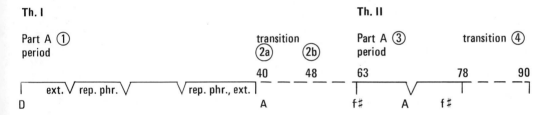

Th. III

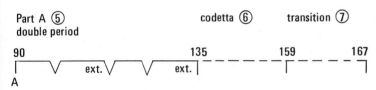

Development

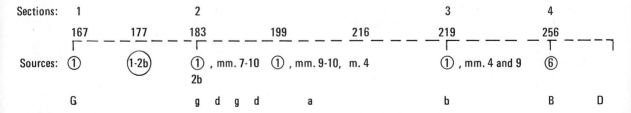

Recapitulation

Th. I   **Th. II**

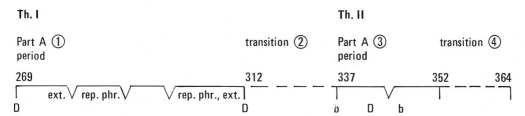

Part A ①   transition ②   Part A ③   transition ④
period   period

269   312   337   352   364

Th. III

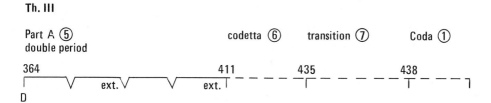

Part A ⑤   codetta ⑥   transition ⑦   Coda ①
double period

364   411   435   438

Ex. 8-16. Beethoven: String Quartet, Op. 18, No. 2, IV.

Exposition

Th. I

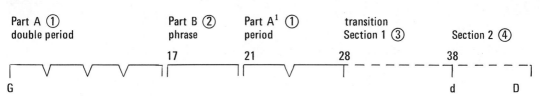

Part A ①   Part B ②   Part A¹ ①   transition
double period   phrase   period   Section 1 ③   Section 2 ④

                    17   21   28   38

Th. II

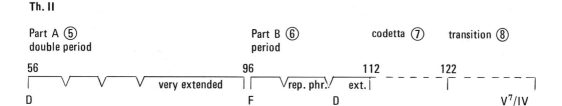

Part A ⑤   Part B ⑥   codetta ⑦   transition ⑧
double period   period

56   96   112   122

Ex. 8-16. (Continued)

Development

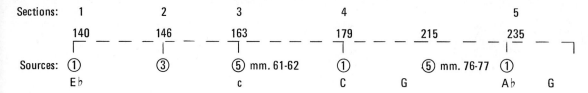

Sections: 1   2   3   4   5

            140   146   163   179   215   235

Sources: ① | ③ | ⑤ mm. 61-62 | ① | ⑤ mm. 76-77 | ①
            E♭   c   C   G   A♭   G

Recapitulation

Th. I

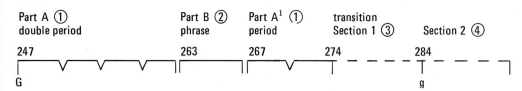

Part A ①   Part B ②   Part A¹ ①   transition
double period   phrase   period   Section 1 ③   Section 2 ④

247   263   267   274   284

G   g

Th. II

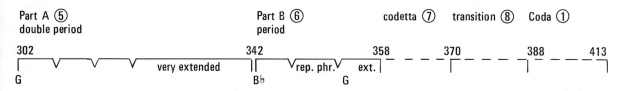

Part A ⑤   Part B ⑥   codetta ⑦   transition ⑧   Coda ①
double period   period

302   342   358   370   388   413

G   very extended   B♭   rep. phr.   ext.
G

Ex. 8-17. Brahms: Piano Quintet in F Minor, Op. 34, I.

Exposition

Th. I   **Th. II**

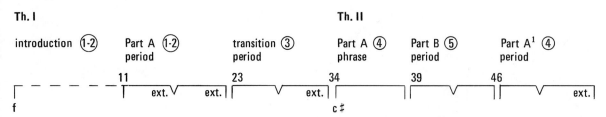

introduction ①-②   Part A ①-②   transition ③   Part A ④   Part B ⑤   Part A¹ ④
                     period   period   phrase   period   period

                     11   23   34   39   46

f   ext.   ext.   ext.   c♯   ext.

Closing Th.

Codetta combines ⑤ , ② and mm. 53-54 of ④   Part A ⑥   transition ⑦
double period   period

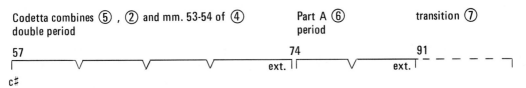

57   74   91

ext.

c♯

Development

Sections: 1   2   3

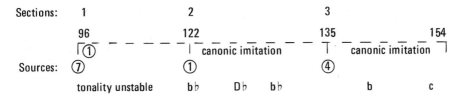

96   122   135   154

canonic imitation   canonic imitation

Sources: ⑦   ①   ④

tonality unstable   b♭   D♭   b♭   b   c

4

154   160   165

canonic imitation

④   ①

f

Recapitulation

Th. I   **Th. II**

introduction ②   Part A ①-②   transition ③   Part A ④   Part B ⑤
period   period   phrase   period

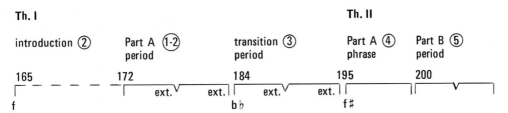

165   172   184   195   200

ext.   ext.   ext.   ext.

f   b♭   f♯

Ex. 8-17. (Continued)

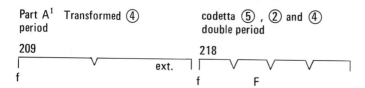

Part A¹   Transformed ④   codetta ⑤ , ② and ④
period   double period

209   218

Closing Th.

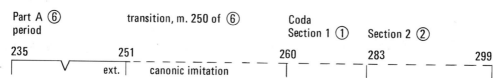

Part A ⑥   transition, m. 250 of ⑥   Coda
period   Section 1 ①   Section 2 ②

235   251   260   283   299

Ex. 8-18. Haydn: String Quartet, Op. 76, No. 4, I.

Exposition

Th. I

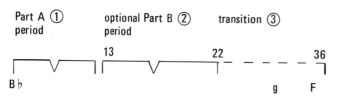

Part A ①   optional Part B ②   transition ③
period   period

                13   22   36

Th. II

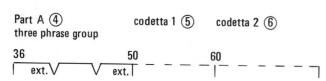

Part A ④   codetta 1 ⑤   codetta 2 ⑥
three phrase group

36   50   60

Development

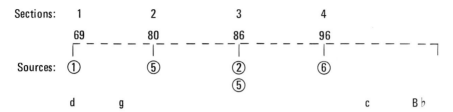

Recapitulation

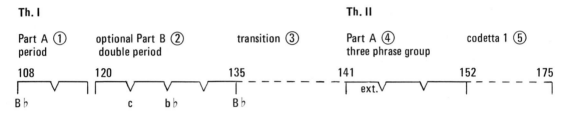

Coda

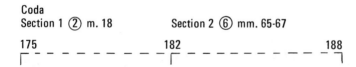

Ex. 8-19. Hindemith: Piano Sonata No. 3, I.

Exposition

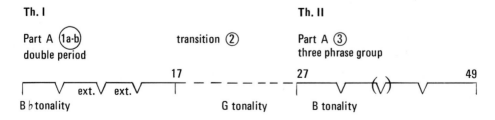

Ex. 8-19. (Continued)

Development

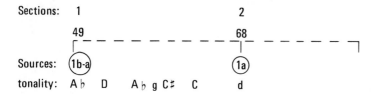

Sections: 1   2

            49   68

Sources: (1b-a)   (1a)
tonality: A♭ D   A♭ g C♯   C   d

Recapitulation

Th. II

Part A ③
three phrase group

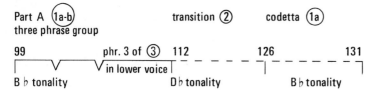

75

A tonality   F♯ tonality   D tonality

Th. I

Part A (1a-b)   transition ②   codetta (1a)
three phrase group

99   phr. 3 of ③ 112   126   131

B♭ tonality   D♭ tonality   B♭ tonality

Ex. 8-20. Mendelssohn: Violin Concerto in E Minor, Op. 64, I.

Exposition

Th. I

introduction   Part A ①   Part B ②
                double period   double period

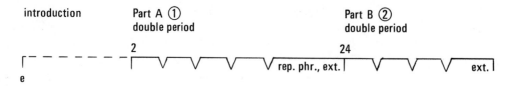

                2   24

e

Transition Th.

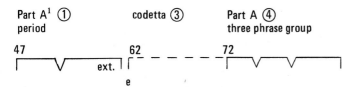

Part A¹ ①   codetta ③   Part A ④
period   three phrase group

47   62   72
⌐___∨___ ext. ⌐ - - - - -   ⌐___∨___∨___⌐
            e

possible Part B ⑤   transition
three phrase group   Section 1 ⑥ₐ   Section 2 ⑥ᵦ

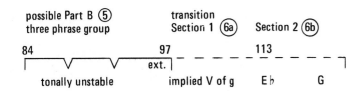

84   97   113
⌐___∨___∨___ ext. ⌐ - - - - -   - - - - -⌐
    tonally unstable   implied V of g   E♭   G

Th. II

Part A ⑦   Part B ⑧   Part A¹ ⑨₁
double period   period

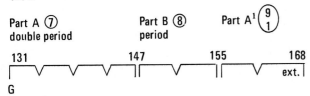

131   147   155   168
⌐___∨___∨___∨___⌐⌐___∨___⌐⌐___∨___ ext. ⌐
G

codetta 1 ①   codetta 2 ⑩   codetta 3 ⑪   transition ①

168   181   197   209   226
⌐ - - - - ⌐   ⌐ - - - - ⌐   ⌐ - - - - ⌐

Development

Sections: 1   2   3   4   5 cadenza
            226   238   255   279   290   298
            ⌐ - - - - ⌐ - - - - - - - - - - - ⌐ - - - - - - - ⌐   ⌐ - - - - - ⌐
                       ④ in diminution   ④ in diminution   motive derived

Sources: ④   ①   ①   from ①   ①
            a   G   E   e   e: V⁷

Ex. 8-20. (Continued)

Recapitulation

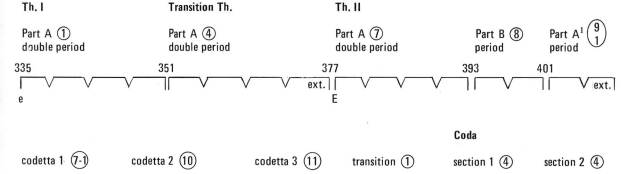

Ex. 8-21. Mozart: Sonata in F Major, K.332, I.

Exposition

Th. I

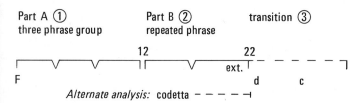

Th. II

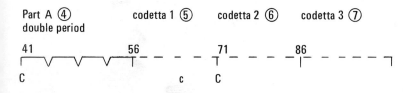

Development

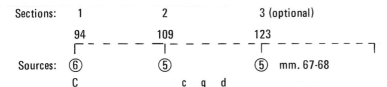

Sections: 1   2   3 (optional)

          94   109   123
          ┌ ─ ─ ─ ─ ─ ┴ ─ ─ ─ ─ ─ ┴ ─ ─ ─ ─ ─ ┐
Sources: ⑥   ⑤   ⑤   mm. 67-68
          C   c   g   d

Recapitulation

Th. I

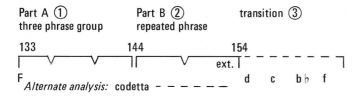

Part A ①   Part B ②   transition ③
three phrase group   repeated phrase

133   144   154
┌ ── ∨ ── ∨ ──┐┌ ──── ∨ ──── ┐
F   ext.┘ ─ ─ ─ ─ ─ ─ ┐
    Alternate analysis: codetta ─ ─ ─ ─ ─   d   c   b♭   f

Th. II

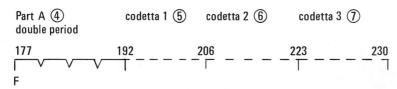

Part A ④   codetta 1 ⑤   codetta 2 ⑥   codetta 3 ⑦
double period

177   192   206   223   230
┌ ─ ∨ ─ ∨ ─ ∨ ─ ┐ ─ ─ ─ ─ ┐ ─ ─ ─ ─ ┐ ─ ─ ─ ─ ┐
F

Ex. 8-22. Prokofieff: Symphony No. 5, Op. 100, I.

Exposition

Th. I

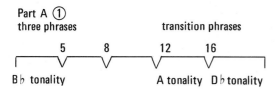

Part A ①
three phrases   transition phrases

          5   8   12   16
┌ ──── ∨ ──── ∨ ──── ∨ ──── ∨ ──── ┐
B♭ tonality   A tonality   D♭ tonality

Ex. 8-22. (Continued)

Part B ② and A ① combined   transition ③

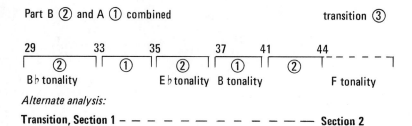

Alternate analysis:

Transition, Section 1 – – – – – – – – – – – – **Section 2**

Th. II   **Closing Th.**

Part A ④   Part A ⑤   codetta ⑥

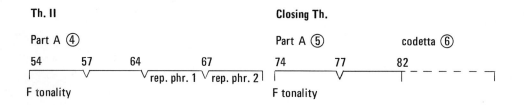

Development

Sections: 1   2

	92	104	106	111	115	119	121	125	130 136
Sources:	①	①	⑤	①	⑥	①	② ⑥	①-⑥	②-⑥

B♭ tonality   F tonality   E♭ tonality

Sections: 3   4

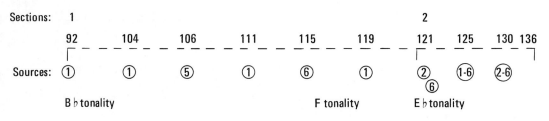

E♭ tonality   C tonality

Recapitulation

Th. I

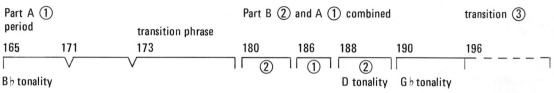

Part A ①   Part B ② and A ① combined   transition ③
period
                    transition phrase

165   171   173   180   186   188   190   196

Bb tonality   D tonality   Gb tonality

Alternate analysis: **Transition, Section 1** — — — — — — — — **Section 2**

Th. II   **Closing Th.**

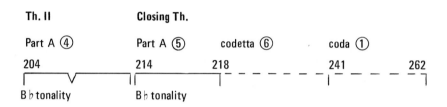

Part A ④   Part A ⑤   codetta ⑥   coda ①

204   214   218   241   262

Bb tonality   Bb tonality

Ex. 8-23. Schubert: String Quintet, Op. 163, I.

Exposition

Th. I

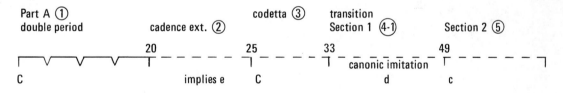

Part A ①   codetta ③   transition
double period   cadence ext. ②   Section 1 ④-1   Section 2 ⑤

                    20   25   33   49

C   implies e   C   canonic imitation
                                                      d   c

Th. II

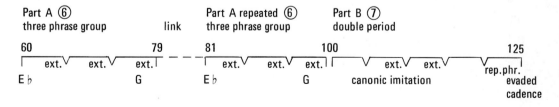

Part A ⑥   Part A repeated ⑥   Part B ⑦
three phrase group   link   three phrase group   double period

60   79   81   100   125

    ext.   ext.   ext.   ext.   ext.   ext.   ext.   ext.   rep.phr.

Eb   G   Eb   G   canonic imitation   evaded cadence

Ex. 8-23. (Continued)

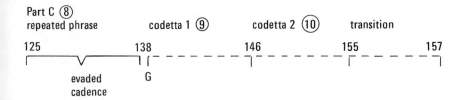

Part C ⑧
repeated phrase   codetta 1 ⑨   codetta 2 ⑩   transition

125   138   146   155   157

evaded   G
cadence

Development

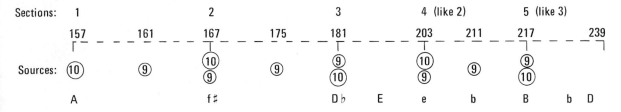

Sections: 1   2   3   4 (like 2)   5 (like 3)

               157   161   167   175   181   203   211   217   239

Sources: ⑩   ⑨   ⑩   ⑨   ⑨   ⑩   ⑨   ⑨
                                           ⑨   ⑩   ⑨   ⑩

               A   f♯   D♭   E   e   b   B   b   D

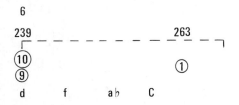

6
239   263

⑩   ①
⑨

d   f   a♭   C

Recapitulation

Th. I

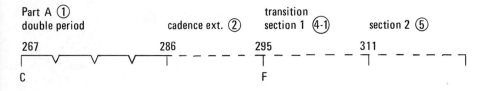

Part A ①   transition
double period   cadence ext. ②   section 1 ④-1   section 2 ⑤

267   286   295   311

C   F

Th. II

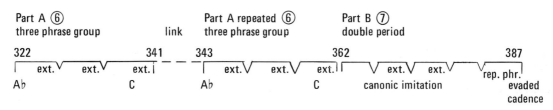

Part A ⑥
three phrase group   link   Part A repeated ⑥
three phrase group   Part B ⑦
double period

322   341   343   362   387
Ab   C   Ab   C   canonic imitation   rep. phr.   evaded
cadence

ext. ∨ ext. ∨ ext.   ext. ∨ ext. ∨ ext.   ∨ ext. ∨ ext. ∨

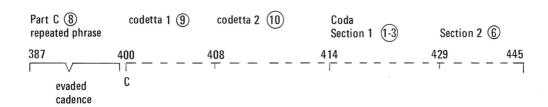

Part C ⑧
repeated phrase   codetta 1 ⑨   codetta 2 ⑩   Coda
Section 1 ①-③   Section 2 ⑥

387   400   408   414   429   445

evaded   C
cadence

Ex. 8-24. Shostakovich: Symphony No. 5, Op. 47, I.

Exposition

Th. I (miniature part form)

Part A ①
phrase   accompaniment   Part B ②
period

4   6   ext.

d tonality

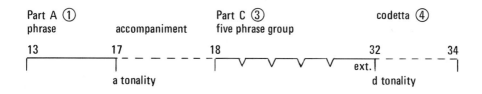

Part A ①
phrase   accompaniment   Part C ③
five phrase group   codetta ④

13   17   18   32   34

a tonality   ext.   d tonality

Ex. 8-24. (Continued)

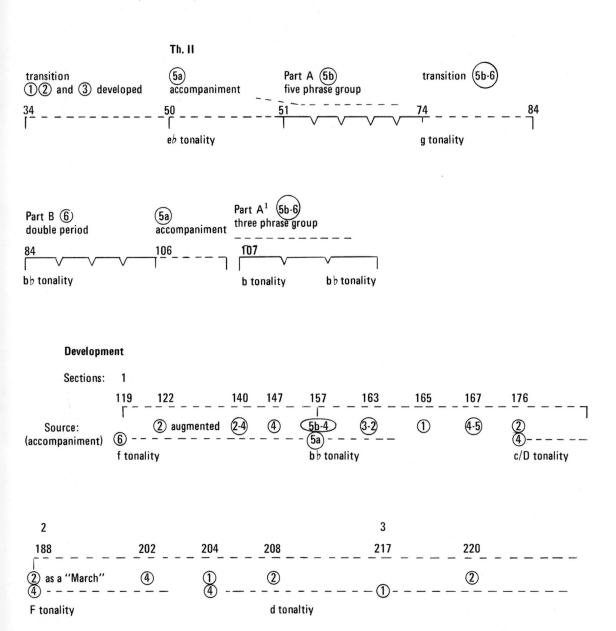

abbreviated Recapitulation

Th. i

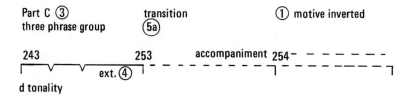

Part C ③   transition   ① motive inverted
three phrase group   ⑤ₐ

243   253   accompaniment 254 ⎯ ⎯ ⎯ ⎯ ⎯ ⎯
                                     ext. ④
d tonality

Th. II

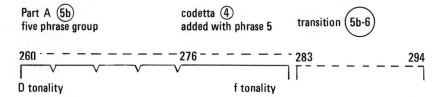

Part A ⑤ᵦ   codetta ④   transition ⑤ᵦ₋₆
five phrase group   added with phrase 5

260 ⎯ ⎯ ⎯ ⎯ ⎯ ⎯ 276 ⎯ ⎯ ⎯ ⎯ ⎯ 283   294
D tonality   f tonality

Coda

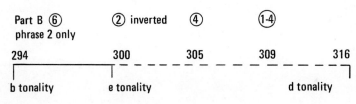

Part B ⑥   ② inverted   ④   ①₋₄
phrase 2 only

294   300   305   309   316
b tonality   e tonality   d tonality

index of musical examples

index

Pages cited may include the musical examples of a discussion